The Design of a Thinking Computer

Robert S. Grondalski

ISBN: 1479113956
ISBN-13: 978-1479113958

CONTENTS

Robert S. Grondalski

PREFACE

A computer that thinks like a person has long been the dream of computer designers. The author uses his 35 years of computer design experience to describe the mechanisms of a thinking computer. These mechanisms include recall, recognition, learning, doing procedures, speech, vision, attention, intelligence, and consciousness. This is a book of science, and as such describes reproducible experiments that demonstrate the operation of the mechanisms described. These experiments use software that the reader can download from www.rgrondalski.com and run on his or her personal computer. The software includes a large engram file containing knowledge we use on a daily basis. Additional experiments allow the reader to write and run new engrams. An effort has been made to make this book readable by a general audience, not just computer designers.

The computer architecture of the human brain is first described. Standard methods of computer design are next used to convert this architecture into thinking computer implementations spanning a range of performance levels. Lastly, the operation of a thinking computer is presented.

The author has received the first patent for a conscious, thinking computer: Method and system for the architecture and implementation of a conscious machine, US Patent number 7,370,042. This patent may be viewed at www.uspto.gov. This book describes the invention in detail.

INTRODUCTION

As we read this, we are conscious and use our brains to understand what we have read. Our brains have a structure to allow this consciousness and understanding to occur. To design a thinking computer, we must first understand the computer architecture of this structure and then implement it using standard methods of computer design.

Chapter 1 provides an overview of the computer architecture of the human brain. It is shown how this architecture uses many copies of a simple structure called a cognitive link. The use of millions of copies of this cognitive link to perform all of our cognitive functions is described. These functions include recall, recognition, learning, doing procedures, understanding and generating speech, vision, attention, intelligence, and consciousness. Input and output structures are described along with implementations and results. After reading Chapter 1, the reader will have a good understanding of the design of a thinking computer.

Although the computer architecture of the brain is described in this book as factual, it is actually a theory. It would be redundant and tedious to constantly be referring to the architectural features as a proposal, so this statement will have to suffice. The experiments described in chapter 11 attempt to provide proof of the proposed theory. These experiments use an engram containing over 10,000 cognitive links storing knowledge we use on a daily basis. The experiments include reading a short story, automatically learning knowledge structures of the story, and being able to interactively answer questions about the story. Other experiments demonstrate learning new cognitive links and answering questions related to a wide range of subjects. Until medical technology allows the actual architecture and connections between the cells of the brain to be determined, this theory of the architecture of the brain will remain unproven.

Chapters 2 through 9 describe the computer architecture of the human brain in more detail. Some of the information from chapter 1 is repeated in chapters 2 through 9, but is used as an introduction to a more detailed description.

Chapter 10, the detailed implementation section, describes how to build a thinking computer by implementing the computer architecture of our brains using standard methods of computer design. The first and simplest implementation described uses simple existing hardware (a personal computer) and thinking computer software to implement the thinking computer architecture. After the personal computer implementation, faster and more complex implementations are described.

Chapter 11 describes the operation of thinking computers. Numerous experiments demonstrating the operation of a thinking computer are provided, starting with simple operations, advancing to very complex operations. The experiments are contained in software that the reader may download from www.rgrondalski.com. Chapter 11 describes how to install and run the software. The reader can run this software and observe, step by step, the mechanisms involved in common thinking activities, such as reading, understanding, and answering questions related to a wide range of subjects.

1 The Computer Architecture of the Human Brain

Our brains are composed of billions of interconnected neurons [10]. A neuron is a single living cell with many inputs and one output that can connect to the input of many other neurons. For thinking to occur, these neurons cannot be connected randomly, but must have a connection structure. When we activate an idea, the neurons associated with the idea activate. For example, if we know someone named Bill, then when we activate the idea "Bill", the neurons associated with the idea "Bill" activate. A group of neurons associated with an idea will be referred to as a node. When we activate the idea "Bill", the "Bill" node activates.

Nodes are connected by cognitive links. Each cognitive link has three connections: a source node, a relation node, and a destination node, as shown in Figure 1. Each of the three nodes is associated with an idea. This chapter will show how all of our thinking capabilities: recall, recognition, learning, doing procedures, understanding, speech, vision, attention, intelligence, and consciousness, result from millions of copies of cognitive links.

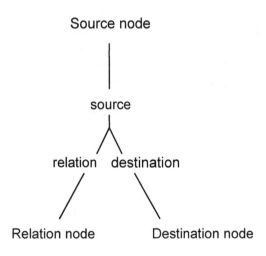

Figure 1: A cognitive link in the human brain

An example of the use of a cognitive link (which will be referred to simply as a link) being used to store the fact that "Bill's uncle is Ed" is shown in figure 2. Bill is a node, Uncle is a node, and Ed is a node.

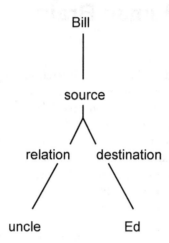

Figure 2: A cognitive link that stores the fact "Bill's uncle is Ed"

Our memory is full of millions of these links, which store all that we know. For example, besides knowing Bill's uncle is Ed, we may also know Ed's uncle is Jim and Ed's sister is Sue. The link structure for these three facts is shown in Figure 3. The source connection for each link will be abbreviated "s", the relation connection will be abbreviated "r", and the destination connection will be abbreviated "d". It is important to note in Figure 3 that a node can be used as a source node for some cognitive links, a relation node for other cognitive links, and a destination node for even other cognitive links. For example, "Ed" is a destination node for link1, and a source node for links 2 and 3.

Although we have millions of links in our memory, we cannot be thinking of everything we know at once. For example, we cannot be thinking of people related to Bill at the same time we are thinking about people related to Ed. We only have one active source node (for example "Bill"), which will be referred to as the current data source (DSRC); we only have one active relation node, which will be referred to as the current data relation (DREL); and likewise with the current data destination (DDST). As we activate each of the three nodes, we put attention on the idea associated with each node. We can have attention on only one node at a time. For example, as we access

"Ed", we no longer have attention on "Bill". The current idea we are holding attention on will be referred to as the hold idea (HOLD).

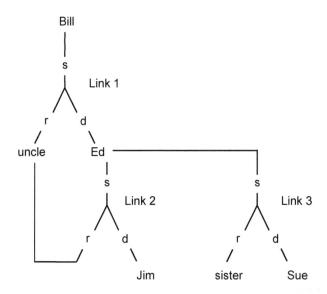

Figure 3: Three facts stored using three links

Ideas can also be activated from external inputs, such as when we hear a word, and ideas can activate outputs, such as when we speak a word. Although we may know many people named Bill, the Bill node in the above example is for a specific person named Bill. We may select this specific Bill node from other persons named Bill by moving to it though the array of cognitive links, like we moved to Ed in the above example.

When implementing the above structure using a traditional computer, a unique number is assigned to each node. The millions of cognitive links may then be stored in an array in the computer's memory. Each cognitive link's array entry in the computer's memory therefore has three node numbers associated with it: the source node, the relation node, and the destination node. There is a computer register (or memory location) associated with each active node: a current data source register (DSRC register), current data relation register (DREL register), and current data destination register (DDST register). The HOLD register contains what we have attention on. We recall, recognize, and learn data links using these registers. It is important to keep in mind that although registers are being referred to, they are actually groups of active neurons in the brain. When a register loaded, neurons are being "set".

The software associated with this book, available at www.rgrondalski.com, includes an engram file containing thousands of cognitive links along with other software that processes the engram as described above. This software can interact with the user by answering questions related to a wide range of subjects. It can also read text and answer questions related to the text.

The human brain has two major sections, the data section and the control section. The data section uses cognitive links to store factual information. The control section uses cognitive links to store procedural information. The control section output instructions to control the data section. First the data section will be described and later the control section will be described.

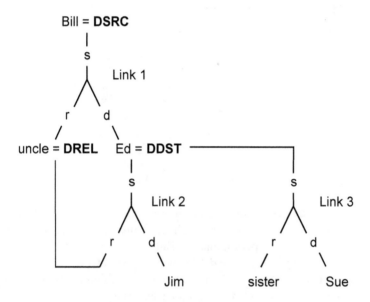

Figure 4: Recalling the uncle of Bill using the data section registers (Bill = DSRC)

1.1 Recall

To recall the uncle of Bill, the DSRC register is set to "Bill", the DREL register is set to "uncle", and then we perform the "data relation access" (DRELACC) instruction, which looks for a link where the source of the link equals the DSRC register, and the relation of the link equals the DREL register. All links are checked simultaneously in the human brain. If a match is found, the destination of the link is loaded to the HOLD register and the DDST register. In Figure 4, the destination of the link "Ed" is loaded to the HOLD register and the DDST register. We can then load the HOLD register to the DSRC register to access information about Ed, such as Ed's uncle is Jim, as shown in Figure 5. In this way, attention flows from idea to idea (data node to data node). We can also leave the DSRC register set to "Bill" and access other facts about Bill. The setting of registers and accessing results is controlled by instructions from the control section, described in section 1.4 and chapter 3 of this book. The "set data source" (SETDSRC) instruction loads the DSRC register from the HOLD register, SETDREL loads the DREL register from the HOLD register, and SETDDST loads the DDST register from the HOLD register. Note that although we may know many people named Bill, the Bill node in the above example is really for a specific person named Bill. We select this specific Bill node from other persons named Bill by moving to it though the array of cognitive links, like we moved to Ed in the above example.

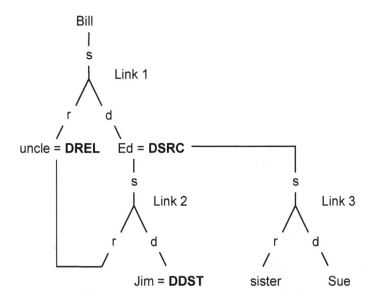

Figure 5: Once we recall Ed, we can then set Ed as DSRC, and recall the uncle of Ed

The DSRC register is actually an active node in the brain; the same for the DREL register. The brain looks for a match to the DSRC node and the DREL node by selecting a cognitive link with an active source and relation. The destination node connected to that link activates when the DRELACC instruction activates. During recall, we move downwards in Figure 5.

Nodes can also be activated from external inputs, such as when we hear a word or look at a word, and nodes can activate outputs, such as when we speak a word. Each sense has its own computer architecture, which are described in chapters 6 and 7 of this book.

The data section links store all the factual information that we know. The relations are not just relations between people. The relations can be relations between any data nodes (ideas). Table 1 is an example of many types of useful information being stored as links, including facts about people and places, math tables, sentences, alphabets, animals, visual information, English words, and foreign language words. The links can be in any order. Every fact that we know can be expressed as a relation between two ideas, with the relation also being an idea. For ease of reading, a tabular format is used instead of the stick drawing, but the structure is the same. Words are in parenthesis because these refer to sounds, as will be described in chapters 6 and 7 of this book. Note that the nodes for the English and French words for "dog" are not the same as the node for the idea "dog". The node for the idea "dog" activates regardless of language.

| | | | | (continued from below left) | |
Source	Relation	Destination	Source	Relation	Destination
Bill	uncle	Ed	tree	made_of	wood
Ed	uncle	Jim	alphabet	start	a
Ed	sister	Sue	alphabet	a	b
Bill	age	40	alphabet	b	c
Bill	lives_in	Kansas	2	+	2+
Bill	works_at	factory	2+	2	4
Bill	fav_color	red	2+	3	5
Bill	isa	person	2	x	2x
Bill	word	(Bill)	2x	2	4
Bill	wordtype	noun	2x	3	6
Ed	age	42	Italy	capital	Rome
Ed	lives_in	Ohio	Italy	isa	country
Ed	word	(Ed)	Nile	isa	river
Ed	wordtype	noun	Nile	location	Africa
Kansas	capital	Topeka	Africa	word	(Africa)
Kansas	isa	state	Africa	isa	continent
Kansas	location	central-USA	Africa	wordtype	noun
Topeka	isa	city	jump	word	(jump)
sky	color	blue	jump	wordtype	verb
cow	sound	moo	picture1	top_right	cloud
horse	eats	hay	picture1	top_left	sun
horse	eats	oats	picture1	bot_left	tree
sentence5	subject	Mary	tree	top	branches
sentence5	verb	had	tree	bottom	trunk
sentence5	object	little_lamb	dog	word	(dog)
mountain	size	big	dog	French-wd	(chien)
(continued above right)					

Table 1: Example of data links

1.2 Recognition

We store the information that we know about a red tomato in the data section, as shown in Figure 6. The relation node and destination node of each cognitive link form an attribute of the source node.

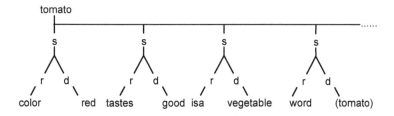

Figure 6: Data section example

We may be asked the question: "What is red and tastes good?". We are able to recognize an object, such as a "tomato", as follows. Each node has a sum associated with it. First the control section outputs the "clear sums" (CLRSUM) instruction, which sets all the millions of sums associated with data nodes to zero. Then the control section sets the DREL register to "color", using the SETDREL instruction, and the DDST register to "red" with SETDDST. Then the control section activates the "sum attribute" (SUMATR) instruction. The "tomato" node sum and any other red object's sum, such as a fire truck, are set to 1. Then the DREL register is set to "tastes" and the DDST register to "good", and another SUMATR is activated. The "tomato" node will now have a sum of 2. Then the "select maximum sum" (SELMAX) instruction is activated and the "tomato" node may be selected for attention, and loaded to the HOLD register. If there is a tie, such as with "apple", then the strongest source node based on recency and frequency of use is selected. Later, with each SELMAX, the next node with the same sum is selected, by blocking each node after it is selected with a large negative sum. For example, if we then decide that "tomato" is not the object we are looking for, we can SELMAX to find "apple", and on to other red objects (strawberry...) that taste good. The first SELMAX requires the sum to be equal to the number of SUMATR instructions so we do not find objects that do not match all attributes. The brain implements the summing mechanism by using different levels of neuron activation.

Once the "tomato" node is found, the "word tomato" may be recalled to say the answer. Words in other languages may also be recalled. Words may also be used to recognize nodes such as during listening or reading. During recognition we move upwards in Figure 6, during recall we move downwards.

11

Once recognized, we may use "tomato" in another recognition, such as finding a picture with a tomato. In this way, during thinking we continually move through the array of data links, sometimes upwards, sometimes downwards.

1.3 Learning

Learning in the data section occurs when the "data learn" (DLEARN) instruction is performed, which takes whatever has been set in the data registers, and uses it to create a new link in the array of data links. The neurons of the brain form a massively parallel interconnection network [6, 7] which is used to connect nodes to the new link. Neurons move from being unused to become part of the nodes connected to the new link. During forgetting, neurons move back to being unused.

The brain actually has two sets of the three data registers described above. Instead of just a "current data source register" (DSRC), there is also a "temporary data source register" (TMPSRC). Likewise, there is a "current data relation register" (DREL) and a "temporary data relation register" (TMPREL). The same with the destination registers (DDST, TMPDST). These two sets of registers are needed when we are asked a question, because one set is used with the question sentence, and the other set is used to access the answer. This will be explained in section 1.5 of this book: parsing sentences.

To correct a data link that has been learned incorrectly, or keeps changing (which car in is first place in a race), DLEARN will overwrite the old data link. In cases where there is more than one correct result, such as when Ed has more than one uncle, the "data learn multiple" (DLEARNML) instruction is used.

1.4 The Control Section of the Brain

The structure described so far is the data section of the brain. The data section of the brain stores factual information and the control section of the brain stores procedural information (sequences of steps). All computers have a control section and a data section. First the control and data section of a traditional computer will be described. This will help with the understanding of the control and data sections of a thinking computer.

The block diagram of a traditional computer [8] is shown in Figure 7. The data section performs operations on data, such as arithmetic operations (add, subtract, multiply …), logical operations (AND, OR, SHIFT …), and other types of data operations. The data is stored in a hierarchy of speed and capacity memories, such as registers, cache, RAM, and disk. From an architectural viewpoint, the memories may be viewed as a single large array of data that is part of the data section. The control section feeds the sequence of instructions to control the data section (read operands from memory, perform data operations, and write results to memory), control the control section itself (branches, subroutine calls and returns, jumps), and control the input and output. The control section's instructions are stored in various computer memory structures, such as microcode memory, cache, RAM, and disk. From an architectural viewpoint, the sequence of instructions may be viewed as a single large program that is part of the control section. The instruction set of a traditional computer is the list of possible instructions output by the control section. The control section receives branch status information from the data section. This allows branching in the instruction sequence, such as looping in the control section while the data section counts the number of loops, or comparing data in the data section. The control section receives interrupts to allow it to service peripherals. The data section receives input data from peripherals, such as when we type on a keyboard, and it outputs data, such as sending data to a computer display.

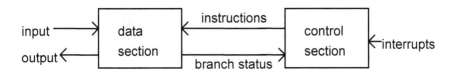

Figure 7: Block diagram of a traditional computer

The architecture of the human brain is very similar to the architecture of a traditional computer. Like a traditional computer, the human brain has a data section and a control section, where the control section of the human brain outputs a sequence of instructions that are processed by the data section. The list of possible instructions is the instruction set of the human brain, which will be described. Unlike a traditional computer, the control section of the brain is able to learn new sequences of instructions. The data section of the human brain does not perform arithmetic and logical operations like a traditional computer; it performs recall, recognition, and learning. The control section of the human brain receives branch status information from the data section, but the branch information is related to operations the data section performs, such as during recognition the control section can branch on whether something is recognized or not. The control section receives interrupts, but these are from the senses, such as a loud sound, or a flash of light. The data section can input data, but this is also from the senses, such as hearing words or reading. The data section can output data, such as speech.

In a traditional computer, the data section performs arithmetic and logical operations. It uses complex circuitry, such arithmetic and logical units made from various transistor structures and gates, such as AND, NAND, OR, NOR, and XOR. The data section of the brain does not perform these operations, and these circuits would be too complex for nature to evolve. For example, nowhere in nature is a 32 bit binary adder found (or even a 2 bit adder). To a skilled computer designer, the data section arithmetic units would clearly be too complex for evolution. The simple cognitive link structure of the thinking computer evolved and we can use it to add binary numbers once we have learned the control procedures to do this. In this way, the architecture of a thinking computer is actually much simpler than the complex structures of a traditional computer. Nature excels at making many copies of simple structures. The architecture of a thinking computer also has better redundancy than a traditional computer. If a cognitive link fails, it can be relearned. If a bit in an adder fails, the adder is permanently broken.

The control section of the brain will be next described. Instructions are required to load the various data registers, access answers, and to perform all the other data section functions we are capable of doing, such as recognition, recall, and learning. These instructions come from the control section, which contains cognitive links that activate instructions that control the data section. The organization of the control section is similar to that of the data section in that it contains millions of cognitive links, with only one active at a time. The control section of the brain is likely much smaller than the size of the data section, because a single control procedure can be used over and over to process different data.

Figure 8 shows the control section of the brain controlling the data section of the brain. Link 4 and link 5 are links storing control section procedural information. As previously described, the data section of the brain has a data source register (DSRC), a data relation register (DREL), and a data destination register (DDST). Likewise, the control section of the brain has a procedure source register (PSRC), a procedure relation register (PREL), and a procedure destination register (PDST). The nodes of the control section are states. Each state can be associated with one or more instructions to control the data section. The registers of the data section are loaded under control of the control section. The registers of the control section are loaded automatically as the instructions associated with a state are completed, and the control section moves to the next state. The control section relation NEXT moves the procedure source register to the next state when an instruction completes. The relation can also be a node other than NEXT, which allows conditional branching from state to state. The program counter of a traditional computer causes the movement from instruction to instruction in a traditional computer. The human brain does not need a program counter, it just moves from state node to state node. A program counter and the associated address decoder would be too complex for nature to evolve.

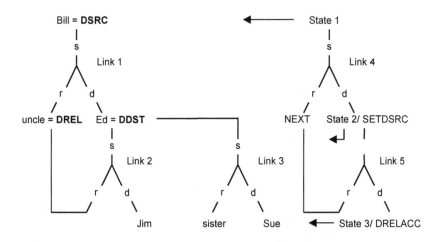

Figure 8: The states of the control section of the brain control the data section of the brain

In Figure 8, the PSRC register is initially set to "STATE1". The PSRC register automatically moves to "STATE2", which causes the "set data source" (SETDSRC) instruction to activate. This sets the DSRC register to the value "Bill". When this is complete, the PSRC register moves to "STATE3", which causes the "data relation access" (DRELACC) instruction to activate, and attention moves to "Ed". Subsequent states could set "Ed" as the data source, allowing subsequent states to access information related to "Ed".

The control section procedures (sequences of states) can be accessed as data. In this case, the same node is used as a node in the data section and a state in the control section. This allows recalling a procedure as data and then executing it. The control section automatically learns a step (state) in a new procedure every time it executes an instruction or existing procedure from the HOLD register. For example, we can learn how to add two numbers for the first time. First we recall from the data section the idea "get operand 1", which loads "get operand1" to the HOLD register. Then the control section activates the EXECUTE instruction. This executes the procedure "get operand 1", which performs the sequence of steps to get the first operand, when adding two numbers. The EXECUTE instruction executes the procedure or instruction in the HOLD register. A new step is automatically learned in a new procedure, at the same time. We then execute the procedure to "get operand2", then we execute the procedure to access the data section and find the sum. As we do this, we learn the new procedure "add", and later we can just execute this new procedure to do all the steps we have just learned, without thinking about the individual steps, such as "get operand 1". This new procedure looks like a sequence of calls to the procedures (subroutines) or instructions that were executed. At each EXECUTE, a new state is created in a new procedure that is being learned, and it is linked with the relation NEXT to the previous new state. The control section has a second set of registers to keep track of the new states being learned: the "procedure learn source register" (PLSRC), the "procedure learn relation register" (PLREL), and the "procedure learn destination register" (PLDST). In this way we learn the new procedure "add", as we do it the first time. We can then use this new procedure "add" to form even more complex procedures, such as when we learn how to add a column of numbers. In this way, the control section automatically learns more and more complex procedures to handle the complexity of the environment. The "create new control state node" (CRCTL) instruction is used to start learning a new procedure, and creates a node that is a starting state in the control section and an idea of the new procedure in the data section. Successful procedures are reused. Those that are not successful are forgotten because of lack of use, resulting in a type of natural selection [1] for the control section.

A relation between states, other than NEXT, can be loaded by using the PLREL register. This allows branch conditions to be added between states. For example, to branch from state-x to state-y when the idea "tomato" occurs, and activate the SETDSRC instruction, the PLSRC register is set to state-x, the PLREL is set to "tomato", the PLDST register is set to state-y, and the PLOUT register is set to SETDSRC. To learn this branch condition, the PLEARN instruction is activated by the control section. In this way the control section has both automatic and manual learning.

The control section can output constants. To answer a question, the control section can output the constants "subject", "verb", etc, to learn or recall the various words in a sentence. Constants are indicated in square brackets. These constants are learned with the "constant learn" (CLEARN) instruction, which learns a new state with the idea in the HOLD register as the state output, which is a constant. All modern computer architectures allow constants in the instruction stream (sometimes referred to as literals).

When a procedure ends (no next state), return is automatic. There is no return instruction required. The control section does not have a subroutine return stack, but it is able to call and return from subroutines like a traditional computer. Like an adder or program counter, a subroutine return stack would be too complex for nature to evolve. When the output of a state is not an instruction and not a constant, the control section performs a subroutine call. Once the subroutine is completed, the control section accesses the return state by selecting the most recent calling state, then moving to the next state. Once found, this calling state is blocked until it is again used to call a subroutine, and if there is another return, return is to the next most recent calling state. In this way, nested subroutines are performed without a subroutine return stack. The mechanism for this is similar to the way we move from tomato, to apple, to strawberry in the data section, selecting the most recent and blocking those that have been found. We "recognize" the return state in the control section like we recognize objects in the data section. A minor limitation is that a particular calling state cannot be used for multiple nested returns.

The control section of a traditional computer can be interrupted. For example, when a peripheral device needs servicing, it will produce an interrupt, and the traditional computer will proceed to service the interrupt. In a similar way, the control section of the brain can be interrupted with a loud sound or flash of light, and we proceed to think about the interrupt. In both a traditional computer and the brain, the interrupt priority level can be set and low level interrupts ignored.

The links from Figure 8 are listed in tabular form in Table 2. Data links are link type 1, control links are link type 2.

```
Link Type  Source    relation  destination  instruction output
---------  ------    --------  -----------  ------------------
    1      Bill      uncle     Ed                              ;
    1      Ed        uncle     Jim                             ;
    1      Ed        sister    Sue                             ;
    2      state1    next      state2       SETDSRC            ;
    2      state2    next      state3       DRELACC            ;
```

Table 2: Data and control links

The control section learns what instructions it is capable of performing with the SPASM operation. This randomly executes instructions infrequently, and procedures are initially learned in this way. Useful procedures are kept as a result of being reused and are not forgotten. The emotion section, described in section 1.10, selects useful procedures. It is likely that the control section of

17

the brain has some built in procedures that it uses to initially help get started.

It is important to note that the data section of the brain and the control section of the brain are copies of the same basic structure. Each is an array of links. Nature makes copies of successful structures [1]. It is likely that nature started with a control section made of one or a few source/relation/destination links. When these were successful, more copies of links were made, and the millions of links in the human brain evolved. The data section was likely a copy of the control section, because a control section can function without a data section. Also, it is likely the there was initially a single set of registers, and nature copied them to make the two sets of registers in both the data section and the control section.

1.5 Parsing Sentences

When the sentence "Ed's uncle is Jim" is input, the control section first creates a new node with the "create new data node" (CRDAT) instruction, and sets it to DSRC to store the sentence. Although this is just a new node number, in Table 3 it is listed as "sentence1", for ease of explanation. The control section inputs each word, and based on the word type (noun, verb, preposition, etc.) determines the sentence part.

As the sentence is input, either by reading or listening, the links that store the sentence are learned with the DLEARN instruction, as shown in Table 3.

```
Link Type  Source      relation   destination
---------  ------      --------   -----------
    1      sentence1   subject    Ed               ;
    1      sentence1   relation   uncle            ;
    1      sentence1   verb       is               ;
    1      sentence1   object     Jim              ;
```

Table 3: Sentence links

Once the sentence has been parsed, the control section then proceeds to learn the fact that the sentence is describing. DSRC is set to "sentence1". The control section sets DREL to "subject", then outputs the DRELACC instruction, which accesses "Ed". The control section outputs the "SETTMPSRC" instruction, which sets TMPSRC to "Ed", then sets DREL to "relation" and accesses "uncle" and sets TMPREL to "uncle" with SETTMPREL, then sets DREL to "object" and accesses "Jim", and sets TMPDST to "Jim". Then the control section activates the DLEARN instruction, which creates the new link: Ed/uncle/Jim. In this way a new fact is learned, which can be recalled later when asked "Who is Ed's uncle?". Note that two sets of registers are required, one set to access the sentence and one set to learn the new fact. The DLEARN instruction uses whichever of the two sets of registers has been most recently loaded for learning. The CRDAT instruction is frequently used, such as whenever we encounter a new object and want to link to it, whenever we hear a new sentence, and whenever there is a new event in a story. Sentences describing a sequence of events can be linked with the relation "next_event" as follows: source=sentence3, relation="next_event", and destination=sentence4. In this way, semantic and episodic information is stored in the same data structure.

```
Link  Source     relation   destination  instruction output
Type
-----  ------     --------   -----------  -------------------
  1    Bill       word       (Bill)                    ;
  1    Bill       wordtype   noun                      ;
  2    parse1     next       parse2       CRDAT         ; new sentence
  2    parse2     next       parse3       SETDSRC       ;
  2    parse3     next       parse4       EXTINP        ; input word
  2    parse4     next       parse5       SETTMPDST     ; word -> TMPDST
  2    parse5     next       parse6       [word]        ; constant [word]
  2    parse6     next       parse7       SETTMPREL     ; TMPREL = [word]
  2    parse7     next       parse8       SUMATR        ; sum attribute
  2    parse8     next       parse9       SELMAX        ; recognize input
  2    parse9     next       parse10      SETDDST       ;
  2    parse10    next       parse11      [wordtype]    ;
  2    parse11    next       parse12      SETTMPREL     ;
  2    parse12    next       parse13      TRELACC       ; access wordtype
  2    parse13    noun       parse14      [subject]     ; branch noun
  2    parse13    verb       parse15      [verb]        ; branch verb
  2    parse13    adjective  parse16      [adjective]   ; branch adj
  2    parse14    next       parse17      SETDREL       ; learn subject
  2    parse17    next       parse18      DLEARN        ;
```

Table 4: Control sequence for learning the subject of a sentence

Part of the control section sequence of states to input a sentence is listed in Table 4. This sequence shows how a word, such as "Bill", is input, how it is determined if it is the subject of a sentence, and how it is learned in the data section. For homonyms, such as run-verb (as in "run" home) and run-noun (as in home "run"), there is a separate data node for each idea.

1.6 Instantiation

When we learn about a specific tomato, we do not have to link all the facts about a tomato to the specific tomato. We just link "is a" tomato, abbreviated "isa". For example, we may observe a specific tomato that is yellow. We would create a new data node for the new tomato. Here it is named tomato1 but tomato1 is just the name of the idea for the specific tomato. Any new name could be used. This is referred to as instantiation. An instance of a general concept is created. If we are asked about tomato1, the control section first looks for the answer at the level of tomato1, and then it moves to tomato using the "isa" link to see if the answer is at that level. These procedures we learned at an early age.

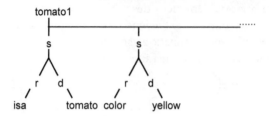

Figure 9: Creating an instance of a general idea

Another example of instantiation is how we learn about people. We learn that people move, see, talk, breathe, etc. Each time we learn about a new person, we do not have to learn all of these facts. We just link isa/person and when asked questions about a specific person, the control section knows to first check for an answer with the specific person set as the data source; then using the "isa" link, moves to the general person node to look for an answer at that level. For example, if we are asked "Does Bill breathe?" we first check at the Bill level and do not find an answer, then we use the "isa" link to move to the person level (person is set as the data source) and we find the answer and can say "yes, because people breathe".

1.7 Input and Output

The thinking computer input/output paths receive and send data to the outside world, as with a traditional computer. The human brain receives input data from the eyes, ears, and other senses and sends output data to move muscles.

We input visual information which allows us to recognize objects. An object is recognized visually by taking the pieces of the image and using the same recognition mechanism described in section 1.2. For example, we may have looked at a picture with a cloud at the top left, the sun and the top right, a house at the bottom left, and a house at the bottom right. This picture would be stored as shown in Table 5.

```
Link Type Source      relation       destination
--------- ------      --------       -----------
    1     picture1    top-left       cloud          ;
    1     picture1    top-right      sun            ;
    1     picture1    bottom-left    house          ;
    1     picture1    bottom-right   tree           ;
```

Table 5: Visual links

If we are asked to recall a picture with a house at the bottom left, and a tree at the bottom right, we actually first recognize it using the recognition mechanism described in section 1.2, as if we are looking at a picture and recognizing it. Once we have found the picture, we can recall the rest of it (cloud at the top left) using the recall mechanism described in section 1.1. We can recall a picture with a house and a tree without knowing the relation by using a wild card relation, which is described in chapter 2.

We may notice that the house is a specific house, Bill's house, which is green. We would use the links in Table 6. As we recognize an object in more detail, first a house, then Bill's house, we form the additional links. The data is stored in a hierarchical fashion. Stories are stored in the same way.

Link Type	Source	relation	destination	
1	picture1	bottom-left	Bill's_house	;
1	Bill's_house	color	green	;
1	Bill's_house	owner	Bill	;

Table 6: Visual links linking Bill's house to the picture

The image primitive section of the brain generates simple pieces of a picture and these are used to recognize images in more and more detail. First a simple shape, such as a left curve or circle is recognized, and this is then used to recognize an object. This is described in more detail in section 6.6.

The sound section works in a similar way, using links to store the sequence of sounds (phonemes) that make up words, as described in chapters 6 and 7.

It is important to note that any two nodes of a cognitive data link can access the third. For example, we can access the bottom-left of picture1 by setting DSRC=picture1, DREL=bottom-left and doing the instruction DRELACC to find Bill's_house. We can access the picture1 by setting DREL=bottom-left and DDST=Bill's_house and doing the instructions SUMATR and SELMAX and picture1 will activate (or other Source nodes that match). If we want to find where Bill's_house is located in picture1 we set DSRC=picture1, DDST=Bill's_house and do the instruction DDSTACC to find bottom-left.

1.8 The Basic Instruction Set of the Human Brain

The basic instruction set of the human brain is shown in Table 6. The instruction set of the human brain is very simple, with instructions for loading registers, learning, recall, recognition, and control. This basic instruction set does not include instructions that control the peripheral sections (sound input, speech output). These peripheral instructions are described in chapters

6 and 7 of this book and the complete instruction set of the brain is listed at the end of chapter 3.

Data section instructions:

```
SETDSRC: HOLD -> DSRC          SRCTOHLD: DSRC -> HOLD
SETDREL: HOLD -> DREL          RELTOHLD: DREL -> HOLD
SETDDST: HOLD -> DDST          DSTTOHLD: DDST -> HOLD
SETTMPSRC: HOLD -> TMPSRC      TSRCTOHLD: TMPSRC -> HOLD
SETTMPREL: HOLD -> TMPREL      TRELTOHLD: TMPREL -> HOLD
SETTMPDST: HOLD -> TMPDST      TDSTTOHLD: TMPDST -> HOLD
```

DRELACC: access the array of data links and look for a match to the DSRC and DREL registers. If a match is found, activate the idea "find" for branching, and load the destination of the link to the DDST register and to the HOLD register

TRELACC: same as DRELACC but uses the temporary data registers

DDSTACC: same as DRELACC but uses DSRC and DDST and finds DREL

TDSTACC: same as DDSTACC but uses the temporary data registers

DLEARN: learn a new link in the data section using the current or temporary registers, whichever was loaded last

DLEARNML: learn multiple links with the same source and relation.

CRDAT: create a new data node

CLRSUM: clear the sum associated with each data node

SUMATR: increment the sum of source nodes that have a link that match the DREL and DDST registers

SELMAX: select the maximum sum (Note that with SUMATR/SELMAX, DRELACC, and DDSTACC, any two nodes of a link can find the third node)

Control section instructions:

CRCTL: create a new control state node   CLEARN: learn a constant

EXECUTE: execute the procedure in the HOLD register and learn a new state using the procedure learn registers

```
SETPLSRC: HOLD -> PLSRC                  SETPLDST: HOLD -> PLDST
SETPLREL: HOLD -> PLREL to add a branch condition between states
SETPLOUT: HOLD -> PLOUT
```

PLEARN: procedure learn, learn a new control link using the procedure learn registers

I/O instructions: described in chapters 6 and 7

Table 6: The basic instruction set of the human brain

1.9 Unification of the Data Section Structure and the Control Section Structure of a Traditional Computer

As has been described, the data and control sections of the brain are copies of the same structure: each is a large array of cognitive links. The data and control sections of a traditional computer may look like completely different structures, but they are also fundamentally the same. This is important to computer architects. We normally think of the data section of a traditional computer as being made of data units (adders, logical units, and multipliers), registers, and data stored in memory. We think of the control section as being made of a microcode memory, a microsequencer, a subroutine return stack, and a program stored in memory. The data section of a traditional computer is fundamentally a structure to access the source, relation, and destination between operands/operations, which are fundamentally data nodes. The control section of a traditional computer is fundamentally a source, relation, destination structure between lines of instructions, which are fundamentally state nodes. For example, an adder in the data section of a traditional computer that adds 2 + 3 = 5, can be viewed as a source, relation, destination structure with the source = 2+, the relation = 3, and the destination = 5. We learned these single digit relations when we learned math tables in elementary school (all the 2+ answers, all the 3+ answers, all the 2x answers, all the 3x answers, and so on). A sequence of instructions in a traditional computer, such as instruction 1, branch if negative, instruction 2, can be viewed as a source relation, destination structure with the source = instruction 1, the relation = negative, and the destination = instruction 2. The relation between data nodes in the data section is equivalent to the branch condition between states in the control section.

1.10 The Emotion Section

The block diagram of the computer architecture of the human brain is shown in Figure 10. It is the same as that of a traditional computer, with the addition of the emotion section [4]. The data and control sections of the brain determine how we think. The emotion section of the brain determines why we think about the things that we do. Computer programs run with no reason why. The emotion section receives external pain and pleasure information and links it to the data and control sections, where it can be recalled to help determine what procedures to do, and to activate important data. The emotion section prevents us from touching a hot stove, and helps us select useful things to do.

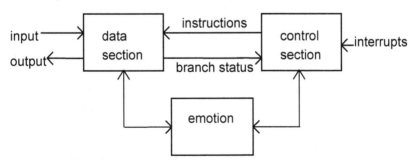

Figure 10: Block diagram of the computer architecture of the human brain

1.11   Implementation of the Computer Architecture of the Human Brain Using a Traditional Computer

To implement the computer architecture of the human brain, a custom hardware implementation would provide the best performance; a massively parallel implementation [6, 7] would provide very good performance; but a traditional computer can provide good performance at low cost. Using a traditional computer, a unique number is assigned to each unique node. The millions of cognitive links can then be stored in an array in the computer's memory. Each data link's array entry in the computer's memory therefore has three node numbers associated with it: the source node, the relation node, and the destination node. Each control link's entry has four numbers, the source state node, relation state node, destination state node, and the output (instruction, constant, or subroutine call). There is a computer register (or memory location) associated with each register that has been described: DSRC, DREL, DDST, HOLD, and so on. A program can then be run on the traditional computer that loops through a sequence of traditional computer instructions that performs the instruction output from the cognitive control section, each time it moves to a new instruction. For example, if the instruction is SETDSRC, then the traditional computer register (or memory location) storing DSRC is loaded with the value in the traditional computer register (or memory location) storing HOLD. The DRELACC instruction searches the array of links for a match to DSRC and DREL, and loads the result to DDST and HOLD. Various techniques to improve the performance of searches have been described [11]. The HOLD register is very similar to the ACCUMULATOR of early computers in that results of operations were stored in the ACCUMULATOR.

Each data node has an associated sum that is stored in an array in memory. When the CLRSUM instruction is performed, all of these sums are set to 0. When the SUMATR instruction is performed, any source node that has a link that matches the TMPREL and TMPDST registers has its sum incremented. At SELMAX, the node with the maximum count is loaded to the HOLD register. It there is a tie, the node with the most recency and frequency is selected. Recency and frequency are stored in memory arrays.

The emotion section is implemented by storing externally input pleasure levels, associated with each node, in an array in memory. When looking for things to do, these good data nodes and procedures are automatically activated.

New data nodes and new control nodes are constantly being created. For example, every time a new sentence is input, a new data node is created for that sentence. Every time a procedure is executed, a new state node is created

24

to record that step. Eventually, memory is full. Forgetting (freeing up memory) is based on frequency and recency of use. The least recently used node with the least frequent use is selected for forgetting. Forgetting is described in detail in chapter 5 of this book.

1.12 The Mechanism of Consciousness

The automatic movement of the control section state node to state node, controlling the data section movement of attention from data node to data node (idea to idea), along with biasing from the emotion section, produces conscious thought. Intelligence is having and using many useful cognitive data and control links.

1.13 Results

A program [5] that implements all of the described computer architecture and instruction set of the human brain has been written for a traditional computer. The program is written in the computer language C and the executable file runs on a PC (Windows). An operational engram file [5] containing over 10K control and data links, storing knowledge we use on a daily basis, has been written and run using the program. The program and engram are able to read and correctly answer questions related to a wide range of general knowledge, learn new procedures, and learn new facts. The program and engram are also able to read simple children's stories, and answer questions related to the stories. Table 7 is a sample of actual input and output. The short story is from a children's book named "The Little Farm" by Lois Lenski [12]. Only part of the full interaction is shown. The experiments described in chapter 11 describe how the reader may run the full story. Performance is good, with answers to questions requiring approximately the same time a person would require to answer.

```
I: Farmer Small lives on a farm .
I: He gets up early in the morning .
I: He goes to the barn to feed the animals .
I: They are all very hungry .
I: When does Farmer Small get up ?
O: early
I: Where does he go ?
O: to barn
I: What does Farmer Small feed ?
O: animals
I: Why does Farmer Small go to the barn ?
O: feed animals
I: He milks the cows .
I: What does Farmer Small milk ?
O: cows
I: He strains the milk into the milk cans .
I: Where does he strain the milk ?
```

```
O: milk cans
I: He sets them in the cooler .
I: What does he set ?
O: milk cans
I: Where does he set the milk cans ?
O: cooler
```

Table 7: Sample of actual input(I) and output(O) of the operational engram file and program

The executable program described above was written in C because of its high performance. Most computer aided design tools are written in C (or some version of C) for this reason. Another potential language is Prolog. This language has some features that would make programming easier. For example, there is a fact statement with the following format "predicate (argument1, argument2, argument3 ...)". An example is "age(Bill, 40)". This allows checking the fact "Bill's age is 40" or accessing Bill's age or "Whose age is 42" Unfortunately, if asked "What is the relationship between Bill and 42, the relation "age" cannot be accessed because there is not a command to do this (like the DDSTACC instruction). The arguments beyond argument2 do not make sense for a relationship between two ideas. Prolog is a declarative language (no steps), while a procedural language, like C, is a better implementation choice because the control section is inherently procedural. Prolog runs much slower than C. Please note that Prolog is a computer language", not a computer architecture, as is being described in this book

1.14 Overview summary

The computer architecture for the human brain has been described. The architecture is similar to that of a traditional computer in that it has a data section and a control section. The two sections have been shown to be based on a simple cognitive link structure that connects a source node, a relation node, and a destination node. The data section of the brain has been described including mechanisms to recall, recognize, and learn. The data section has been shown to store factual information using a specific structure of links connecting data nodes (ideas). The instruction set of the brain has been described. The automatic learning of sequences of these instructions by the control section has been described. These new sequences of instructions can be used in even newer sequences, resulting in more and more complex procedures being learned automatically over time. These control sequences result in automatic learning in the data section. Significantly, the data and control sections of the brain have been shown to be copies of the same structure, and the data and control sections of a traditional computer can be viewed the same way. Until now, the data section and the control section of a traditional computer have been viewed as two completely different structures.

Besides the data and control sections, a new section, the emotion section, has been described, which helps the data and control sections decide what to do. The emotion section biases cognitive links. The mechanism for attention and consciousness has been described. Speech and vision mechanisms have been introduced. It has been shown how the architecture of the human brain may be implemented using traditional computers and using more advanced hardware.

The preceding discussion has been an overview of the major sections of a thinking computer. In the following pages of this book, these sections will be described in detail. Chapter 2 describes the data section in detail including how we recall, recognize, and learn in the data section. Chapter 3 describes the control section in detail including all the instructions the control section can output to control the data section along with actions that control input and output. This list is the instruction set of the brain. Chapter 3 also describes control section output of constants and control section learning. Chapter 4 describes the emotion section. Forgetting is described in Chapter 5. Chapter 6 and 7 describe sensory input and output functions.

2   Detailed Description of the Data Section

The chapter provides a detailed description of the data section of a thinking computer. As described in the overview, the basic structure used in the data section is shown in figure 11. Each data source node is the source node of one or more links. The relation node and a destination node of each link form an attribute of the source node. For example the source node "apple" would have an attribute with the relation node "color" and destination node "red". It will be shown how this structure can be used for recall, recognition, and learning.

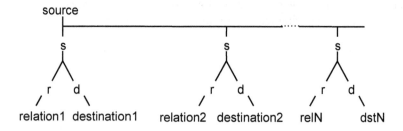

Figure 11: Basic structure of the human brain data section

A specific example of the use of the data section is shown in figure 12.

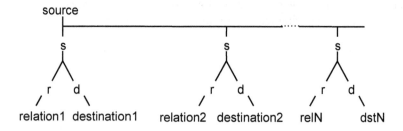

Figure 12: Data section example

The data section contains millions of these links, storing all the factual information that we know. As previously discussed, the data section also contains a few registers. We recall, recognize, and learn data links using these registers. The first register is the HOLD register, which contains what we currently are holding attention on. There is a group of three other registers - the current data source register (DSRC), the current data relation register (DREL), and the current data destination register (DDST), that we use for data link recall, recognition, and learning. To recall an item from the data links, we first put attention on something by loading it to the HOLD register. This attention item can be externally input, such as when we are looking at an object, or it can be accessed from a previous data recall. Once we have attention on something, we can load it from the HOLD register to the current data source register, the current data relation register, or the current data destination register.

- Recall in the data section

To recall the color of an apple, we first set the current data source register to "apple", then we set the current data relation register to "color", then we access the destination using the instruction "data relation access" (DRELACC). We move downward in Figure 12 during recall. This and all other instructions are activated by the control section, which will be described in detail in chapter 3. The DRELACC instruction uses the registers to access the millions of data links stored in the data section and puts the result in the HOLD register, which holds what we have attention on. Once we put attention on the answer, "red", we can then load it from the HOLD register to the current data source register, for example, to say the word "red" by accessing the destination with the data relation set to "word". All this loading of registers is controlled by the control section, as it controls all data section operation.

- Recognition in the data section

We may be asked the question: "What is red and tastes good?". We recognize "apple" as follows. First we do the instruction "clear sums" (CLRSUM is the abbreviation), which sets all the millions of sums associated with data nodes to zero. We set the current data relation register to "color", and the current data destination register to "red". Then we do the data instruction "sum attribute" (SUMATR). The apple node sum and any other red object (such as a fire truck) sum will have a value of 1. Then we set the data relation register to "taste" and the data destination register to "good" and do another sum attribute. "Apple" will now have a sum of 2. We then perform the instruction "select maximum sum" (SELMAX) and "apple" can be selected for attention and be loaded to the HOLD register. From the

HOLD register, it can then be used to load to another data register if desired. If there is a tie, such as with "tomato", then we pick the strongest source node based on recency and frequency of use of the data node. Later, with each SELMAX we select the next node with the same sum if there is one and if not we move to finding nodes with the next lower value and so on until there are no more nodes with a sum greater than 0. As each node is found, it is blocked with a large negative sum so it is not found again. This allows us, for example, to access "apple", then, if we decide that is not the object we are looking for, we can step to "tomato", and on to other red objects (strawberry...) that taste good. The first SELMAX requires the sum to be equal to the number of SUMATR instructions so we do not find objects at first that do not match all the attributes. Each subsequent SELMAX allows objects with lower sums to be found. For example, we can find "fire truck" using subsequent SELMAX instructions even though "fire truck" only matches one attribute (color/red). During recognition we move upward in Figure 12.

- The current and temporary registers

We actually have two versions of each of the three data registers described above. Instead of just a current data source register (DSRC), we also have a temporary data source register (TMPSRC). Likewise, we have a current data relation register (DREL) and a temporary data relation register (TMPREL). The same with the destination registers (DDST, TMPDST). When we are asked "What is the color of an apple?", it has been shown how we load the DSRC register with "apple", the DREL register with "color" and access the answer. Where does the idea "apple" come from to load the DSRC register? As we hear the sentence, "What is the color of an apple?", we parse the sentence and store it as shown below. The sentence structure of links is shown below. For ease of reading, a tabular format is used below instead of the stick drawing above, but the structure is the same. The 1 at the beginning of the line indicates it is a data type link; later control, sound, and constant types will be described (link types 2-4).

```
  source      relation    destination
  ------      --------    -----------
1 story1      subject     apple          ;
1 story1      adjective   color          ;
1 story1      verb        is             ;
```

To answer the question, we need two source registers at the same time, one to recall the sentence (TMPSRC), the other to find the answer (DSRC). First we set TMPSRC to "story1", which is a source node we created when we input the sentence, then we set TMPREL to "subject" and so the instruction "DRELACC", which accesses "apple". We set "apple" to DSRC so we can work on accessing the answer. Next we set TMPREL to "adjective" and access "color" with DRELACC. We set "color" to DREL. Then we access the answer "red". In this way we use two sets of data registers to answer a question.

The control section knows how to answer the question by setting "story1" as the temporary data source register (TMPSRC) by using the instruction SETTMPSRC, then setting "subject" to TMPREL and finding "apple" by using the instruction "temporary data relation access" or TRELACC. The result, if found (apple), is stored in the HOLD register. The control procedure receives the branch status "find" and then moves the HOLD register to the current data source register (SETDSRC), then sets "adjective" to TMPREL and accesses "color" using TRELACC and sets it as the current data relation register (SETDREL). Finally, the answer "red" is accessed with the current data registers by using the instruction "data relation access" (DRELACC). In this example, the use of the current and temporary registers is interchangeable. The control section produces the "subject" and "adjective" ideas as constants, which will be described later in the control section discussion (chapter 3). The control section learned this procedure and other procedures through trial and error and later through manual learning, once we learned how to learn procedures. Successful procedures are reused, the result of a control section natural selection [1]. Control procedures that work we reuse; those that do not are forgotten because of lack of use.

In the tabular format above, there is a separate attribute pair stored for each use of an attribute. For example, the attribute pair color/red is not used for each object that is color/red; a new attribute is stored for each one. This speeds recognition because there is no need to search for and find an attribute pair during recognition. It should be noted that storing attributes instead of relation and destination could be used to save memory space in an implementation, but for now there will be a separate attribute stored for each use of an attribute.

To load the HOLD register to the various data registers, we use the following instructions:

set current data source register (SETDSRC)
set current data relation register (SETDREL)
set current data destination register (SETDDST)
set temporary data source register (SETTMPSRC)
set temporary data relation register (SETTMPREL)
set temporary data destination register (SETTMPDST)

To load the various data registers to the HOLD register, we use the following instructions:

current data source register -> HOLD register (SRCTOHLD)
current data relation register -> HOLD register (RELTOHLD)
current data destination register -> HOLD register (DSTTOHLD)
temporary data source register -> HOLD register (TSRCTOHLD)
temporary data relation register -> HOLD register (TRELTOHLD)
temporary data destination register -> HOLD register (TDSTTOHLD)

The instruction DSRCTSRC loads the current data source register to the temporary data source register.

Another example of the use of the current and temporary data registers follows:

Assume that we have four groups of data; each group is a data source node.

```
group1          group2          group3          group4
 976             824             396             585
```

All groups are stored in the data section, where we can randomly access the first, second, and third elements of each group as follows:

```
  source      relation   destination
  ------      --------   -----------
1 group1      first      9              ;
1 group1      second     7              ;
1 group1      third      6              ;
1 group2      first      8              ;
.
.
```

To add the second element of group 3 to the third element of group 4, the following sequence of data section operations is used. First, the temporary data source register is set to "group 3" and the temporary data relation register is set to "second". Next, the instruction TRELACC is used to access the second element 9, which is then saved in the current data source register. Then "+" is loaded to the current data relation register and the current data registers are used with the instruction DRELACC to recall 9+, which is then set as the new current data source register value. Then "group 4" is loaded to the temporary data source register and "third" is loaded to the temporary data relation register and the temporary registers are used to recall "5". The "5" is then loaded to the current data relation register and the instruction

DRELACC accesses the answer "14". All of this is done in the data section and is controlled by the control section.

- Data section learning

Data section learning is done manually. There is no automatic data section learning because the control section must determine when it is appropriate for the data section to learn. The control section has automatic learning, which helps learn complex procedures. Manual learning is when we decide to learn something, such as apple/color/red (this is an abbreviation for source/relation/destination of a data link).

We manually learn in the data section by using the instruction "data learn" (DLEARN), which takes whatever has been set in the data registers and uses it to create a new link in the array of data links. The most recently loaded of the current or temporary data registers is used. Only the temporary data registers are used for recognition. We can recall with both the current and temporary data registers.

We manually create a new data node with the instruction "create new data node" (CRDAT), which places the new data node into the HOLD register where it can then be loaded to other registers. We use this instruction, for example, when we encounter a new object and want to link attributes to it, or when we need to create a new event in a story. Each time we hear a new sentence we create a new data node for the new sentence.

If we try to learn a data link where the data source register matches an existing data source, and the data relation register matches an existing data relation, and the data destination is different from the existing data relation, then we overwrite the existing data link. For example, if we have stored in our memory the data link:

```
  source      relation   destination
  ------      --------   -----------
1 apple       color      orange              ;
```

We may want to correct the above link:

```
  source      relation   destination
  ------      --------   -----------
1 apple       color      red                 ;
```

We overwrite the existing data link with the new information. This is useful in situations where facts keep changing. For example, a car race where the car in first place keeps changing. Initially it may be:

```
  source     relation  destination
  ------     --------  -----------
1 story4     frstplace red_car                    ;
```

Later it may change to:

```
  source     relation  destination
  ------     --------  -----------
1 story4     frstplace blue_car                   ;
```

At any point in time, we will access the correct answer when we access which car is in first place. To recall the order of the different cars in first place, we recall events stored in the data section.

During recognition, we store the attributes we are using for recognition. Later we can learn all of the stored attributes with a single instruction. For example, if we are looking to recognize what is color/red and sound/siren, we will recognize a fire truck. But if we input different attributes and we do not recognize anything, then we may want to create a new data source node and link it to all of the attributes we have just input. We can perform this with the instruction "learn attributes" (LRNATRS). Instead of using LRNATRS, we may perform the instruction "DLEARN" after each SUMATR. If we do recognize the object, the attributes we have learned will be soon forgotten because we will not be recalling those attributes once the object is recognized.

- Instantiation

The "apple" link to "fruit" in the "apple" example above is an example of instantiation. This data link is the same as other data links, but the control section knows to use "is a" (abbreviated "isa") relations to move up and down the data links to access attributes. We do not want to store all we know about fruits with the apple node. We just link rel=isa/dst=fruit and the control section knows when accessing relations to move up the hierarchy of "isa" relations to access information. (In the following discussion when we refer to an attribute the first item is the relation, followed by a "/", and the second item is the destination.) We may have a specific apple and we do not want to store color/red with the source node of each specific apple we know. We solve this problem by just linking "isa/apple" to every specific apple, and if we are asked what is the color of a specific apple we can answer "probably red". We know to answer "probably" because the control section knows it had to move up the data links to answer the question.

- Storage of sentences and event sequences

The data links can store sentences. For example, the sentence "the man went to the movies" is stored as follows:

```
  source      relation   destination
  ------      --------   -----------
1 event2      subject    man              ;
1 event2      verb       went             ;
1 event2      object     movies           ;
```

We can recall or recognize the sentence using the same techniques we used for the "apple" example above. Groups of sentence information form stories. Whenever we learn a new piece of a story, we create a new source node - in this case with a default name event2. We link event2 with the rest of the story events using data links. For example, if we first stored "the man went to the movies", then we stored "he then went to the store", we would create an event3 node to store the second sentence and link it to the first event with nxt-evnt. In this way, semantic and episodic information is stored in the same structure.

```
  source      relation   destination
  ------      --------   -----------
1 event2      nxt-evnt   event3           ;
```

- Storage of words

We link the sound of words to the idea associated with a word. This way, when speaking, we can recall a word associated with an idea and when we hear a word we can find the idea associated with it. For example:

```
1 dog-idea    word       (dog)                        ;
```

In the above, (dog) represents the sound dog. Homonyms, such as to/too/two, are stored as follows:

```
1 to-pr-idea     word       (to/too/two)      ;
1 to-pr-idea     wordtype   prepositn         ;
1 two-adj-idea   word       (to/too/two)      ;
1 two-adj-idea   wordtype   adjective         ;
1 too-adv-idea   word       (to/too/two)      ;
1 too-adv-idea   wordtype   adverb            ;
```

When we hear the word to/too/two (all pronounced the same), we determine which one it is by the type of word we are expecting, and we use

SUMATR/SELMAX to sum the sound and the wordtype to recognize the correct idea.

The word "to" can also be used as an adverb and the word "two" can also be used as a noun, therefore the following links also exist:

```
1 to-adv-idea    word       (to/too/two)        ;
1 to-adv-idea    wordtype   adverb              ;
1 two-noun-idea  word       (to/too/two)        ;
1 two-noun-idea  wordtype   noun                ;
```

We use other sentence information to distinguish between to-adv and too-adv. Since we work with ideas more than words, the -idea suffix is eliminated in the engram listings and is implied. Items in parenthesis indicate sounds.

- Data section block diagram

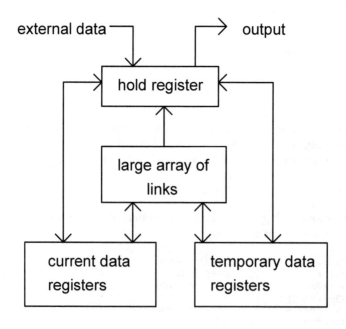

Figure 13: Data section block diagram (the data paths)

Figure 13 is a block diagram of the data section and summarizes the register and data link array connections. The current and temporary data registers access links in the large array of data links. The result is output to the HOLD register during recall and recognition. The result is also output to the temporary data source register during recognition. The HOLD register can be written to the data registers and the data registers can be written to the HOLD register. Input and output is through the HOLD register. The current data registers can write (learn) a new link in the array of links.

- Relations

We can store family relations as shown in figure 14, but this structure does not allow direct access of the family structure. The way it is more typically stored is shown in figure 15.

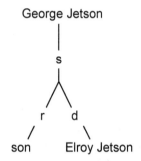

Figure 14: Family relation data structure

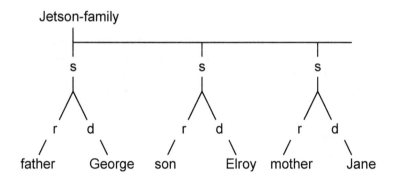

Figure 15: Family relation data structure improved

In this way, all the relations can be accessed, and any single person can be used to activate the family data source node.

We can recall the relation given the source and destination. In the above example, if we wanted to recall what position in the Jetson family is Elroy, we would set a data source register (either current data source or temporary data source) to Jetson-family and set the destination to Elroy and do the instruction "current data destination access" (DDSTACC) or "temporary data destination access" (TDSTACC) depending on which registers we were using. In normal use, the data relation access operations are used much more frequently than the data destination access operations.

Therefore, given any two out of three registers, we can use them to access the large array of links to find the third. Given a source and a relation, we can access the destination by using DRELACC or TRELACC. Given a source and a destination, we can access the relation by using DDSTACC and TDSTACC. Given a relation and a destination, we can access the source by using SUMATR and SELMAX.

- Other data operations

There are times when we want to block certain ideas from being selected by SELMAX. For example, we may be asked to name all trees except pine and oak trees. In this case, we set the temporary data relation register to "isa" and the temporary data destination register to "tree", and then we do SUMATR. We can then put attention on pine, and before we do the instruction SELMAX we can perform the instruction BLOCKSUM, then we can put attention on oak and do the instruction BLOCKSUM. This sets a large negative number in the sum for pine and oak, so at SELMAX a tree type other than pine or oak will be selected. As described earlier, each subsequent SELMAX allows us to step through different tree types. This is done in a way similar to BLOCKSUM where the sum associated with the node we put attention on as a result of a SELMAX is reduced in value so it is not found again unless a future SELMAX finds it as the next best sum.

Sometimes, we want to select the most recent results of a SUMATR operation. Other times, we may want to access items we have not accessed recently. For example, we may be asked to name trees we have not named recently. We can perform this by doing a SUMATR as above, and then doing the instruction SUBRCNT, which reduces the sum of data sources that have been recently activated.

Sometimes, we just want to select random results of a SUMATR operation. For example, we may want to name all colors in any random order. We use the instruction "select maximum sum randomly" (SELMAXR). In the case of naming trees, there are many sums with the same maximum value. The SELMAXR instruction will select from these randomly. The SELMAXR instruction is also used with the random instruction mechanism used to initially find useful sequences of instructions, which is described in the control section below.

If we are asked "what is not red and is a fruit?", we use the instruction "subtract attribute" (SUBATR). This instruction reduces the sum by 1 for any source that matches the attribute set in the temporary data relation register and temporary data destination register. This is used less frequently than the SUMATR instruction, but it is nevertheless needed. We first set color/red and do SUBATR, and then we set isa/fruit and do SUMATR, and then SELMAX to find an answer.

- Bi-directional nature of data section links

Each data type link is composed of three connections. These connections are bi-directional as shown in figure 16. They can be used for recall and recognition. As mentioned previously, any two can access the third.

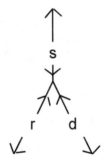

Figure 16: Bi-directional nature of data section links

We can recall and recognize with only a relation register set or with only a destination register set. The instruction "drop temporary registers" (DRPTMP) sets the temporary relation register and the temporary destination register to a wild card value that matches anything. We can then set the temporary relation or destination register to a value and then do SUMATR and SELMAX for recognition with a wild card, or TRELACC or TDSTACC for recall with a wild card. This is useful, for example, when we want to access the last time we recalled an apple, or the last time we accessed a specific relation.

An example of the use of DRPTMP is as follows:

The man went to the store. (subj/man, verb/went, obj/store)
The car is stopped.
The dog is running.

If we are asked "Where have you heard the word "store" recently?", we are able to answer by just setting a wild card relation, destination=store, and selecting a recently accessed data link using SUMATR and SELMAX. TMPSRC is loaded with the source node that we find. We can then recall subj/man and verb/went. Wild card values also work with DRELACC, TRELACC, DDSTACC, TDSTACC.

Note that a node can be the source node of many links that have different relations, but have the same destination. For example, if we are looking at a page (referred to as page_n) with letters on it and there is an x at the top left, a y at the bottom left, and an x at the bottom right, then we will store it as page_n/top-left/x, page_n/bot-left/y, page_n/bot-right/x. If asked to recall where is an x, then we set x as destination, relation=wild card, and do SUMATR/SELMAX. We first find the most recent case of an x as a destination (unless we do SUBRCNT or BLOCKSUM) because it is the strongest link. We can continue to do SELMAX to see if there are any more cases of x as a destination. Each time we need to check if we are still finding the x's on page_n. The idea "find" activates as we find each x.

- Data storage of sequential information

Normally, the data section stores non-sequentially ordered information (sequentially ordered information is typically stored in the sound data section, explained in section 7.1), but partially and fully ordered information can also be stored in the data section. When we visually recognize an object, there is no exact order that the information is input (we can start looking at any place on the object). When we recall an object visually, there is no order. When we recall a story, we can recall (or recognize) in any order. All of these types of information are stored in a form that allows any order. When we recognize words, there can be missing pieces and the phonemes are associated with their relative positions. In this case, the data section stores partially ordered information. The data section can also store fully ordered information. When we learn the letters to the alphabet we link each letter to the last one. For example, we have the links alphabet/A/B, alphabet/B/C, and so on. In this way we can start recalling at any point in the alphabet.

- Recognition of sequential data

When we receive input from our senses, we are able to recognize objects with only partial attributes of the object, such as recognition of a car that is partially obscured by a tree. We can also recognize words that are partial (OPULAR STRONOMY). The recognition based on partial information occurs even though the data is input in a serial fashion, as it is with words.

The data link structure allows recognition of strings of data. To recognize a piece of the word POPULAR, such as OPULAR, the attributes are stored as location/syllable pairs as shown in figure 17. The relation "start-word" is associated with the destination POP. The relation "location1" is associated with the destination U, and the relation "location2" is associated with the destination LAR. The control section keeps track of the location and sets the relation register. If just a few relative syllables are correct, it is enough to have the correct word have the highest sum. Other information, such as syntax or situation information, can also be summed. Words are stored as phoneme sequences to make recognition of speech possible. The sound data section is able to associate a phoneme with a location to allow it to be summed by the data section.

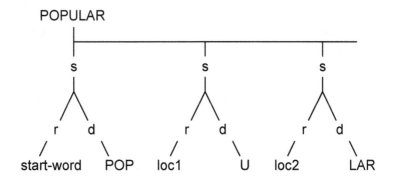

Figure 17: Recognition of strings of data

When we say words, we typically do not say them from the data section; we just activate the idea of the word and load it to the sound data section. We can say just a word, or a whole song, with just one idea activating it.

Although we could store the word "popular" as shown in figure 18, we would not be able to determine during recognition if just the first syllable were missing, or two syllables were missing. Therefore, it is important to have location information as the relation for word recognition. Note that the data section storage of information, with the items relative to each other as shown in figure 18, is useful for some types of data. For example, the sequence of numbers 1 2 3 4..., we can be given any number and access the next. We access src=number-sequence/rel=3/dst=4 to find the number after 3.

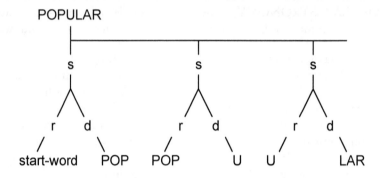

Figure 18: Less useful storage of a word

- Long sequences

Long sequences, such as the ABC's, are normally stored in the sound data section, described in section 7.1, but we can also store them in the data section using a relative structure for the information. For example, to store the ABC's, the structure shown in figure 19 would be used:

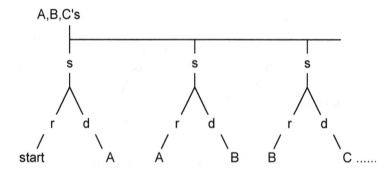

Figure 19: Storage of long strings

Note that we can recognize the A,B,C's from just a few pairs: if we are input C/D, J/K, X/Y we can easily recognize the A,B,C's. This is accomplished by the summing capability of the data section described above. We can store 1 2 3 4 ... the same way. This relative structure storage technique is useful only where there is no repeat of an item. For sequences with repeated items, we use the sound data section, described in section 7.1.

We recall a long string by accessing an element with SETDREL, followed by DRELACC. Since the result is put into the HOLD register, we can continue with another SETDREL, followed by DRELACC, and so on.

To determine if one is using the sound or data section to access a string, one can try to look around and recognize an object visually while recalling the string. If there is a slow down, then the data section is being used to recall the string. Note that we cannot look and recognize objects while recognizing speech because speech needs parallel recognition of partial word input.

- Recall of phoneme sequences

The data section can recognize sequences of phonemes because each phoneme has a relation of its position. We can recall these phonemes by stepping through their positions, although we normally do not use the data section for phoneme recall, we use the sound data section. Note that when we use the sound data section, we can stop and hold the sound sequence being recalled at any point, and then think of ideas, without losing the sequence. For example, we can say 1 2 3 4, then look around, then say 5 6 7.

- Foreign words and idea nodes versus word nodes

We frequently recognize an idea associated with multiple words, not a specific word. For example, the idea dog is associated with the English word "dog" and the Italian word "cane". The same idea must activate from both words. This is handled by having a group of English syllables (or untagged if English is our first language) and a group of Italian syllables, and linking all the syllables to the same idea as follows:

```
  source      relation   destination
  ------      --------   -----------
1 idea-dog  syllabl-1  (dog)               ;
1 idea-dog  syllabl-2  (blank)             ;
1 idea-dog  syll-it-1  (ca)                ;
1 idea-dog  syll-it-2  (ne)                ;
1 idea-dog  syll-it-3  (blank)             ;
1 idea-dog  sound      (bark)              ;
```

In the above example, (dog) represents the sound of the syllable dog. This syllable is actually a sequence of phonemes, which is described later in the

43

sound section. It is important to note that we may just want to recognize the word "dog", not the idea "dog". Therefore, for each word, we also have just a word node. The node for the word dog would just have the links to the sound dog as follows:

```
source      relation  destination
------      --------  -----------
1 word-dog  syllabl-1 (dog)            ;
1 word-dog  syllabl-2 (blank)          ;
1 word-dog  isa       word             ;
```

During normal speech, we are not often concerned with the word nodes. For example, "sound/bark" is not associated with the word node "dog"; it is just associated with the idea node "dog".

We do not have a separate image recognition section or word recognition section because we can select pieces of information from many senses, and they are all summed together in the data section. For example, we may hear "the -obin flew to a tree", and we would assume the word is "robin" because we would sum the sound "-obin" with isa/bird.

- Translation of words into a foreign language

The data section is used for translation. We translate the same way we access, for example, the color of an object. If we want to translate "two" into Italian, we set DSRC to "two", we set DREL to "Italian word", and we access the destination word "due" (pronounced do-ay).

- Detection of repeats of source and destination

We detect a repeat at DLEARN if we have a source and destination that matches an existing link, but a different relation. For example, if we have learned that there is an X in the top left of a picture, and we learn X also in the top right, then we notice a repeat of a source and destination. The branch status RPEATSD activates.

- Detection of repeats of a relation

We can detect the repeat of a relation. For example, if we learn about a new object and are told the object is red, big, furry, and brown then at brown, we immediately notice an error. This error occurs when we set a relation "color" and then try to learn "brown". When this happens, we detect that there is an existing link (object/color/red) that matches the source and relation being learned. An unexpected repeat occurs, the idea RPEAT activates, and the control section learns to respond by knowing it is a repeat of a relation. Even if we were to input red, big, furry, red, we would notice the repeat. With number or word sequences, we can use this to signify that it is time to create a new data source, although normally phrasing of a sentence is enough to signify it is time for a new data source. The control section receives the unexpected repeat and can handle it by indicating an error has occurred, or in some cases can create a new source.

As previously described, the instruction DLEARN overwrites an existing link if one exists. For example, if we know that we have learned an incorrect color of an object and want to correct it, then DLEARN will overwrite the color with the correction. There are times we do not want to overwrite, but to create more than one destination with the same relation. For example, if the Jetson's have two sons, Elroy and Bill, we want to be able to recognize the Jetson family with son/Elroy or son/Bill, therefore we need to be able to learn both. We use the instruction "data learn multiple" (DLEARNML) to learn multiple destinations with the same source and relation. Other than not overwriting, DLEARNML operates the same as DLEARN. Most learning is done with DLEARN. During recall, when we do the instruction TRELACC, at each TRELACC we step to the next destination with the same relation, and in this case we are able to recall Elroy and Bill. We can say each word after each TRELACC by setting it as DSRC and setting "word" as DREL and accessing the word with DRELACC. Only SETTMPSRC initializes the TRELACC stepping, therefore SETDSRC or DRELACC does not interfere with what has and has not been accessed with TRELACC.

- Comparing objects

When comparing two objects, such as a red cup and a green cup to see if they are the same color, we can use the following technique. We first access the color of the first cup by setting the source register to be the first cup, then we set the relation register to "color", then we do the instruction DRELACC and we access "red". We then create a new "test" source and link "red" as the relation and "first cup" as the destination and DLEARN it. Then we set the source to the second cup and access the color, in this case "green". We then set the source back to the new "test" source and set green as the relation and do DRELACC. Since we receive a "no find" branch status, the control procedure proceeds and knows the colors are not the same. If the second cup were red, then as we set red as a relation and did DRELACC, the branch status would be "find", and we would know the cups were the same color.

We can use the data learning repeat mechanism described above to also look for matching. After we access the color of the first cup, we can learn current/red/match, and then we can access the color of the second cup and learn current/green/match. There is no repeat and the control section can branch on this and understand there is no match.

Often when comparing, we not only want to see if the items match, but if they do not match we want to know how similar they are. For example, with heights, if the items being compared were tall and short, then we could set tall as the data source, then use short as the data destination and if we then recalled the relation, it would be "opposite". Many relations have a range of values, such as sizes (small, medium, large). We can answer how close the value of the relation is by first accessing the first value and, for example, assigning a position to it along a range, and then accessing the second item and finding its position. Then by using a control procedure, we can answer how close in value the items are.

Although a relation typically has a range of values, some do not, and there is no real way to access how close the values are. For example, there are many mathematical operations: integration, summing, factorials, and so on, but if we compare them to each other there is no real range. This is merely to point out that a range for values of a relation is not always necessary.

- The HOLD register

Each time we recall or recognize, the result becomes the current item we have attention on. It is stored in the data section HOLD register for use later, to allow it to be loaded to a data section or control section register. Attention is what is held in the HOLD register. The data section can learn by moving the HOLD register value to the data source, relation, or destination registers, followed by a DLEARN instruction.

- Selective attention

We are constantly bombarded with sensory input, but we normally attend to only a small part of this input. For example, we may be listening and ignore visual inputs or vice versa. This selection is performed by the control section selecting a particular external input to load to the HOLD register (sound or visual) from an external input buffer. Note that the control section becomes aware of external input by receiving an interrupt if the external input is loud or bright (or movement). The control section can also test the status of the external input registers.

- Creating new data nodes for situations

If we have a data node of an object, and we learn some temporary fact about the object, we must create a new data node and abstract (relation=isa) it to the data node that it has attributes of. For example, if we have a data node for a particular dog named Spot, if we consider Spot in a particular situation, such as Spot being thirsty, we create a new data node with the instruction

46

CRDAT and link the following attributes: isa/Spot, status/thirsty. CRDAT puts the new node in the HOLD register.

- Control fed by ideas activated by the data section

All ideas as they activate, whether as a result of a source node activating during recognition, or a destination node activating during recall, or from any other source, are fed to the control section where they can be used for branching. During recall and recognition, the idea "find" or "no find" is always activated, and is fed to the control section along with the idea of the data that is found. Often the control section branches just on the fact that we have found something, not on the actual idea that has been found.

- Accessing elements of a group

We can try to access as many elements of a group as we can remember. For example, we can be asked to name all types of trees (oak, pine, elm...), or all colors (red, green, blue...) that we can recall. To accomplish this, we use the recognition mechanism. If we are asked to name all types of trees we first CLRSUM then we set TMPREL=isa and we set TMPDST=tree. Then we do SUMATR, then SELMAX. With each SELMAX we will find at different type of tree. This is similar to the way we access "apple", then "tomato", then strawberry. We also may use links such as source=tree, relation=best_example, and we can find the best example of a tree (possibly oak). Then we can use the relation "moderate_example" to find other examples of a tree.

- Creation of reality and story structures

When we experience things or when we read a story, we create data section structures of the story as the control section activates manual data learning. This creation seems effortless and automatic even though it is the result of complex control procedures understanding what is being input. As we understand a story, data learning occurs. For example, when we are reading, we have structures created of the current word, the current sentence, a structure of the story, and even a structure that we can return to of what we were doing related to the situation in which we are reading the story. This effortless creation is a result of automatic movement of states in the control section. As inputs occur, states move and response states activate, which control how we form the structure in the data section. This state movement occurs as we understand.

We can start a new "situation2" and not confuse it with "situation1". For example, we may input the following sentences:

Create a new situation.
The doctor is in the park.
The lawyer is in the church.
The mailman is in the bank.
Where is the doctor?
Create a new situation.
The doctor is in the school.
The dog is in the park.
The lawyer is in the bank.
Where is the doctor?
Where is the lawyer?
Recall the situation with the doctor in the park.
Where is the lawyer?

As the sentences are input, we form the following links:

```
  source       relation    destination
  ------       --------    -----------
1 sentence10 part_of    situation2        ;
1 sentence10 subject    doctor1           ;
1 sentence10 location   park1             ;
1 sentence11 part_of    situation2        ;
1 sentence11 subject    lawyer1           ;
1 sentence11 location   church1           ;
1 sentence12 part_of    situation2        ;
1 sentence12 subject    mailman1          ;
1 sentence12 location   bank1             ;
1 sentence13 part_of    situation3        ;
1 sentence13 subject    doctor1           ;
1 sentence13 location   school1           ;
1 sentence14 part_of    situation3        ;
1 sentence14 subject    dog1              ;
1 sentence14 location   park1             ;
1 sentence15 part_of    situation3        ;
1 sentence15 subject    lawyer1           ;
1 sentence15 location   bank1             ;
```

In the above sequence of sentence, we are able to answer "church" when asked "Where is the lawyer?". We do this as follows. When asked to recall the situation with the "doctor in the park", we first set TMPREL to "subject" and TMPDST to "doctor1" and do SUMATR. We next set TMPREL to "location" and TMPDST to "park" and do SUMATR. Then we do SELMAX and we find sentence10 and TMPSRC is set to sentence10. Then we set TMPREL to "part of" and access "situation 2". We then CLRSUM, SUMATR, then set TMPREL to "subject" and TMPDST to "lawyer1", and do SUMATR, SELMAX which find sentence11. Finally, we set TMPREL to "location" and access "church". In this way we recall the situation with the "doctor in the park" and then answer the question "where is the lawyer?". We can use the general idea of a character when creating links. For example, we can use doctor instead of doctor1, but we cannot link information specific (such as age) to doctor1 to the idea doctor because not all doctors are the same age.

Note that we use the same doctor, lawyer, nodes throughout the situations because we are assuming all the situations use the same characters. We can start a completely new story with its own set of situations. In this case, we create new nodes for the characters in the story. Instead of lawyer1, we may have laywer2. Instead of bank1, we may have bank2. We can also reuse characters or locations if we decide that is the correct thing to do. To keep the stories separate, we may link all of the sentences in the above example to story/story1 and when we create a new story, the sentences are linked to story/story2. It should be noted that although we are referring to sentence10, sentence11, story1, lawyer1, etc, these are really just nodes and these names are just used for ease of explanation.

It has been shown that the more items with a particular element; the more difficult it is to verify that a statement is true. For example, if we have two statements with "in the bank" such as "The doctor is in the bank" and "The mailman is in the bank" then it takes longer to verify these statements than if only one character is in the bank. If more than one object or more than one location is the same then there is more of a delay for verification. This increased delay is the result of the additional difficulty in selecting one node over another during recognition because multiple nodes have activation. The recognition time is the same whether the subject or the location is used twice (with the other used once). This is reasonable because if the sums are the same during SUMATR and SELMAX, the selection time should be the same.

The data section does not record an exact sequence of events. For example, if we recall going to the store, we can recall it in almost any level of detail we like. We can remember just going to major departments, or we can recall extreme detail of just one event (purchasing an item or picking up an item). This level of detail is a result of our activating sequences in the control section and accessing the related facts in the data section. We can activate just a cursory control sequence (procedure) of going to a store, or we can activate detailed control sequences. This demonstrates that the data section does not record strings of events, but stores the individual events, so they may be accessed to whatever level of detail is required.

A good example of event storage in the data section is to imagine and later recall a car race. We can imagine an event: "car A starts in first place". The next event "car B passes car A". We store the sequence of these events using the relation "nxt-evnt". We can store each of these events in more detail, so that when recalling, we can explain more fully. The linking is done manually. This is necessary so that when recalling the car race we do not recall a recording of the events. We use the control section to step through the race in whatever level of detail we desire. We can recall a quick overview of the car race or details of one car passing another.

The data section stores stories, such as going to see a movie. We activate the "what to do at a movie" control procedure (as explained below in the control section) and fit the ideas as they occur to this procedure. As the control section understands, it creates the data structure of the story.

When we are reading, the exact word sequence that we have input and stored in a data structure of the sentence fades faster than the data structure of the story that we are inputting. This occurs because we refer to the story structure frequently. Once a word sequence has been input, we move on to other sentences, and do not reactivate the sentence data structure. We can recall what a story is about long after we have forgotten individual sentences because we have used (recalled) the story paths many times and therefore stored them strongly, but we have not recalled the sentences. As will be explained in chapter 5, we forget based on recency and frequency of use.

When we verbally describe a story, we first access each idea from the data section, and then we can access the words. By starting with ideas, we can access a word in any language by setting the idea as a data source, then selecting the word associated with the idea using the language we are interested in as a relation. After saying a word, we can move back to the data source of the story that we are accessing. An example of this is when we want to describe: "the man went to the store". We first recall the idea of the subject (man), then we recall the related word in the desired language and we say the word. Next we recall the verb and object ideas, recall the related words, and say them.

A more detailed example of storing a story is as follows:

This is the story of Ed.
He lives in a small house.
One day he went to the library.
He read two books.
Then he walked by the river.
Then he went home.

We form a data structure for each event and we link the events with nxt-evnt:

```
  source        relation    destination
  ------        --------    -----------
1 story1        frst-evnt   evnt1          ;
1 Ed            lives-in    sml-house      ;
1 sml-house     adj         small          ;
1 sml-house     subj        house          ;
1 evnt1         subj        Ed             ;
1 evnt1         verb        went           ;
1 evnt1         obj         library        ;
1 evnt1         nxt-evnt    evnt2          ;
1 evnt2         subj        Ed             ;
1 evnt2         location    library        ;
1 evnt2         verb        read           ;
1 evnt2         obj         two-books      ;
1 two-books     adj         two            ;
1 two-books     subj        books          ;
1 evnt2         nxt-evnt    evnt3          ;
1 evnt3         subj        Ed             ;
1 evnt3         verb        walked         ;
1 evnt3         prepositn   by             ;
1 evnt3         obj         river          ;
1 evnt3         nxt-evnt    evnt4          ;
1 evnt4         Ed          subject        ;
1 evnt4         verb        went           ;
1 evnt4         object      home           ;
```

We form the above type of structure when reading a story or observing a story. When we input another story, we start the new story with evnt5. There is no actual event number stored. The event, such as evnt4 above, is just a source node linked to other nodes. The only way to ever recall it is to access it with SUMATR/SELMAX using its attributes, or with relations from other nodes. For example, if we are accessing evnt3 then we can use the nxt-evnt relation to access evnt4. To start recalling a story, we normally first access the story source node, then access the first event relation.

Every sentence in a story is not an event. Facts can be part of a story. In the above example, "Ed lives in a small house" is a fact. It is not linked with nxt-evnt to other events because it is not an event. If we read the sentence Ed lives in a small house, we do create a new sentence structure as we are reading it, but as we imagine what we have just read, we create a data structure that is a fact.

1 Ed   lives-in sml-house   ;

There are a large number of relations that the control section learns to use. When parsing a sentence, the control section uses subject, verb, object, and so on. When creating facts, it knows to use relations like "location", for where something is, "lives-in", as in the example above, or size, color, and so on.

During recall, the recall procedure knows to access subject, verb, object, location, and so on, and to access nxt-evnt between events. At the last event, when we access nxt-evnt, we do not find anything, so the control section knows it is the end of the story.

- Data section event sequences

We can use the data section to step through a sequence of events, and between the events we can think of other things. For example, if we learn the sequence of events bell->buzzer->press button "A", we can branch from the bell event data node to the buzzer event data node when the sound "buzzer" occurs. Note that we can wait and be aware of our surroundings while waiting between bell and buzzer. When this occurs, we are stepping through a data structure of bell, buzzer, and the control section is running a "look around" procedure during the time between inputs. When an input does occur, the control section returns from looking around to step to the next data node, which may output "press button". We can modify this sequence to form the link light->press button "B" by using the data learn instruction.

- Storing multiplication tables

When we learn multiplication tables, we learn a data structure as shown in the table below and figure 20.

source	relation	destination	
------	--------	-----------	
1 2	x	2x	;
1 2x	2	4	;
1 2x	3	6	;
1 2x	4	8	;
1 2x	5	10	;
1 2x	6	12	;
1 2x	7	14	;
1 2x	8	16	;
1 2x	9	18	;
1 3	x	3x	;
1 3x	2	6	;
1 3x	3	9	;
1 3x	4	12	;
1 3x	5	15	;
1 3x	6	18	;
1 3x	7	21	;
1 3x	8	24	;
1 3x	9	27	;

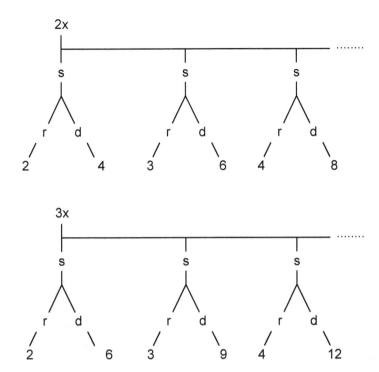

Figure 20: Storing multiplication tables

Addition tables and other arithmetic operations are stored in a similar way.

- Example of storage of general facts

The following list is an example of data section storage of general facts:

```
  source     delation   destination
  ------     --------   -----------
1 sky        color      blue           ;
1 planet     does       orbitsun       ;
1 planet     word       (planet)       ;
1 planet     wordtype   noun           ;
1 orbitsun   verb       orbit          ;
1 orbitsun   obj        sun            ;
1 mars       next       jupiter        ;
1 mars       previous   earth          ;
1 jupiter    next       saturn         ;
1 saturn     next       uranus         ;
1 uranus     next       neptune        ;
1 neptune    next       pluto          ;
1 jupiter    isa        planet         ;
1 uranus     isa        planet         ;
1 neptune    isa        planet         ;
```

```
1 pluto      isa        planet          ;
1 mercury    word       (Mercury)       ;
1 mercuryel  word       (Mercury)       ;
1 mercuryel  isa        metal           ;
1 mercury    isa        planet          ;
1 venus      word       (Venus)         ;
1 earth      word       (Earth)         ;
1 mars       word       (Mars)          ;
1 jupiter    word       (Jupiter)       ;
1 saturn     word       (Saturn)        ;
1 andromeda  isa        galaxy          ;
1 milkyway   isa        galaxy          ;
1 carrot     word       (carrot)        ;
1 europe     word       (Europe)        ;
1 asia       word       (Asia)          ;
1 carrot     isa        vegetable       ;
1 carrot     color      orange          ;
1 carrot     taste      good            ;
1 europe     isa        continent       ;
1 asia       isa        continent       ;
```

- Visual objects and the data section

The data section can recognize and recall visual objects in a way similar to its recognition and recall of words. Image primitives are grouped similar to the way phonemes are grouped. The data section receives image primitives and groups them to recognize objects. Just as ideas are associated with words, visual recognition activates an idea when we recognize an object, such as a house, from the visual image of it. The visual storage of an object is not very detailed. For example, if we recall a house, we can zoom into parts of the house, such as the details of a window or roof, but at the top level there is not much detail - enough for recognition and for recall.

An important part of image processing is deciding what the current object is. We can look at a page, such as this one, and we can select the page as the current object, with texture areas (paragraphs) stored at locations. As we focus on a paragraph, it becomes the current object (the current data source register) and we can link words to it. We do not have to see all of an object to decide it is an object. For example, we can be facing a brick wall and only see part of it, but we store it as one wall.

When we are confronted with a complex scene, for example an outside yard, we start by trying to identify major objects (house, car, tree, dog...), as we link their locations to the yard data source node. We decide what part of a visual field is each object. Then we can zoom in and access and store details of these objects. Note that we can also focus first on an object and move outward to a larger object. We decide what are objects by using knowledge of lines. Much of this is learned; a baby cannot focus on objects. Control procedures know how to follow lines around an object. For example, by observing the lines in the corner of an object, the orientation of the object can be determined. If the lines are all from the vertex toward us, we are looking into the corner of an object. If they are all from the vertex away from us then we are looking at the corner of an object. This is illustrated in figure 21.

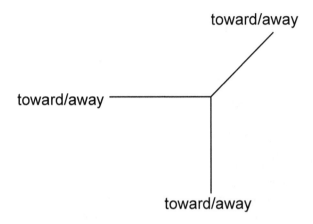

Figure 21: Visual corner recognition

We learn that an object contained in another object, as in the following figure 22, is a different object. A new data source node is created for each new object. An object can be composed of other objects (a group of letters on a page is an object: paragraph). If we see a group of similar objects, we know to group them because the vision control procedure understands that there is a group of similar objects.

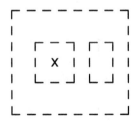

Figure 22: Object within an object

We can even recognize objects that are not made of continuous lines, but we can imagine that the lines are continuous. For example, we can recognize a box made of dashed lines as shown in figure 22, or a negative box within a box as shown in figure 23. Also, when we see a partially obscured object, we can still recognize the object if enough attributes allow it.

Figure 23: Visual recognition of non-continuous lines

We can mentally rotate an object by focusing on end points and assigning new locations. We do this by accessing a recalled object and creating a new object. We move back and forth to form the new object. We do this by moving down the hierarchy to endpoints. We focus on the unrotated one and move down the hierarchy to an endpoint. Then we determine its new location and move down the hierarchy of the new object and assign a new endpoint location. Therefore, control procedures perform rotation by reassigning endpoints of objects stored in the data section. The more the rotation, the more control work and therefore time is required. Experiments [16] have shown this to be the case.

We visually recognize objects by using SUMATR and eventually SELMAX.

When we look at a complex object, we assign perspective to various line intersections and planes. For example, the cube shown in figure 24 can be viewed with "plane a" or "plane b" as the front.

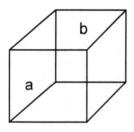

Figure 24: Visual recognition of a cube

Once one assignment is made, all the rest falls into place. The figure cannot be viewed two ways at once and we can feel all the primitives change as we change which plane is in front.

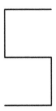

Figure 25: S or 5

Visual information can be combined with information from the other senses by the data section. For example, if we see an object and know it is an animal, but we do not know what type, we can activate the data source "animal". Then if we hear the sound of a "bark", we can use the data section to determine the object is a dog. If we were to see the object below in figure 25, and we were looking for a letter, then "S" would activate, but if we were looking for a number, then "5" would activate.

The letter S has the links shown in figure 26 (along with sound links)

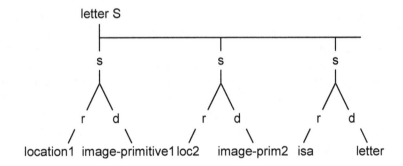

Figure 26: S links

The location of objects is understood by the control section as we move our eyes. The control section stores the appropriate relations for the various locations in the data section. During recall, the control section generates these locations without physically moving the eyes.

Often, we recognize in more and more detail as shown in figure 27.

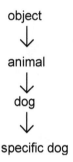

Figure 27: Recognition in more and more detail

We do this by moving the source register (for example, animal) to a destination register and setting relation=isa, which allows for recognition of "dog" when other dog specific attributes are also summed. We then set "dog" from the source register to the destination register, and "isa" as relation, to recognize a specific dog.

Complex images use a hierarchical structure similar to the hierarchy used for storing a story. In the case of a complex image, for example a "dog", we have a general shape stored with the dog idea, and views of parts of the dog that we can zoom in to, such as to the head, or the tail, or a paw, to allow access to more detailed data. We zoom in by setting dog-head as the data source. For example, we can continue to keep zooming in after the head, to the ear or eye. We zoom in by selecting the section we want to zoom in as a relation, and we access the idea associated with the new level and set it as a data source. For example, in the case of "head", we would set "head" as the relation, with "dog" as the source, and we would access the idea "dog-head", which could be set as a new data source.

To imagine a yard with a dog in it, we first create a new data node and learn a data link of source/new node, relation/view/, destination/yard. If we imagine the dog on the left side of the yard, we link source/new node, relation/left side, destination dog. We can zoom in to the dog or zoom out to the yard with the dog in it. To find where the dog is located, we set the source/new node, the destination to dog, and use the instruction DDSTACC to find the relation "left side".

```
   source      relation   destination
   ------      --------   -----------
1  picture1    overall    yard           ;
1  picture1    left       dog1           ;
1  dog1        isa        dog            ;
1  dog         front      dog-head       ;
1  dog         middle     dog-middle     ;
1  dog         back       dog-tail       ;
1  dog-head    top        ears           ;
1  dog-head    middle     nose           ;
1  dog-head    bottom     mouth          ;
```

Stories are stored in a similar hierarchical fashion, allowing us to recall a story in any level of detail that we like. Geographical information is also stored in a hierarchical fashion. This allows us to think of a country, then to access cities in that country, then to access details of a particular city, and so on. We are able to move downward (more detail), and upward (less detail), like zooming in and out of a picture.

- Instantiation/hierarchy

When we recognize an object, we frequently know a lot about the object. If we see a person, we may recognize a specific person or an unknown person. We know what to expect in either case because we can activate "isa" as a relation in the data section to abstract a specific person to a general idea of a person. The specific person is an instantiation of the general idea of a person. An unrecognized person has a new data source node created.

We use up and down relations to manually abstract up and down. "Is a" (or isa) for up and "example of" for down. This allows us to answer: "is a fish a dog ?", or "is a dog an animal ?", or "is a dog a thing ?", and so on. If we know Spot is a dog and Spot cannot bark, we answer the question "can Spot bark ?" at the first level and we do not move up a level. Therefore, we use a combination of data information and control procedures. There is no automatic abstraction; the control section controls when we move up a level.

Computer designers work with instantiation and hierarchy every day. The top level hierarchy schematic typically shows a box with the pins of the computer chip. When this box is selected and "push down" is selected, then multiple boxes of the major sections of the computer are shown. For example, data and control boxes are shown, along with all of the pins for each section and the interconnection wires. One can keep pushing down, finding boxes of the data or control sections. There are often a dozen levels of hierarchy in modern computers. Computer designers are constantly pushing down and popping up the hierarchy to work on some part of the design.

Some parts of a computer are repeated. For example, an adder my have 32 bits. The computer designer does not draw each bit of the adder. Usually, only one bit is drawn or 4 bits are drawn, and this is instantiated many times. When instantiated, each box has a different instance name, but when pushing down, the same circuit is found. Instead of drawing the same circuit many times, the computer designer draws it one time then uses instances of the design. Each instance has its own connections to other instances. The RTL (register transfer language) for a computer, typically written in verilog, likewise uses hierarchy and instantiation.

- Doing more than one thing at once

We can be driving and talking. We focus on only one thing at a time and we switch attention between driving and talking. We have all of our control branches set up for driving so it requires little attention. We only focus on driving when there is a situation for which we do not have a preplanned response. Since the speaking information is probably all new, we focus mostly on it and learn what we are talking about. There is no new learning of driving routines most of the time.

When reading, we may forget our surroundings and have difficulty reactivating them if they have not been used for a while, but we always know we are reading while reading because the reading is done by reading control procedures.

- Checking age

We can tell how long ago we did something. For example, if we go someplace and later recall it, we can access how long ago we did it. We can tell if we just did it, or did it a while ago, or long ago. When we create a node (data, sound, or procedure), we link the current cycle count to it as lastuse. Later if we access it, we can recall this lastuse and determine how long ago it was by using the instruction CHECKAGE, which activates a branch status of recent, medium, or old. Then we update the lastuse to the current cycle count so we can recall later that we accessed it more recently than when it was created. A future improvement can be to keep track of the creation of all nodes and be able to access the last use age and the creation age.

- Selecting a piece of a string of words for recognition

We can be recalling a sequence from the sound data section and also try to recognize pieces of it. For example, "the square root of 2" can be recalled, i.e.

1.4142135, and we may want to recognize 2135. We access the element 2 from the sound data section then we do SUMATR in the data section with "start/2". We return to the sound data section to select the next element "1", and SUMATR "second-position/1". We proceed until we have summed the attributes of the four numbers 2135, then we use them to try to recognize 2135. We may recognize 2135 as a room number or something else.

- External input

When external inputs first occur, there are no links to them to activate in the data or control sections. The instruction "external to HOLD" (EXTHLD) is used to bring external data into the HOLD register, where links can then be formed.

- Detecting fitting to a data source

We can have a source node active for an object, and we can fit each attribute to it as we recognize it by using the instruction "fit source" (FITSRC). If an attribute does not fit, then we receive a "no find" branch status. For example, if we see a dog and it has two eyes, ears, and says "meow" then we receive a "no find" branch status as we try to fit "sound/meow" to dog.

The "no find" branch status allows us to keep the source active, and to see if the item keeps getting "no find" branch status. For example, if we see a car that we know, but it has just been painted a different color, we can still hold its data source active to see if anything else has changed. The control section knows it is not an exact fit because it received a "no find" branch status.

- Review of data links

In review, all of the factual information that we know is stored in millions of cognitive data links in our memory. Each link consists of connection to a source node, a connection to a relation node, and a connection to a destination node.

The data section cognitive links in memory are recalled, learned, and recognized using the current data and temporary data source, relation, and destination registers. During recall and recognition, any two of the three registers can activate a link in memory and find the associated third node. Using wild cards, only a single relation or destination register is needed. We learn a data link in memory by setting the current data source, relation, and destination to what we want to learn and then asserting DLEARN.

Summary: human brain data section
function: stores factual information
input: receives instructions from the control section and receives external input
output: outputs status information to the control section and outputs to the external output
learning: CRDAT creates a new data node. Learning occurs at DLEARN, which creates a new link using the data source, relation, and destination registers. At DLEARN, if the source and relation exist, then we overwrite the destination. DLEARNML learns multiple destinations with the same source and relation.

instructions that control the data section:

basic instructions:

SETDSRC - loads the HOLD register to the DSRC register
SETDREL - loads the HOLD register to the DREL register
SETDDST - loads the HOLD register to the DDST register
SETTMPSRC - loads the HOLD register to the TMPSRC register
SETTMPREL - loads the HOLD register to the TMPREL register
SETTMPDST - loads the HOLD register to the TMPDST register
DRELACC - access the destination node associated with the DSRC and DREL
    registers and load it to the HOLD register
TRELACC - access the destination node associated with the TMPSRC and TMPREL
    registers and load it to the HOLD register
DLEARN - learn SRC/REL/DST – overwrite/correct
DLEARNML – learn SRC/REL/DST – do not overwrite
SRCTOHLD - loads the DSRC register to the HOLD register
RELTOHLD - loads DREL to the HOLD register
DSTTOHLD - loads DDST to the HOLD register
TSRCTOHLD - loads the TMPSRC register to the HOLD register
TRELTOHLD - loads TMPREL to the HOLD register
TDSTTOHLD - loads TMPDST to the HOLD register
DSRCTSRC - DSRC moved to TMPSRC
DDSTACC - access the relation between DSRC and DDST
TDSTACC - access the relation between TMPSRC and TMPDST
data recognition related instructions:
CLRSUM - clear sum array getting ready for recognize.
SUMATR - increment all source nodes that match the attribute in TMPREL
    and TMPDST

SELMAX - select maximum sum - if more than one equal to maximum then pick most

recent - the result is loaded to TMPSRC and to the HOLD register

SELMAXR - select maximum sum - if more than one is equal to the maximum then

pick randomly from the maximum group - the result is loaded to TMPSRC and to

the HOLD register

BLOCKSUM - block HOLD register value from being found with SELMAX(R)

SUBRCNT - block recently activated nodes from being found with SELMAX(R)

SUBATR - subtract an attribute from the sums before doing a SELMAX(R) -

select maximum sum as HOLD and as TMPSRC - used for recognition.

DRPTMP - sets TMPREL and TMPDST to 0 for wild card recognition. Used for wild

card recall and recognition, such as the last relation of "big" or the last destination

of a particular book - at DRELACC if DSRC=0 then we find the most recent use of

the current DREL.

other data instructions:

CRDAT - create new data node, such as in a new situation; we use

SUMATR/SELMAX to reactivate it from rel and dst information

LRNATRS - learn the current group of atrs stored during a sequence of SUMATR. We

do not learn at each SUMATR because we may be just reactivating an existing data

node. We store when we try to recognize and receive no find we manually

activate LRNATRS.

FITSRC - look for a match to current source/ relation/destination to answer, for

example, "is the sky blue".

CHECKAGE – determine how long ago we accessed something: recent, medium, old.

3 Detailed Description of the Control Section

The second major section of the human brain is the control section. The control section is used to store and execute procedures, which are sequences of states (cognitive links) that activate individual instructions, procedure calls, and constants. The individual instructions control the input of data, the processing of data in the data section and other sections, and the output of data. Procedure calls activate other procedures in a hierarchical fashion. When performing instructions in the control section, we are not focusing on the instructions - these occur as we automatically move from state to state; we focus on data. Besides individual instructions and procedure calls, the sequences can directly activate ideas (constants).

An example of the operation of the control section is adding. The first adding state is a procedure call to the procedure "select next digit", the next state is a call to "add it to total". When executing the first state, the control section activates the procedure "select next digit", which is a sequence of states that includes procedure calls which activate lower level procedures until we reach a level that operates internal registers (individual elemental instructions). This pushing down is automatic when we encounter a procedure call. Returning (popping up) is automatic when we finish the last state in a procedure. Note that when adding, we do not focus on the instructions of adding, but on the data (for example 5 + 2=).

We automatically learn a new step (state, link) in a procedure whenever we manually start a procedure, perform an elemental instruction, or set a constant. For example, we learn the above adding procedure by first manually activating the procedure "select next digit", followed by manually activating the procedure "add it to total". The steps in these two procedures had been already learned. This way, we are constantly building up more and more complex procedures to handle life's situations.

Once a procedure is started, the only way to stop it is to interrupt out of the procedure or for the procedure to finish, since we automatically move from state to state and automatically push and pop. There are many interrupts, such as "loud sound", pain, boring, and so on. These activate control section service procedures where we can decide what to do. The decide procedure is one of the most frequently used procedures. It is used to determine what to do next based on goals, plans, data and procedure emotion levels, and so on.

The control section is based on states. At any one time, only a single control state is active (single control section cognitive link). The most common relation between states is "next". This moves us from state to state as each instruction is performed. Ideas can also cause states to move. For example, branch status information from the data section, such as finding a destination during recall. Any data in the HOLD register can be used to move from state to state. For example, when we recognize input data in the HOLD register, it can be used for moving from state to state. As we move to a new state, one or many outputs can activate. These outputs can be instructions, constants, or procedure calls.

The structure that allows this is shown in figure 28.

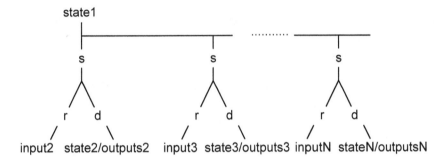

Figure 28: Basic cognitive links structure of the control section

The inputs above can be from an internal branch status (for example "find" or "no find"), the HOLD register, or the default idea "NEXT".

The following is an example of the use of the above structure. If we want to activate the instruction SETDSRC if a noun is input, then we first input the word, then set the relation to wordtype, then do DRELACC, and if it is a noun, as shown below in figure 29, then we activate the instruction SETDSRC and move to state wd-st2. If it is a verb, we activate the constant "subject-verb" and move to state wd-st3. Constants are described in detail below. If it is not a noun or a verb, then we take the "next" branch to do the procedure subr1 to access another word. The first branch taken has priority over subsequent branches (from left to right in figure 28 and figure 29). This example illustrates the three types of outputs from the control link: elemental instruction, constant, and procedure call. There can also be no output from a control link – we may just want to branch from state to state before doing

65

anything else. Note that different inputs can result in movement from a source state to the same destination state, but with different outputs (Mealy machine).

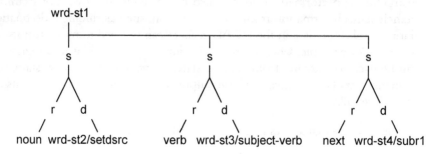

Figure 29: Control links example

The control structure is very similar to the data structure. In the data structure we have source, relation, and destination data section cognitive links. In the control structure, we have a source state, a relation between states, and a destination state cognitive links. In the control section, we also have an additional item, the output. This output is optional and can be an elemental instruction, a procedure call, or a constant. Multiple outputs from a state are allowed. The data structure operates based on instructions from the control structure, while the control structure always moves from state to state. This movement can be based on what we have attention on (the HOLD register), internal status, or the value "next". It should be noted that the control section states only flow in one direction – downward in figure 29; there is no upward path in the control section like the SUMATR path in the data section.

We must have a way to return from procedure calls - to pop after we are done a procedure that we have pushed to. We store which procedure is currently running, and to pop/return we access the state that most recently activated that procedure. We are able to recall the most recent state that activated a procedure - this is similar to the data section where we can overwrite a relationship, such as 2+2=5, we correct it to 2+2=4. (In an implementation, we can actually use a small procedure (subroutine) stack for simplicity although a data type structure allows jumping out of an execution and returning to it later, while a stack must be used in a carefully controlled manner).

An automatic low level procedure continually moves the control section from state to state if there are elemental instructions or constants, and automatically pushes down to procedures and automatically pops when done a procedure (no next state). The push and pop instructions are "procedure push" (PPUSH) and "procedure pop" (PPOP). PPUSH and PPOP are used by the automatic low level procedure and allow mixing of elemental instruction state outputs and procedure call outputs in a string of states. States can move based on data or just "next", which occurs when a state is finished its output.

When pushing down to levels of procedures, the automatic low level procedure must test at each level if the instruction is an elemental instruction. For example, when pushing down from "add", to "add column", to "select a number", to an elemental instruction, it automatically tests at each level if the output of a state is an elemental instruction. If it is then it executes that instruction (or if a constant it loads it to the HOLD register), otherwise it pushes down. The low level procedure knows to pop when there is no next state.

If we encounter a state, and no next state activates when we are done the current state, then we assume it is the end of a procedure and we return to the state in the calling procedure. If we are at the top of the procedure (subroutine) stack, then there is no place to return to, and we activate the interrupt "procedure pop pointer negative" (PPOPNEG). This activates the interrupt service state, where we can branch to the PPOPNEG control service procedure to determine what to do next.

As with the data section, for ease of reading the control section links can be listed in a tabular format. A "2" at the start of a line indicates it is a control section link (procedure step). In the following example, we set what is in the HOLD register to the data relation register, then DRELACC, and then load the result to the data source register.

```
2 ex-stp1   next    ex-stp2  setdrel  ;
2 ex-stp2   next    ex-stp3  drelacc  ;
2 ex-stp3   next    ex-stp4  setdsrc  ;
```

The output of a state can be a constant. This constant is loaded to the HOLD register and can be used the next cycle to load to a register. A "4" at the start of a line indicates it is a control type link with a constant as the output, as shown below.

```
4 ex1-stp1   next    ex1-stp2  sky      ;
2 ex1-stp2   next    ex1-stp3  setdsrc  ;
4 ex1-stp3   next    ex1-stp4  color    ;
2 ex1-stp4   next    ex1-stp5  setdrel  ;
2 ex1-stp5   next    ex1-stp6  drelacc  ;
```

We first perform procedures manually using the data section to determine what instruction to do next. We record these instructions and data in a new state sequence using the procedure learn registers, and this sequence can later be accessed to execute the instruction sequence without thinking about each instruction. It is interesting that the control section learns to control itself. We learn a new control state automatically when we execute an instruction; we can also learn manually by directly loading the procedure learn registers. There is also a random instruction/spasm mechanism that must be used when a thinking computer with no learned procedures first activates. This mechanism uses the SELMAXR instruction to pick random instructions and random branches to form sequences of simple and complex instructions. These random instructions/spasms are learned as if they were manually activated. The emotion section helps pick good procedures to reactivate. At first, these procedures will have been learned as the result of random instructions and branches.

We do not use the control section for storing strings of items, such as a telephone number, because the control section must control the recall of strings, and it cannot perform control and also store what is being recalled at the same time. The sound data section is normally used for storing strings of sounds (speech, music, environmental sounds) or sequences of words. The data section can also store strings by using one item as the relation to access the next, as described previously. Most data section items are not strings, but are non-sequential data items, such as facts.

Multi-way branches are allowed from control states. For example, if we learn a procedure to press "button A" if a red light comes on, and press "button B" if a green light comes on, then we have a single control state branching to two other control states. We can also use the data section, along with the control section, to determine what instruction to do based on a situation. These data procedures use the data section to access the response to stimulus in situations. For example, if we are at the movies and become hungry, we access in the data section: at-movies/hungry and find get-popcorn.

The control section must be separate from the data section so that:

1. it can control the data section

2. state movement does not interfere with data recognition

For example, when we are reading this sentence, the data section is performing recognition of the letters and words while the control section is understanding the syntax (flow of nouns, verbs, and so on, and the order that they occur). When we are listening, the data section recognizes words and the control section understands syntax.

The data and control sections are responsible for what we perceive as consciousness and subconsciousness. We have no way to stop the flow of consciousness; as inputs and data ideas occur, states move; there is no way to stop this movement.

- Passing parameters

When moving between procedures, the data section can be used to pass information. For example, a procedure can select two numbers, and return to allow another procedure to operate on them. In this case the numbers are held in the data section, with the data src, for example, being "current data", and the attributes being rel=firstnum/dst=5, rel=2ndnum/dst=3.

- Interrupts in the control section

Although control states normally activate based on the previous state, interrupts can occur that disrupt the normal sequence of states and we move directly to the interrupt service state. For example, when we experience pain, we move immediately to the pain interrupt service state, with the HOLD register = pain interrupt. The interrupt service procedure can first do things to handle the interrupt, but when done we usually want to return to what we were doing (we have learned to do this). We accomplish this by checking the goal structure stored in the data section. We may have to repeat some states; for example, if we are half way through adding a column of numbers and we receive an interrupt, we may have to restart the column if we forget where we left off. We keep track of what we are doing and have procedures to help us return to what we were doing. We can also use the data section's goals and plans to help return to what we were doing. For example, when adding, we store the numbers in the data section as we access them and we can then recall the last number to determine where we left off.

- Types of control section learning

There are 3 types of control section procedure learning:

1. Automatic - when we manually activate a procedure with the instruction EXECUTE from the control section then we automatically create a step (state) in the new procedure being learned. This procedure is a sequence of the procedures, elemental instruction, or constants that we manually enable.

2. Manual - when we manually load the procedure learn registers and use the procedure learn (PLEARN) instruction.

3. Spasm - when a random instruction or random branch occurs (this allows us to initially learn the instructions and branches we are capable of doing)

During automatic learning, the control section learns whenever we manually activate an instruction (when we EXECUTE what is in the HOLD register). It learns like the sound data section learns by recording a sequence. The control section records sequences of instructions, which can then be played back. Initially, these are random instructions and branches that are recorded and then auto selected (best is selected) at a PPOPNEG interrupt. The control section learns how to activate data section learning. The automatic and random instruction learning of procedures along with the emotion section help the control section learn how to learn procedures manually.

A more detailed example of how automatic procedure learning is very similar to learning sound sequences (which are learned in the sound data section described in section 7.1) is as follows. We may at some time randomly make the sound "tone1". We store this as a one step sound sequence in the sound data section. We can recall it as many times as we like. Later, we may make the sound "tone2". If tone2 occurred close to tone1, we may create a tone1-tone2 two step sequence. If tone2 occurred by itself, then we may create just a single step sequence of tone2. Later, we could recall tone1 manually, then tone2 manually, and create a tone1-tone2 two step sequence. We create procedures in the control section the same way we create sound sequences in the sound data section, as demonstrated with the example above. If we randomly do SETDSRC then SETDREL (or any sequence of instructions), then we form a procedure. Breaks, where we start a new procedure, can be done manually, or automatically. Breaks are automatic if a long time has passed since the last manual execution, or if the current procedure gets too long, or if we reactivate the current new procedure.

If a new procedure produces a good result, the emotion section links "goodgoal" to it, biasing it for future recall. We normally create many not useful procedures for every eventually useful procedure. This is described in more detail in the emotion section, chapter 4.

To help with initially learning what we are capable of doing, there must be ease in forming control compounds from the elemental instructions. This automatically occurs as we manually execute elemental instructions and also occurs when random elemental instructions and branches activate. This causes us to form new procedures, which can be recalled. This results in our forming more and more complex procedures with a minimum of storage space. Note that we can mix procedure calls, constants, and elemental instructions in a single procedure.

We create a new control procedure for learning when:

1. the instruction "create new control" (CRACTL) is asserted by the control section

2. or when we manually execute an instruction and have not done a manual execution in a while

3. or the current procedure is getting too long (over a certain number of steps)

The first state of the new procedure is stored in the "procedure learn source register" (PLSRC). At each new manual execution a new state is learned - the new state becomes the new PLSRC and it is linked with "next" to the last state. When a new procedure is created, we automatically learn it in the data section with the link: source = (the new procedure)/relation = isa/destination = procedure. This allows us to select it as a procedure in the data section for linking attributes, such as what it is good for. A register named "control start" (CTLSTART) is loaded with the first state of a new procedure. We can access this register in the data section to link more data information to the start of the procedure, such as if the procedure is a good procedure, to help recall it if we are trying to decide on something good to do. To re-execute a newly learned procedure, we can execute STRTCTL, which loads CTLSTART, the start of the new procedure, to the "procedure source register" (PSRC), which starts it running. This STRTCTL instruction is useful to redo a procedure that produced a good result. The PSRC register stores the current state that is active in the control section.

- Procedure learning example

Procedure learning straddles the line between the data and control sections. Information moves back and forth between the two, which makes procedure learning more difficult to understand than simple data section operation or control section operation. We put attention on a data item associated with an instruction, for example, "select a number", when preparing to add. We focus on it as data, then we execute it by the control section outputting the instruction EXECUTE, along with the HOLD register holding "select a number". Whenever we execute something, it is learned as a procedure step. This automatic mechanism for learning is necessary otherwise procedures would never exist because non automatic procedure learning requires procedures to learn other procedures. We must also have mechanisms to add branches to a procedure, correct a procedure, and put constants in a procedure. To do so requires accessing procedural information as data. When we access procedural information as data, we use other procedures to do so. When we have the new procedure the way we want it, we can select the start of it as data, then execute it.

An example of learning a procedure is to read a number then say it. We execute the procedure step to read the number. This causes the first step to be learned. We then execute the procedure to speak it, and this step is learned. We can now redo this new two step procedure at any time by focusing on the start of it (which puts it in the HOLD register) and executing it. Often, the sequence of steps for a new procedure is worked out first as a data sequence, and then we recall the sequence from the data section and execute each step. As we do this, we create the new control procedure.

When learning a procedure, we may want to add a branch. An example of a branch is when reading a number, and if it is 3 then say it, otherwise add 5 then say it:

with 7 we would say 12

with 3 we would say 3

When learning a branch, we must be able to do two things:

1. Set the relation between states - in the above case we compare what we read to 3, then branch if "find" or "nofind". Therefore, we must be able to change the relation between the states, which is normally "next", to "find" or "nofind'

2. Save the branch point, and after we learn what to do at one leg of the branch then return to the branch point to learn another leg (we can have many branches from a branch point, if desired).

We learn the branch by holding the branch point state as data. We do this by accessing the procedure learn registers, which are updated as we learn each step in a procedure. We can access the last step, the relation between the steps (next or some other relation), and the destination step. To add a branch, we normally use the instruction "procedure learn source to HOLD" (PLSRCTOHLD). In the above example, we can first learn the "branch if 3" by comparing the input to 3, but as we start down this branch we save the branch point as data so we can go back to it later. We save it by creating the link: current/branchpt/(what we accessed with PLSRCTOHLD). We start down the branch path by setting the procedure learn relation register PLREL with the instruction SETPLREL. We set PLREL to "find" and do the instruction "block new state" (BLKNEWST), which is used to fix a procedure step. We do not want to learn the procedure that accessed the branchpt because this procedure is only used to learn the branch - not for later executing it. We set the PLREL to "find" because normally the relation is "next", so to change it we need to "fix" it. We then learn to say 3, which overwrites the procedure we used to do SETPLREL and BLKNEWST. We then go back to the branch point by accessing the saved branch point and setting it as the procedure learn source register PLSRC with the instruction SETPLSRC. We then set PLREL to "nofind" with the instruction SETPLREL (or we can just set it to NEXT, which is the default branch if it is the last one in the priority of branches – top to bottom in tabular form). Then we can learn the steps associated with adding 5. Note that we again overwrite the procedure that sets PLREL to "nofind" because we only do this procedure when learning the branching procedure - we do not want to do it when we later execute the new procedure learned above. We normally learn by executing, and we need the BLKNEWST instruction to correct a new procedure so that we do not do procedure steps that were only needed to learn a new procedure.

- Constants

There are times when we need a constant as part of a procedure (procedures are not just instructions and procedure calls). For example, we may always want to input a number and then add 5 to it, as in the above example. We need to recall the constant 5 at this point in the procedure. We learn constants in a procedure by using the instruction "constant learn" (CLEARN). When this instruction occurs, we learn a new procedure step that is a constant, with the constant output of the step loaded from the HOLD register. This constant is set in the HOLD register when the procedure step is later executed (from there it can be loaded to any register). The constant does not have to be a number; it can be any data item. For example, we may have a procedure where we must activate the idea "tree", in which case "tree" would be set as a constant.

Often, we must first execute a procedure at to access the constant, and we do not want this procedure to become part of the newly learned procedure. For example, to access 5 the first time above, we need to access it from a data structure that was created as we decided what to do. But once we find 5, we do not want to each time execute the "find" procedure, we just want the constant 5 to pop up as we become ready to add it. In this case, we want to correct the find 5 procedure step that was automatically learned as we executed the find 5 procedure. We can do this the way we learned a branch - by overwriting the procedure step. We do this by executing the instruction BLKNEWST, as we did with branches above, then getting the constant, then executing CLEARN. We can also fix the output of a state with the instruction "procedure learn fix out" (PLFIXOUT), which overwrites the current procedure learn step in memory after we have set PLOUT with the constant using the instruction "procedure learn HOLD" (PLRNHLD), which causes type 4 (constant) learning.

The first digit in each line is the link type. A "4" is a control link with a constant at the end. A "2" is a control link with either an elemental instruction or procedure call at the end. If it is not an elemental instruction then it is assumed to be a procedure call. If it is a procedure call, then when the procedure is done there is an automatic return to the next step in the calling sequence.

```
4 sayisa7    next        sayisa8     a          ;
2 sayisa8    next        sayisa9     speakb     ;
4 sayisa9    next        sayisa10    subject    ;
2 sayisa10   next        sayisa11    speak      ;
4 sayisa11   next        sayisa12    verb       ;
2 sayisa12   next        sayisa13    speak      ;
4 sayisa13   next        sayisa14    answer     ;
2 sayisa14   next        sayisa15    speak      ;
```

In the above example, we say a sentence based on the recall of an event. We select the subject, verb, and answer, with a constant. Note, the procedures "speak" and "speakb" are not described here, but are detailed in the file engram_main.txt at the website www.rgrondalski.com.

- Data Procedures

We can learn procedures by first creating a data structure of the steps we want to do, then starting a procedure that picks each step and executes it. This procedure will be referred to as a data procedure. For example, we may have already learned a procedure to examine two 3 digit numbers and pick the last digit from the first number and middle digit from the second number, then add them.

358

239

We would pick 8 and 3, then add them to select 11. We may want to learn a new procedure, such as: pick the middle number from both and subtract them. With the above numbers, this would be 5 - 3 = 2. Try doing this procedure. We set up data links, for example, first-number/position/middle, second-number/position/middle. We execute the data procedure type of procedure, which uses data to pick each step and execute it. As we execute it, we record the new procedure in the procedure learn registers - select the first middle number, select the second middle number, then subtract them. Once we have done it once, it is learned and we can then execute it at any future time (unless we forget it). This is how new procedures can be learned. To modify a new procedure, we normally just modify the data that the data procedure accesses to include the modification. We then execute the data procedure, which picks up the modified steps, and they are learned as we execute them. When done, a newly modified procedure is available for use.

When we are finished learning a procedure, the data procedure code can find no more steps and executes CRACTL, so anything we do next is not linked to the newly learned procedure. Often in a situation where we have just learned a new procedure, we will want to try it out to make sure it works. The data procedure code sets the current situation to donedatpro, which can be used by the goal code to test the current situation to decide what to do. In the past, we may have learned the data link donedatpro/situation/do-newpro, which can be used to decide to do the new procedure.

We are also able to learn manually with the PLEARN instruction, which learns what is in the HOLD register as a step. We are also able to step manually in a procedure using the instruction "procedure learn step" (PLSTEP) to reach the point to modify a procedure. We modify it by setting the "procedure learn output register" (PLOUT) with the instruction "set procedure learn output register" (SETPLOUT), then we execute the instruction "fix procedure learn output" (PLFIXOUT), which causes a new output from the state to be learned. It should be noted that the control section therefore not only controls learning in the data section, but is able to manually learn itself.

The instructions that control manual learning are:

1. start new control learn sequence (CRACTL).

2. learn a new step (PLEARN).

3. step to the next state (PLSTEP).

4. link the HOLD register to current control learn state output - this can be an elemental instruction or procedure call (SETPLOUT then PLFIXOUT) or constant data (PLRNHLD)

5. link the HOLD register to the current control relation - so we can branch (SETPLREL)

Control learning can allow manually adding a new branch between an existing source state and an existing destination state by:

1. grabbing an existing procedure source state (we PLSTEP to it).

2. grabbing an existing destination state (we can PLSTEP to it, or recall it from the data section if it was stored there during an earlier PLSTEP or when it was created).

existing source--> existing destination

$$\wedge$$

x

j

For example, if we have two states where the idea x or j (from the HOLD register) will allow us to move between them, and we want to add y as another branch, then first we must grab both states before linking the new relation y between them. This is done with the PLSTEP instruction. We PLSTEP until the source state above is PLDST, then we activate x and PLSTEP, which sets PLSRC to the existing source and PLDST to the destination above. We then access the data section to select y and we set y to PLREL. Then we activate PLEARN. Once a procedure has been learned, we can then execute it and it proceeds automatically until done (when we may go to the interrupt service state because we tried to pop negative - HOLD in this case is PPOPNEG) or an interrupt occurs (when we go to the interrupt service state with the HOLD register set to the type of interrupt). Note that after a PLEARN, the PLDST is set as PLSRC so that we can keep plearn-ing and learn a sequence of steps of a procedure.

Automatic procedure learning is effortless: we learn states as we manually enable (EXECUTE) instructions. The control section eventually learns to learn data structures as we experience them, and we then create levels of data structures as we understand them. The automatic learning of new procedures is similar to a computer with an instruction set that keeps expanding and improving.

As described above, control procedures are learned with registers PLSRC, PLREL, PLDST, and PLOUT. These registers are separate from the other control and data section registers because there can be no interference with state movements and, for example, recognition in the data section. Once learned, control procedures can operate automatically and sub-consciously. The control section is always learning a new sequence of control states as we manually enable steps. This sequence is soon forgotten if we do not recall it.

We automatically learn a control procedure while using another existing control procedure to manually access the instructions and data to do an operation. Once it works, we can execute the new control procedure and not think about the instructions. We do this by learning in the background. While the current executing control procedure runs, the learn (background) control procedure is learning. The current procedure registers are PSRC, PREL, PDST, and POUT. The procedure learn registers are PLSRC, PLREL, PLDST, and PLOUT. The current procedure registers update as we move from state to state. The procedure learn registers update only when we learn a new step or when we recall a procedure step.

We can start a procedure by accessing the data section to select the data node of the procedure, then activating the instruction EXECUTE. This takes whatever is in the HOLD register and uses it as a control sequence starting point. The low level procedure starts a procedure with "set procedure source" (SETPSRC), which loads the procedure source register (PSRC). SETPSRC is like a jump. To be able to return, the instruction "set procedure/push source" (SETPPSRC) is activated and pushes the calling location on the stack where it can be used for a later return. The paths from the data section to the control section used to execute a procedure identified by a data section node are the symmetric dual of the instruction paths from the control section to the data section.

Multiple outputs can be associated with a single state. For example, we may have a constant and the instruction to load it to a register. Both can be outputs from the same state. Early implementations will only have one output per state and a type variable to indicate if it is an instruction or a constant. If it is an instruction, it can be checked if it is an elemental instruction or a procedure call.

- Control section block diagram

The control section uses the same large array of links that the data section uses. With reference to figure 30, the connections to the large array of links are in addition to the connections shown in figure 13, but the connections shown in figure 30 are used by the control section while the connections used in figure 13 are used by the data section. The procedure registers access links each cycle in the large array of links to move from state to state. New control links are learned by using the procedure learn registers to write to the large array of links.

Referring to figure 30, during each cycle, the procedure source register (PSRC) is used to find the next state for the currently running procedure to move to. The procedure source register (PSRC) is used to access the large array of links along with the procedure relation information, which can be of three types: branch status, HOLD register, or "next". This relation information is used along with the PSRC to search through all the control type links in the large array to determine what the next state will be. If there is a match to PSRC and the relation information, then the link found in the large array will have a destination of the next state and it becomes the new PSRC. The output of the link found in the large array is activated if it is an elemental instruction, or called if it is a procedure, or loaded to the HOLD register if it is a constant.

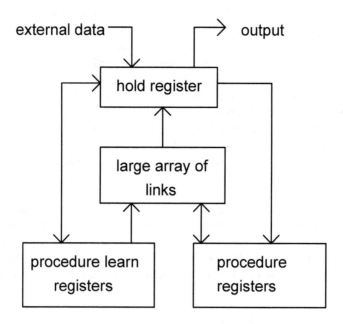

Figure 30: Control section block diagram (the control paths)

Note that the path in figure 30 from the procedure learn registers to the large array is unidirectional because the procedure learn register can only learn a new state. The path from the large array to the procedure registers is bi-directional because the procedure registers are used to find the next state and this next state is loaded back into the procedure registers. The path from the HOLD register to the procedure registers is unidirectional because these registers are constantly changing as states move and the only path is from the HOLD register to the PSRC register to set the start of a new procedure.

- Learning to talk and read

We learn to talk and read by slowly getting all of the states of the control section and the data in the data section properly arranged. In the data section: words, their parts of speech, and meaning must be learned. In the control section, the movement of states associated with words, parts of speech, and meaning must be learned. Once we have learned to read and talk, these procedures proceed with little effort because understanding in the form of state movement occurs with no effort. If a noun has been input, we cannot help but know it because state movement occurs. The knowing happens so automatically it is generally difficult for us to describe how we know.

- Control section control of syntax

Syntax is handled by the control section. When we speak, the control section selects the words in the proper order for syntactically correct sentences. When we listen, we use the data section, under the control of the control section, to select the proper meaning of words, based on their position in the sentence and on meaning. For example, "one" and "won" sound the same, but the first is an adjective, the other a verb. In the case of to/too/two, an idea is first activated for the sound to/too/two, and then the data section under the control of the control section selects the correct meaning by summing the sound with the expected word type. A single data source associated just with the sound could also be activated and the relation of the word type could select the correct idea. A faster way is to sum the sound and the word type together in one operation.

During input of sentences, the control section keeps track of the section of a sentence being processed. The control section activates states for subject, verb, object, and so on. It should be noted that a word type, such as noun, can input to multiple syntax states, although only one activates (noun can activate subject and object). Normally the syntax control procedures know what type of word is occurring.

Listening is a two stage process: syntax processing and imagining. Control states activate to understand syntax and will recognize a noun/verb mismatch (the dogs eats the food). The control states select the correct meaning based on syntax. The sequence of active control states generates a composite data source of a sentence, such as subject (relation)/ man (destination), verb (relation)/ went (destination), object (relation)/ store (destination), with all linked to a single data source. After syntax processing, control states activate to see if it makes sense (we imagine a man going to the store). When listening, we rapidly move back and forth between syntax and imagination. This two stage process is evident when we read something, but cannot remember what we read. We may have processed the syntax, but we did not imagine what was read.

It takes a long time for us to build up the control structures to understand speech. We learn the normal order of word types in sentences. We learn singular and plural nouns and the correct verbs to go with each. We learn to go back to try to understand some sounds. For example, "the "og" went outside and barked"- we assume it is "dog". When we do this, we go back to "og" and correct it. Often, we must go back when parsing to set or correct items as we understand them. This going back is part of the complex control structure we build up to understand what we listen to. We learn what ideas are associated with what words. We learn that words such as "run" can have a noun meaning and a verb meaning. We do this by linking the sound idea to a multiple data sources, such as run-noun and run-verb.

It has been shown that certain words can "prime" the detection of certain other words. For example, if we try to access the idea "nurse", then the response time will be faster if the word "doctor" is first activated; in this case "doctor" would be used to activate a data source that can access associated ideas. This occurs in the data section, where some of the activation of nurse activates doctor nodes because of the many links between them, making it easier for doctor to activate.

- Complex parsing of verbal input

Most verbal input does not have clear word boundaries; these must be determined based on complex procedures stored in the control section. For example, if we input to-day- the next syllable could be "in" for "today in", or it could be "ton" for "to Dayton (Ohio)". We parse this by creating a first word node "to-day", and at "ton" we receive an error (no find), so we move back and parallel access start/day, day/ton, and we find it and link it to the sentence structure. Then we move back to "to" and link it to the sentence structure.

- Control section recognition of words

The data section is normally associated with word recognition because of its summing capability allowing it to recognize the best possibility for a word by combining sound with other attributes. For example, the data section can combine the sound "-obin" and the attribute "isa/bird" to recognize "robin". The control section can also perform word recognition by associating a string of phonemes with a word. Each phoneme can cause a state to move to the next state until a word is recognized. These strings can be used for recognition of words, but not for recalling because there is no way to control the speed of recall with a string of control states.

- Procedures for translating languages

A complex ability that we have is the ability to recall an English word sequence and translate it to another language. We do this by recognizing the word that is input and activating the related non verbal idea associated with the word node. We can then use the idea to load to a data source register and, for example, use the relation "Italian word" to access the Italian word. We can then load the word to the sound data section to say it.

For example, if we translate "the man went to the store", we first input the English sentence and create a data source node along with links to the subject, verb, and object. Then we can output the sentence in Italian by first accessing the subject idea, which is then set as a data source, and the word in Italian is accessed by the control section selecting the relation "Italian word". Using "subject" as the relation accesses the "man" idea, which is then set as a data source and the relation "Italian word" is used to recall the word "uomo". This word "uomo" can then be used to access the sound sequence in the sound data section, which then allows access to the phonemes associated with the word. We then move back to the data source to access the verb. Note that each language has its own control procedures that are a result of the differences in each language (such as the order of adjective and noun).

- Attention and ideas

The current item held in the HOLD register is what we have attention on. The control section does not have to respond to every external input because the control section only responds to the HOLD register, branch status, and interrupts. We can ignore sounds, visuals, or other senses and only bring in to the HOLD register what we want to think about. We can enable certain senses to interrupt when they occur. For example, we can set the sound section to interrupt as soon as a person starts talking, which allows us to think of other things while waiting for the sound section to interrupt.

- Conscious and subconscious processing

If we try to recall, for example, how our foot felt while we were reading this, we cannot. Why is this? We must have been processing information from our foot because if someone stepped on it, we would immediately know. This is not pain interrupt based, because even if someone just touched our foot we would notice it. The answer is that we can set a threshold for our senses to interrupt our conscious processing of data. For information to be consciously processed, it must be loaded to the HOLD register or there must be an interrupt.

In the case of reading a book in a noisy environment, we can ignore the external sound input. But if our name is said we may notice it. This occurs because we may notice a voice in the background noise because it has a different sound spectrum, and we can interrupt our conscious processing with a different sound spectrum.

When we are driving a car and talking, we rapidly switch back and forth for conscious (control and data section based) processing, but we can use motor sequences to allow us to control the car, even when talking. When we are talking, we use the sound data section, which can independently control speaking.

- Repeats

External senses activate ideas and are able to become attention (HOLD register). When the same idea keeps occurring, the control section knows it is twice, three times, and so on. Eventually, the control section loses count when the same idea keeps occurring.

- Limited capacity

We can often be doing many things at once, such as walking, tapping a finger, humming a tune, and so on, but we can focus only on one thing at a time. For example, if we are doing all of these things, we cannot be focusing on our finger while we are focusing on the words to the song. When we focus on something, we input it to the data and control sections. Other activities, such as humming a tune, are using the peripheral sections such as the sound data section described in chapter 7.

We can be reading this and decide to focus on our foot, or ear, or arm, but we have to stop reading. When we are doing addition, we can focus only on the numbers. All of this is a result of the HOLD register being able to hold only one thing - what we have attention on.

The control section also has one state active at a time, but the motor section can operate independently and the sound data section (speaking or humming) can operate independently. It takes attention to learn in the motor and sound data sections, but once learned these sections can operate independently from the others. For example, when focusing on our foot, we set input/foot as an attribute, then SUMATR, and only foot sensory data will activate when we do SUMATR/SELMAX with external inputs. Of course, other areas we are not focusing on (ear, arm, and so on) can interrupt. When focusing on words being input, we set "word" as the relation, the sound input as the destination, and then we do the instructions SUMATR and SELMAX, and only a word will activate. Inputs feed to the thinking computer (through the HOLD register), the motor section, and the sound data section, but the control and data sections can select from a particular group of inputs (figure 31). There is a single control procedure and a single sound sequence active, but there may be multiple motor sequences (walk, turn head, and so on).

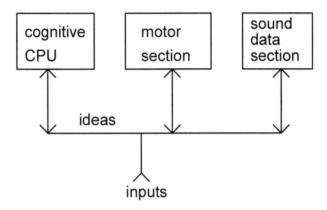

Figure 31: Input to thinking computer, motor, and sound data sections

- Restoration of data registers when returning from a procedure or an interrupt

When we return from a procedure (subroutine), we must manually restore the various registers. We use control procedures that recall what we were doing from the data section and reload the registers. For example, we frequently have to stop what we are doing, then do something else, and then return to what we were doing. While adding, we may have to sharpen a pencil then return to adding. Normally, we save our current goal in the data section and we recall it when we want to restore it. A possible future addition is to add automatic restoration of the various registers.

As with returning from a procedure, when we return from an interrupt, we must manually restore the various registers that were corrupted by the interrupt service procedure. Although automatic register restoration exists in some computer architectures, it is too complex for nature to evolve. When we first learn how to use elemental instructions, such as SETDREL, DRELACC, etc., the registers that we are working with must remain intact, otherwise we would lose what we were thinking about between, for example, the SETDREL and the DRELACC. The way this is accomplished is that the elemental instructions are linked to isa/easygoal and the code to decide what to do next often selects an easygoal to do next. When we are not doing anything specific, the goal code activates and can pick SETDREL, which is then executed and the step is learned, then the goal code activates again and may pick DRELACC, which is then executed and the step is learned. The goal selection mechanism does not corrupt the data registers. It relies on the emotion section and SPASM mechanism. In this way, we learn simple procedures without losing the settings of the data registers.

- Hierarchical data

Often the control section down the hierarchy of "isa" links to access information. For example, when adding, the control sequence must operate with numbers. If a letter occurs, we notice it and know we cannot add it. This occurs by first the idea of a particular number activating (for example 2 in 2+2). Then the control sections sets this as a data source and the control section selects "isa" as a relation and does the instruction DRELACC which allows "number" to activate if it is a number and the control section branches on "number". If it is a letter, then the control section branches to control procedures that can handle variables. This manual abstraction under control of the control section is necessary because many control states will respond to the idea of the original number (some control procedures respond to "2"). Therefore, abstraction cannot occur automatically because in some cases there will be a branch for "2" and a branch for "number", and the least abstracted branch must be taken. The control section first tries to find a branch for the input number is if no branch then the control section accesses the "isa" relation and branches on "number". For example, we may learn that if "0" is added then "sum remains the same". In this case, if "0" occurs, we do not want to take a "number" branch.

- Procedures for data fitting

If we are asked "is the sky blue ?", we can set DSRC to "sky", DREL to "color", and DDST to "blue" and activate the instruction FITSRC. We can then branch in the control section when "find" activates. We can also perform this function by first creating the link current/blue/matches. Then we set TMPSRC=sky and TMPREL=color, and we do TRELACC and find "blue". We return to current=DSRC and use blue from TRELACC as DREL. We then do DRELACC, which activates "matches", which feeds to the control section, which becomes aware of the match.

Another match example is: look at a list of letters and find N, P, or L. We could create a group of "matches" links associated with each letter that we are trying to find using the data section. This would use a single control sequence that branches on "matches". We could also use the control section, but this would require learning the control states in figure 32. Using the data section is preferable because the same control sequence could be used for any time we are looking for items in a list.

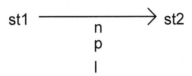

Figure 32: Control learning

The technique shown in figure 32 can handle complex state sequences as shown in figure 33. This would be difficult to do with the data section.

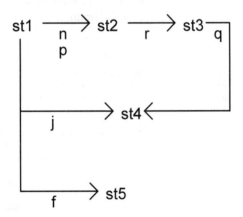

Figure 33: Complex state sequences

- Similarities between the data section and the control section

The structures of the control and data sections are quite similar. Both have a source, a relation, and a destination. A destination state is activated in the control section when a control section source and associated relation are activated. A data section destination is activated when a data section source and associated relation are activated and the destination is accessed. The data section is likely an evolutionary mutation copy of the control section, since the two sections are so similar and that a control section can exist by itself, but a data section needs a control section to operate it.

Summary: thinking computer control section
function: procedural information storage and execution
input: HOLD register, status, interrupts
output: instructions, constants
learning: automatic (at manual execute), manual (at PLEARN), and spasm (for initial learning of the instructions that are available).

The following is a list of instructions produced by the control section. These instructions are the elemental instructions that all complex procedures are built from (note that some instructions control the control section). Also included is a list of branch status information and interrupts. These elemental instructions are really the instruction set of the brain.

Basic data section related instructions:

```
SETDSRC - loads the value in the HOLD register to the DSRC register
SETDREL - loads the value in the HOLD register to the DREL register
SETDDST - loads the value in the HOLD register to the DDST register
SETTMPSRC - loads the value in the HOLD register to the TMPSRC
register
SETTMPREL - loads the value in the HOLD register to the TMPREL
register
SETTMPDST - loads the value in the HOLD register to the TMPDST
register
DRELACC - access the destination node associated with the DSRC and
        DREL registers and load it to the HOLD register
TRELACC - access the destination node associated with the TMPSRC and
        TMPREL registers and load it to the HOLD register
DLEARN - learn SRC/REL/DST - overwrite/correct
DLEARNML - learn SRC/REL/DST - do not overwrite
SRCTOHLD - loads the DSRC register to the HOLD register
RELTOHLD - loads the DREL register to the HOLD register
DSTTOHLD - loads the DDST register to the HOLD register
TSRCTOHLD - loads the TMPSRC register to the HOLD register
TRELTOHLD - loads the TMPREL register to the HOLD register
TDSTTOHLD - loads the TMPDST register to the HOLD register
```

DSRCTSRC - loads the DSRC register to the TMPSRC register
DDSTACC - access the relation between DSRC and DDST
TDSTACC - access the relation between TMPSRC and TMPDST

Data recognition related instructions:
CLRSUM - clear sum array getting ready for recognize.
SUMATR - increment all source nodes that match the attribute in
     TMPREL and TMPDST
SELMAX - select maximum sum - if more than one equal to maximum then
     pick most recent - the result is loaded to TMPSRC and to the
     HOLD register
SELMAXR - select maximum sum - if more than one is equal to the
     maximum then pick randomly from the maximum group - the result
     is loaded to TMPSRC and to the HOLD register
BLOCKSUM - block HOLD register value from being found with SELMAX(R)
SUBRCNT - block recently activated nodes from being found with
     SELMAX(R)
SUBATR - subtract an attribute from the sums before doing a SELMAX(R)
     select maximum sum as HOLD and as TMPSRC - used for
     recognition.
DRPTMP - sets TMPSRC and TMPDST to 0 for wild card recognition. Used
     for wild card recall and recognition, such as the last relation
     of "big" or the last destination of a particular book - at
     DRELACC if DSRC=0 then we find the most recent use of
     the current DREL.

Other data instructions:

CRDAT - create new data node, such as in a new situation; we use
     SUMATR/SELMAX to reactivate it from rel and dst information
LRNATRS - learn the current group of atrs stored during a sequence
     of SUMATR. We do not learn at each SUMATR because we may be
     just reactivating an existing data node. We store when we try
     to recognize and receive no find we manually activate LRNATRS.
FITSRC - look for a match to current source/relation/destination
     to answer, for example, "is the sky blue".
CHECKAGE - determine how long ago we accessed something: recent,
     medium, old.

control related instructions:

EXECUTE - manually starts a procedure - sets PSRC from HOLD and
     causes autolearning of a new procedure state
BLKNEWST - block the automatic creation of a new state - used for
     adding branches to a procedure
PLSTEP - step PLEARN during recall/modify of procedure - the
     instruction associated with the new step (PLOUT) is loaded to
     the HOLD register, but the instruction is not executed
PLFIXOUT - overwrite and fix a PLOUT
PLEARN - learn a new procedure step - PLOUT is loaded from the HOLD
     register - PLSRC and PLDST are automatically updated as we move
     to a new procedure state - PLREL is set at the end to "next",
     but we can overwrite this before the next PLEARN - we learn
     constants with CLEARN
CLEARN - constant learn - creates a new procedure step and sets the
     type to constant and the output from the HOLD register
PLRNHLD - loads the HOLD register to PLOUT and sets typelrn to
     constant - used for constant learning when a new constant step

should not be created; for example it is used with PLFIXOUT to
only fix a step. With CLEARN a new step is created
PRELACC - procedure relation access - causes to step to the next
procedure
step - only used by the low level push/pop procedure
SETPSRC - loads the HOLD register to the procedure source state
register (PSRC) - used to jump to a procedure (no push)
SETPPSRC - loads the HOLD register to procedure source state and also
push the current state on the stack so we can return from this
manually activated procedure. Cannot use PPUSH for this because
PPUSH uses POUT for what is pushed, SETPPSRC uses HOLD
SETPLSRC - loads the HOLD register to procedure learn source register
- for procedure learning
SETPLREL - loads the HOLD register to procedure learn relation
register - for procedure learning
SETPLDST - loads the HOLD register to procedure learn destination
register - for procedure learning
SETPLOUT - loads the HOLD register to procedure learn output register
- used for learning a new step
PLSRCTOHLD - procedure learn source register copied to the HOLD
register - used for adding branches to a procedure
PLRELTOHLD - procedure learn relation register copied to the HOLD
register
PLDSTTOHLD - procedure learn destination register copied to the HOLD
register
PLOUTTOHLD - procedure learn output register copied to the HOLD
register
CRACTL - start a new procedure learn - select a newnode and set it as
PLSRC and link it to a new data source, which is set as HOLD so
we can link it to other things
CSTRTHLD - loads the start of the current control procedure being
learned to the HOLD register
CURGOALHLD - loads start of the current procedure to the HOLD
register - used to allow linking pnpl to it - this is only used
in the automatic pnpl code
STRTCTL - re-execute a newly created procedure
PPUSH - if a state output is not an instruction or a constant we
automatically ppush - only used by the low level push/pop
procedure
PPOP - procedure pop back to where we were before the most recent
procedure was called - this is used only by the low level
push/pop procedure
RETURN - manually pop one level (normally return is automatic when
the last state in a sequence is reached)

emotion related instructions - explained in chapter 4:
OVERRIDE - override pain so we can force ourselves to do something
TSTORIDE - test if override is set; find if override is not set
PNPLTOHLD - loads HOLD with the current pain/pleasure level - this is
only used in the automatic code that links the pain/pleasure
level to the current goal
SETPNPL - loads pain/pleasure level from hold - this is only used by
the automatic decide procedure to recall the pain/pleasure
level associated with a procedure

sensory and output related instructions:

ACCN - access the north character in vis.txt relative to the current
position

```
ACCS - access south
ACCE - access east
ACCW - access west
READPL1 - read the next line in vis1.txt and load it to the top line
      in vis.txt(read plus 1)
READMN1 - same as readpll, but reads the last line (read minus 1)
EXTHLD - look up next word from top line of vis.txt and move it to
      the HOLD register (eventually need sound input and visual
      input).
PRINT - look up the word in HOLD and print it to vis.txt (equivalent
      to speaking)


(Sound related instructions - explained in chapter 7)

PROBEPHR - to probe a phrase for a match
SETSNDSTA - loads the HOLD register to sound state for recall
SETSNDINT - set sound intr enable - used when we want to continue
      thinking yet switch to listening when an input occurs
CLRSNDINT - clear sound intr enable
SETVISINT - set visual intr enable
CLRVISINT - clear visual intr enable
SNDSTATOHLD - loads the current sound state to the HOLD register - to
      allow data to recognize a song or a state in a song
SSTRTHLD - loads the start of the current learning sound string to
      the HOLD register
SNDSTART - clears sndsum array and sets all start of sound strings
      to 1
SNDSTEP - for recognize - looks for a match to external input
SNDMAX - used for sound sequence recognition - similar to SELMAX for
      the data section
CRASND - start a new sound sequence - select a newnode and set it as
      lrnssrc and link it to a new data source, which is set as HOLD
      so we can link it to other things
SNDNEXT - recalls next sound (also a relation that links sounds)

miscellaneous instructions:

TSTTIRED - test if we are tired
TSTVTIRED - test if very tired
NEXT - for procedure step - automatically set each cycle to move
      states linked with next
ENTMPO - enable tempo
TEMPOEND - stop the current tempo
TSTRCNT - during SELMAX test if the result has been recently accessed
      (most recent 200 cycles)


Branch information for the control section:

The control section receives status information from the data section
and input/output sections to control branching. The following is a
list of this status information.

FIND - used for branching when we find something
NOFIND - used for branching when we do not find something
RPEATSD - when we learn something that matches an existing source and
      Destination the idea RPEATSD activates, such as when the letter
      x is at two locations in a picture
RPEAT - if we try to learn something that matches an existing source
```

```
        and relation then the idea rpeat activates
MOVEMNT - idea if visual change
DNINTAC - idea activated every cycle to step low level push/pop
        states
NOFITSTAT  -  if  instruction  =  FITSRC  and  no  fit  then  the  idea
nofitstat is activated
READEND - idea that is activated if we read beyond the end of a line
SNDMATCH - idea set at SNDNEXT if the recalled sound matches external
        input
LOWLEVEL - idea set if the state output is a lowlevel instruction
        (not a procedure) - this is used only by the low level push/pop
        procedure
NOTLL - idea set if the state output is not a level instruction (not
        a procedure) - this is used only by the low level push/pop
        procedure - constants are not notll - notll indicates a
        procedure
LLNOFND - did not find a new state to move to - used by low level
        code to indicate need to PPOP
RECENT, MEDIUM, OLD - age branch status set by the CHECKAGE
        instruction


fixed data values:

START - linked to beginning of sound strings
GOODGOAL - if a goal is a good goal
VGOODGOAL - if a goal is a very good goal
GOALTYPE - data used to select goal type
ISA - for learning isa procedre (abbreviated spelling)
PROCEDRE - for learning isa procedre
SITUA - used for linking attention data found with SELMAX to the
current situation
```

interrupts:

Each sense has its own interrupt when its normal range is exceeded - loud sound, bright light, bad smell, too hot feeling, taste strong. The interrupts force the control flow to the interrupt service state where we branch on the interrupt type to handle the various interrupt types.

```
VISINTR - interrupt that occurs if visintren=1 and there is movement
LOUD - interrupt that occurs when a loud sound occurs
NEWWDINTR - interrupt that occurs if sndintren=1 and there is a word
        input, if sndintren=0 then branching on newwdintr is still
        allowed
PPOPNEG - interrupt that is activated when we pop and there is no
        place to pop to(when we pop from the top level procedure)
INTPN/INTRPLS - interrupts of pain or pleasure - pain can be
        overridden
INTPNPL- interrupt if had pleasure, but ended in boring
INTLOWPN - low level pain often from boring
```

TABLE OF ELEMENTAL INSTRUCTIONS (THE INSTRUCTION SET OF THE BRAIN)

	data reg	tmp reg	recog	recall	other
d	SETDSRC	SETTMPSRC	CLRSUM	DRELAACC	CRDAT
a	SETDREL	SETTMPREL	SUMATR	TRELACC	LRNATRS
t	SETDDST	SETTMPDST	SELMAX	DDSTACC	FITSRC
a	SRCTOHLD	TSRCTOHLD	SELMAXR	TDSTACC	CHECKAGE
	RELTOHLD	TRELTOHLD	BLOCKSUM		
i	DSTTOHLD	TDSTTOHLD	SUBRCNT		
n	DLEARN		SUBATR		
s	DLEARNML		DRPTMP		
t	DSRCTSRC				

	procedure reg	procedure learn reg	other
c	SETPSRC	SETPLSRC	EXECUTE
o	SETPPSRC	SETPLREL	CLEARN
n	PRELACC	SETPLDST	BLKNEWST
t		PLSTEP	CRACTL
r		PLFIXOUT	CSTRTHLD
o		PLRNHLD	STRTCTL
l		SETPLOUT	PPUSH
		PLSRCTOHLD	PPOP
i		PLRELTOHLD	RETURN
n		PLDSTTOHLD	TSTRCNT
s		PLOUTTOHLD	
t		PLEARN	

emotion	vision	sound	misc
OVERRIDE	ACCN	PROBEPHR	NEXT
TSTORIDE	ACCS	SETSNDSTA	ENTMPO
PNPLTOHLD	ACCE	SETSNDINT	TEMPOEND
SETPNPL	ACCW	CLRSNDINT	
TSTTIRED	READPL1	SNDSTATOHLD	
TSTVTIRED	READMN1	SSTRTHLD	
	EXTHLD	SNDSTART	
	PRINT	SNDSTEP	
	SETVISINT	SNDMAX	
	CLRVISINT	CRASND	
		SNDNEXT	

4 Detailed Description of the Emotion Section

The third and final section of the thinking computer is the emotion section. It is not only important to understand how we think, but to understand why we think about the things that we do. The emotion section is responsible for our thinking about useful things, for self-organizing, and for our being functional. Without emotions, there would be no way to initially determine what we should do from the myriad of things we are capable of doing. Everything would be equally important. Actions would be without reason. There would be no desire to understand. Once we organize our thoughts, we have less need of emotions as we can rationally decide to do things, but this rationality is a result of emotions biasing our early thoughts. The emotion section, along with our control and data sections, is responsible for our judgment, our sense of free will, and our ability to decide what to do.

Doing good things produces pleasure, doing bad things produces pain. Pain interrupts our thoughts and interferes with getting pleasure. Emotions bias the selection of good procedures. Random new procedures that we learn that do not produce a good result are not biased and thus not reactivated, and are eventually forgotten. This natural selection results in the retention of only useful procedures. When we are confused, we receive no pleasure and pain eventually occurs. This biases our activation of procedures that organize our thoughts.

When we evaluate doing a procedure, we evaluate its result versus its effort. If multiple procedures produce the same result, then we pick the easiest first because we receive pleasure from the result and there is the least pain in the effort doing it. As a result of this, if we pick apples from a tree, we first pick the easiest to get, even though the result is the same for all apples. Note that we can force ourselves to do the most difficult first if we decide there is a reason to do it (for example, more exercise if exercise is the goal). Evaluation of result versus effort is learned as a result of the pain and pleasure emotions.

Before we start a procedure, we evaluate how tired we are. If very tired, we just rest. If we are somewhat tired, we evaluate the effort of doing a procedure versus our tiredness. Since doing a procedure makes us tired, the result is that we tend to do short easy procedures and to pick the most efficient procedures to reach a goal.

- Emotion mechanisms

The main mechanisms for emotions are various levels of pain interrupts and pleasure interrupts and their associated interrupt service procedures. We have an internal pain/pleasure level and when it reaches the pain interrupt thresholds or pleasure interrupt thresholds we receive either a pain or pleasure interrupt. Pain and pleasure occur in a number of ways. The most obvious way is externally - we feel external pain (something hurts) and we feel pleasure (warmth, good taste, and so on). Pain and pleasure occur internally also. If we access data that we have not accessed in a while, or execute a procedure that we have not executed in a while, we receive pleasure. As we receive pleasure, it moves the pain/pleasure level toward pleasure, and if it reaches a pleasure interrupt threshold then we receive a pleasure type of interrupt. Internal pain occurs when we become bored with what we are doing. This happens because every so often we increase pain and if there is not pleasure from what we are doing we will eventually receive a pain type of interrupt (intlowpn) as the pain/pleasure level reaches the boring pain threshold. Executing procedures that do not produce pleasure eventually causes pain, and the effort of starting a procedure increases the pain level. In general, work increases pain unless there is a corresponding reward. Recalling painful data increases the pain level.

At pain and pleasure interrupts, our flow of thought is interrupted and we automatically link the pain/pleasure level to the current procedure being executed. This is used to later inhibit the re-executing of painful procedures. Whenever we attempt to execute a procedure, the pain/pleasure level is restored and can interrupt immediately. We use the instructions "current goal to hold" (CURGOALHLD) and "control start to hold" (CSTRTHLD) to access the current procedure being executed and the current procedure being learned. We also automatically link goodgoal or badgoal goal types to a procedure. After linking the pain/pleasure level and the goaltype, we proceed to the decide procedure, which decides what to do next. The decide procedure uses these goaltype values in its decision process. Note that there are many interrupt types, but only pain and pleasure types produce goal type links.

We can force ourselves to do painful procedures by using the OVERRIDE instruction. This allows us to do procedures that would normally be inhibited by our getting a pain interrupt as we try to start them. We can only OVERRIDE for a short time or until the pain level gets too high. Once we OVERRIDE, we must wait for a while before we can OVERRIDE again - otherwise we could just keep overriding painful procedures. We experience disappointment when we OVERRIDE and no pleasure results, only the pain that was being overridden. An example of the use of OVERRIDE is when we are reading - we may become bored doing it and stop after we receive a pain interrupt. Later, we may want to start reading again. We must OVERRIDE to start reading again because it ended with a boring (pain) interrupt the last time. As long as we start getting pleasure from what we start reading then there will be no other boring (low pain) interrupts.

The pleasure interrupts are not actual interrupts because we do not want to stop a good procedure with an interrupt. When pleasure occurs, we wait until we are finished with what we are doing before we go to the pleasure procedure, which links goaltype/goodgoal to the procedure that just finished. This goaltype/goodgoal is used later by the decide procedure to help decide what to do.

The decide procedure is built into the thinking computer and cannot be deleted. It picks the best procedure to do based on what has resulted in good results in the past, and based on the current situation. In other words, if we are eating candy, we do not pick any good procedure - we keep picking the eat candy procedure because of the current situation. It should be noted that the decide procedure can activate other procedure that are learned that help with deciding what to do.

The automatic activation of the decide procedure that selects the best procedure in a situation is important for survival. For example, if we are being chased by a wild animal we must quickly select the best response for this situation. This is a survival instinct. Also, since we must always have a procedure running, it makes sense that we auto select a procedure that selects the best procedure for a situation. It is also important for us to think about things related to our situation.

- Boredom and getting out of loops

Our control section is constantly running because we are continually conscious. But what if we become stuck in a loop? For example, we may read a sentence over and over. The way we avoid being permanently in a loop is that we eventually receive a boring (low pain) interrupt when no pleasure occurs for a long time. Every number of cycles, the pain level increases, and if nothing pleasurable occurs, then eventually we interrupt when we reach the pain interrupt threshold. The pain interrupt procedure automatically selects the decide procedure that tends to select good procedures. Even if we decide to do a bad procedure by using the instruction OVERRIDE, this only works up to a certain pain level (the instruction TSTORIDE is used to test if override is set). The pain interrupt procedure also automatically links goaltype/badgoal to the current goal so we do not select that goal over and over. If all we can find are bad goals then we use the instructions TSTRCNT (test recent) and SUBRCNT to find bad goals that have not been executed recently. Once a procedure gets a pain interrupt, it not only is not selected by the decide routine, but if we do try to it again, we automatically restore the pain/pleasure level when we start a procedure, and this would tend to cause another pain interrupt.

When a boring interrupt (INTLOWPN) occurs, the procedure that caused it may still be a good procedure. For example, if we are looking at a good view or reading a book, then the procedures may eventually become boring, but they produced pleasure at first and we may want to find this type of procedure later. If a procedure produces pleasure, but eventually gets boring, we receive a "pain/pleasure interrupt" (intpnpl). This is used to link "sometimes a good goal" (somegoodgl) to a procedure so it can later be reactivated when trying to find something to do.

Ideas occasionally randomly activate, and if we are getting bored with what we are doing and the random idea is interesting, then we start thinking about the random idea. In this way, we can become distracted from a boring task and not loop. When we become bored, we can just wait for one of these random ideas to activate (explained below in the data emotion links discussion).

Pain can occur when we try to learn data that we already know, such as when the source and relation and destination of what we are learning match a link already in memory. When this happens, the pain level moves up, and if it reaches the pain threshold we receive a pain type interrupt. Note that it is not boring if we write the same source/relation with a new destination, such as a new total when adding numbers, a new first place person during a race, or even a new pain/pleasure level associated with a goal. In all of these cases, we overwrite with a new destination. At boring, we interrupt (low pain) and the first part of the service procedure automatically updates the pain/pleasure level associated with the goal (we use CURGOALHLD to access the most recent goal) and sets its pain/pleasure level. We use the instruction PNPLTOHLD to move the pain/pleasure level to HOLD for use setting it as DDST.

- Data emotion links

We link the pain/pleasure level to data as well as procedures. Whenever we receive a pain or pleasure interrupt, we link the emotion level to the data that is in the HOLD register. Later, when we recall the data, the pain/pleasure level is recalled. We receive an internal pain or pleasure interrupt because it is recalled internally.

The data link to the pain emotion is useful in the example of touching a hot stove. We receive pain and link it to the data "hot stove". We also link the emotion level to the touching procedure, but the link is soon forgotten as we override and execute touching and receive pleasure. The pain link to the hot stove is permanent – it is not something we can manually control; we cannot manually DLEARN a correction. We have limited control over the emotion section. If we later encounter a hot stove, we receive an internal pain interrupt to warn us to be careful. This type of internal pain interrupt can be considered a danger interrupt. It can reoccur, but is disabled from reoccurring with a recall of hot stove for a period of time so it does not keep interrupting. If we encounter a cool stove, we create a new data source that does not have the pain emotion linked to it. We do not link emotion to a data source whenever we DLEARN because if, for example, we link color/black to the stove, we do not want to forget the pain link to the hot stove.

The data link to the pleasure emotion is useful in the example of eating candy. We receive pleasure and we link it to the data candy. We also link it to the eating procedure, but the link is soon forgotten as we sometimes eat good things and other times eat bad things. If we recall candy, we activate internal pleasure. At first, for example, before we know how to move our arms to reach for candy, we may look at candy. Eventually, we learn to reach for things and when we encounter candy, we receive internal pleasure, and then we look for procedures of how to obtain the candy, and activate them to reach for the candy. Eventually, we form more and more complex procedures, such as going to work to obtain money to buy candy, or going to school to find a good job to obtain money to buy candy.

When we do not know what to do, there is an automatic mechanism that activates strong emotion data. For example, if we are not thinking about anything in particular, the idea of candy or hot stove may activate and we will think about it.

We can execute the same procedure over and over and not become tired or bored with it, as long as we are recalling good things. For example, if we are adding over and over, there is no pleasure associated with the resulting numbers and we eventually become tired of it. It is work. But if we are daydreaming of sitting on the beach in the sun, we can do it without getting tired of it because the data we are recalling is pleasurable. As with pain, we only recall pleasure with the first access during a period of time. The pain/pleasure level associated with data is not stored as a relation link; it is stored as a number associated with the link itself. The reason for this is that we do not execute a procedure to access the pain/pleasure level when we access data; the pain/pleasure level is immediately available. Note that the pain/pleasure level associated with data is associated with a data node, not with a data source/relation/destination link. Therefore, when we learn a pain/pleasure level associated with a data node, we do not have to link it to all data links with that node, and we just link it to that single data node. The pain and pleasure interrupts store the data pain/pleasure level and the data recall and recognize instructions restore the data pain/pleasure level.

Note that the pleasure of recall is not as good as the actual pleasure of doing something. The level of pleasure is limited at recall. After recall, we may activate the idea to actually do the pleasurable thing (sit in the sun at the beach).

- Getting started and the evolution of complex procedures

Emotions are particularly important when a thinking computer first starts operating and there are no procedures or data learned yet. The emotions help select useful procedures. Eventually, when a thinking computer has learned to organize its thoughts, it can select goals based on reasoning and not emotions, but these reasoning procedures were learned as a result of emotions. For example, when we decide to add some numbers, there is no immediate pleasure or pain to bias our selection of procedures - we already know what to do. Goal structures, which are stored in the data section like any other data, can be extremely complex. The decision procedures know how to access these data structures and to determine what we should do next.

When a thinking computer first starts operating, it randomly does some operations. These are recorded, and if something good results then "goodgoal" is associated with the sequence of operations. For example: set a source register, then a relation register, then do an access. Pleasure and a pleasure interrupt may occur, and if so then "goodgoal" is linked to the new procedure. The automatic decide procedure can later pick this newly learned procedure for reactivation.

A difficult question to answer is how we go from knowing nothing (no data, no procedures) to learning how to decide, activate procedures, learn procedures, learn data, correct procedures, and so on. We first start with single step procedures, which are learned when random elemental instructions occur. We must automatically learn small sequences of instructions for us to eventually go from knowing nothing to knowing how to think. The small sequences undergo a Darwinian type of natural selection where successful procedures are recalled and reused and unsuccessful ones are forgotten because of lack of reuse [1]. The emotion section biases successful procedures for reuse. It is interesting to note that the human brain evolved because of natural selection and the procedures in the control section of the human brain are the result of natural selection. Over time, we gradually build up to more and most complex procedures and their associated data that result in the great achievements of humans:

```
- input external data
- output data
- move letters, visual location
- pairs of letters
- what it means to be done a procedure
- words and word categories
- learn how to learn
- selecting a goal
- self awareness
- learn to speak sentences
- learn to read
- learn to do arithmetic
- learn to handle life's situations
- learn specialties (scientist, engineer, inventor, doctor, musician,
    artist)
```

To quote Charles Darwin: "from so simple a beginning endless forms most beautiful and most wonderful have been, and are being, evolved." He was referring to living things, but it is also true of cognitive procedures.

- Automatic data learning as a result of emotions

Besides automatic procedure learning, we effectively have automatic data learning, but only as the result of a procedure doing manual learning. For example, if we enter a room for the first time, there is no way that we can avoid learning the room (if we leave the room we can recall that we were there). This is a result of the DLEARN instruction producing pleasure (as long as we learn something new) and as a result of the emotion section biasing procedures that cause data learning. We have a pain/pleasure level that moves toward pleasure as we learn new data items manually. If we learn the same thing over and over, such as looking at the same object continuously when we enter a room, we move the pain/pleasure level toward pain. Eventually, this would cause a pain type interrupt. This mechanism causes us to look around and learn about our environment because we receive pleasure with every new thing we learn. Curiosity results from this mechanism. Procedures that cause data learning are auto selected as good procedures. We initially randomly learn "look around and link data" procedures and these produce data learning (without confusion and repeats). These procedures produce pleasure and have "goodgoal" linked to them. Only when we become tired, do we automatically move from good goals to rest procedures.

We do not automatically learn when we sum attributes for recognition. For example, we may be searching for red objects, therefore we set rel=color, dst=red and do the instruction SUMATR, then SELMAX. When we do this, we do not want to data learn. We only want to data learn when we look at an object and do not recognize it. Therefore, when we SUMATR, we store the attributes that we are summing and later we can learn them. We do not want to auto learn at SELMAX with a "no find" because it could be like above, but we may be looking for blue objects, and if we do not find any then we do not want to learn. So data learning results from learning procedures that produce pleasure when we understand what is going on, resulting in self organization. We then reuse these procedures. We eventually learn to data learn when we cannot recognize a new object (the instruction is LRNATRS - learn attributes). Note that when we do recognize an object, we automatically link this object to the current situation along with an emotion link.

If we find something with SUMATR/SELMAX then we receive pleasure (pain/pleasure level decremented by 1). But we could become stuck in a loop if we keep recognizing the same thing and getting pleasure. For example, if we recall trees: pine then oak, we could become stuck in a loop and keep recalling them. The solution to this problem is to only provide pleasure the first time or first few times (during a time period) we recognize a particular object. Otherwise, if we looked at a forest, we would keep recognizing tree over and over. In other words, if the last time we accessed an item was close to the current cycle count, we do not receive pleasure.

- More complex goaltypes and goal links

When we receive a pain type interrupt, we can link different types of goaltypes to the active procedure, depending if it was already a badgoal or a goodgoal. If the current goal was a goodgoal, then we can link goodbadgoal to the current goal. This can be used for the case where we may be reading and become bored, but the reading procedure is still useful. When deciding what to do, we can first look for goodgoals then goodbadgoals. Note that we can have many more levels of goaltypes. For example, if we select a goodgoal once then we can link onetimegood and if twice then goodgoal in case we are not sure it is really a goodgoal, or we can link vgoodgoal (very good goal).

When we receive pleasure, we only link goodgoal to a current goal (curgoal) if it is not a goodgoal. If the current procedure is already a goodgoal, we do not want to relink goodgoal to it, and we do not want to create another goodgoal procedure from the newly learned procedure (ctlstrt) because we would encounter the problem of having the initial goodgoal, then a goodgoal procedure that activates that original goodgoal, then another procedure that activates the procedure that activates the original goodgoal, and so on. Therefore, at the start of the pleasure interrupt, we test if the current procedure is already a goodgoal, and if so we do not link goodgoal to the current procedure, and we do not link goodgoal to the procedure being learned. The above also applies to vgoodgoal if this goaltype is used.

- Deciding to do something

Ideas to do something pop into our head when there is nothing to do. We tend to start the sequence of deciding to do something by imagining a good result, such as something we desire. In a way similar to the way a dog salivates when it sees something it wants, we focus on what we want. Then the idea of working out how to reach our goal pops up because we have learned that to reach a goal we must do certain steps. The decide procedure uses the situation to activate this working out how procedure. This is a goodgoal procedure we have learned and received positive reinforcement for over time. Once we find a goodgoal, we can then activate it. If the initial good result of a goal is difficult to achieve, then we may imagine getting tired and decide not to activate the goal (for example, climbing a mountain).

- Tiredness

Besides pain and pleasure, we have the emotion of tiredness. Pain and pleasure produce interrupts. Tiredness does not interrupt, but it does block activation of procedures if we are too tired. We do not always have to be doing a procedure. There are times when we are tired and just wait. When we focus on a procedure to consider doing it, if it is very interesting it can overcome tiredness. Before we execute a procedure, it must pass the pain/pleasure test and we must not be too tired to do it. Extremely tired is sleep. We become tired when we have performed many procedures. Time (rest) makes us less tired. Tiredness helps us find efficient procedures. The tuning of the tired register is important. Too tired and we do not do enough. Too active and we just do anything and do not learn useful procedures because we just jump from procedure to procedure. Danger eliminates tiredness and we start executing situation based procedures.

- List of human emotions

There are a large number of human emotions. A list of English words associated with emotions [2] is shown below:

Admiration	Gratitude
Affection	Grief
Amusement	Guilt
Anger	Happiness
Anxiety	Hate
Apathy	Hope
Awe	Impatience
Boredom	Inspiration
Cheerfulness	Irritation

Confidence	Jealousy
Contempt	Love
Contentment	Nervousness
Delight	Panic
Depression	Passion
Determination	Pity
Disgust	Pride
Dislike	Relief
Elation	Remorse
Embarrassment	Resentment
Enjoyment	Reverence
Excitement	Sadness
Fear	Serenity
Friendliness	Shame
Frustration	Solemnity
Gaiety	Surprise

All emotions are the result of moving to state nodes (which we have learned) associated with each type of emotion. This movement is directly or indirectly a result of pain and pleasure interrupts. Pleasure interrupts are those that occur at a low frequency and can temporarily block pain interrupts because the pain/pleasure level is at pleasure. Pain tends to be interrupts that can occur excessively and that we cannot ignore. We learn that some stimulation, such as hunger or thirst, if ignored, will become more and more intense until at the extreme will be almost all we can think about (constant interrupts). Throbbing is a group of frequent pain interrupts, followed by less frequent, then returning to frequent. Each of our senses is able to generate pleasure feelings as a result of stimulation, and pain if the stimulation is too intense. Human examples are shown below, but any sensory mechanism can have a good range and pain outside this range:

sense	pleasure	pain
sight	nice scene	flash bulb too close
sound	music	loud sound
taste	good food, candy	bad food
touch	soft touch correct temp	being hit too hard too hot or cold
smell	good smell	bad smell
other	stomach satisfied	hungry thirsty

If we are acclimated to external pleasure and it stops, we receive some pain even though pain is not occurring. This is equivalent to taking candy from a baby. Children have a crying response that is activated by any pain. This is necessary to let adults know that a child is having a problem. All pain interrupts are OR'd and fed to the crying response section for children.

If we imagine getting a good result from a procedure that we have enabled, and then the good result does not occur, then we receive disappointment. This is a result of the imagined good result being used to keep the procedure going by using OVERRIDE. An actual good result is of a higher pleasure level than an imagined result. When we do not receive this higher pleasure level, then we receive a pain interrupt from the effort keeping the procedure going and there is no imagined good result anymore.

We learn to avoid pain because we do not like to be excessively interrupted in our thoughts, while pleasure helps avoid excessive boredom in that its interrupts signal that things are good, which temporarily blocks pain interrupts because the pain/pleasure level is near pleasure.

If we learn a procedure where we must do something dangerous, then we link pain (from danger) to the procedure. Later, when we try to start the procedure, we receive an interrupt. We can still start it, but we know to be careful.

- Dreaming and emotions

Dreaming is imagination with no return to reality. When we imagine, we activate data nodes and control procedures. These can be manually activated, or if we are dreaming or day-dreaming they can spuriously activate. The same mechanism that activates strong emotion data and control procedures (described above) runs continuously when dreaming. Once active, it feels like actively being in a place doing certain things. Even though the data is being recalled, it feels as if it is being experienced. This is a result of non-conscious activation of data nodes, and the activation of control procedures to respond to the data. For example, we can first dream that we are in Africa, and then suddenly a lion appears and chases us. Data structures with highly emotional links tend to have a higher chance of becoming active. In a particular place or situation, emotionally related data nodes tend to spuriously activate (such as a lion, or snake, or quicksand, and so on). Once a data structure is active, we can manually move within it under control of the control section (with spurious emotional data occurring). For example, if we are dreaming of walking down a street, the data structure for the street activates and the control procedure for walking activates. If the activation becomes too weak, some other place activates along with ideas of what to do at that place. Perhaps most important is that even though we are recalling a place, it feels as if we are experiencing it.

Dreaming may have evolved for us to learn to respond to dangerous or other emotionally important situations quickly, because we have already dreamed of the situation and as a result have created response structures.

Daydreaming also may have evolved for a similar reason. We daydream when the external world is not interesting enough. During these times, our cognitive abilities may be better used in terms of survival for considering emotionally strong situations.

The portion of sleep without dreaming may be used to allow nodes that have not been used for a long while to free up to allow more learning to occur. Automatic node free up is part of forgetting described in the next section.

- Comments on the emotion section

The emotion section is used to determine what to do: good/bad - right/wrong. Without the emotion section, the thinking computer is just a self programming machine that just continuously runs, but has no criteria for which goal to seek. The pain and pleasure of the emotion section gives the thinking computer a way to distinguish between goals and pursue happiness. We not only have an inalienable right to pursue happiness, it is built in to us to help us to decide what to do.

Summary: thinking computer emotion section
function: emotion processing
input: external pain and pleasure
output: pain and pleasure interrupts, bias control and data sections
learning: automatic at pain and pleasure interrupts

5 FORGETTING

A thinking computer must have a forgetting mechanism, otherwise storage space would eventually be filled and there would be no place to learn new information. It also takes longer to find a piece of information the more information we have (although the relationship is not linear), therefore getting rid of useless information helps speed up overall operation. To determine what information is least useful, a forgetting algorithm must include recency of use and total use. If we just save information that we have used many times, we will forget all new information. If we just save information that is new, we will forget important old information used many times. A simple example forgetting algorithm would forget items used few times and not used for many cycles: if usecount = 1 and lastuse < current_cycle_count - 1000 then forget.

We are constantly learning new information, often repeats of existing information. Each time we hear a song, it is not known if it is new so a new sound data sequence must be created. If we recognize the song, we can immediately move to recalling it and drop the new sound source without linking it to an idea. This new node, which was being linked to, will never be accessed again and will eventually be forgotten because of lack of use. Any nodes not used for a long while are forgotten. If we learn something and never use it, we forget it quicker than something that we have not used for a while but we use occasionally. We remember source nodes that have been held active longer than others. We remember higher levels of a story better because we refer to them more frequently. When we forget we free up nodes. These nodes can then be used again. During sleep, little learning occurs, so when we awake we have many free nodes and we are ready to start learning. During sleep, when we dream, we refresh important nodes (nodes that have strong emotions associated with them).

We rapidly forget some structures in the data section. For example, we rapidly forget the exact words in the sentences in a book that we are reading. This occurs because forgetting is based on how recently and frequently we have recalled something and we rarely recall the exact words in sentences. We are able to recall the overall story because we do recall the story frequently (total use) as we are thinking about it. The exact word sequences are forgotten quickly due to lack of being recalled. Soon after we read this sentence we forget it. For every piece of information that we keep for the long term, we likely forget thousands of other pieces of information.

We rapidly forget some control section information. If we learn a new procedure and it does not work, we probably will never use it again. Since its total use will be low, then as soon as it becomes non-recent it will be forgotten.

6   SENSORY INPUT

All input we receive is through our senses. Senses can be broadly categorized as external senses or internal status senses. Examples of external senses are hearing, sight, touch, taste, and smell. Internal status senses are hunger, thirst, and non-external pain, such as headache, soreness, and so on. As will be described in the implementation section, sensory structures are implementation dependent. In this section, human senses will be used as an example, but a particular thinking computer implementation can have whatever sensory structure is desired.

The following figure 34 is a block diagram of our cognitive sections. The upper part if the diagram has been described. The lower part, the senses will be described next. In figure 34, the control section sends instructions (abbreviated here as inst) to the other cognitive sections. The image buffer and phoneme section can interrupt the control section (movement, bright light, sound change, loud sound). The emotion section receives external and internal pain/pleasure and uses it to bias the control and data sections. The data section contains the data source, relation, and destination registers (abbreviated here as ds,r,d), and the temporary source, relation, and destination registers (abbreviated here as ts,r,d). The control section contains the procedure registers and the procedure learn registers and the control section can branch to the destination state using "next", the HOLD register value, or branch status information. The HOLD register is what we currently have attention on, and can be used for input from the senses and for output to the sound data section and the motor section. The vision input section receives visual information, which is stored in an image buffer and converted to image primitives by the image primitive section. The sound input section receives sound information, which is converted into phoneme information by the phone section and is stored in the sound buffer. The sound data section is used to recall and recognize sound sequences.

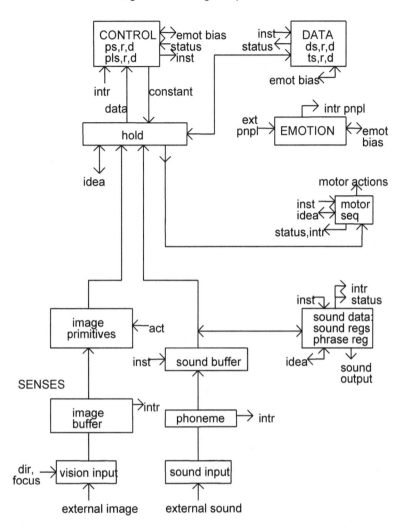

Figure 34: BLOCK DIAGRAM OF THE COGNITIVE
INFORMATION PROCESSING SECTIONS
OF THE HUMAN BRAIN AND OF THE
THINKING COMPUTER, INCLUDING INPUT
SENSES AND OUTPUT

6.1 SOUND INPUT SECTION

Processing of sound information starts in the ear at the neuron structure receiving sound. Sounds we hear are converted by our ear into their associated frequency spectrum. This is accomplished by sound vibrating the eardrum, which causes a membrane (basilar) to vibrate. This membrane is tapered so that its resonant characteristics vary over its length. Sensory hairs detect the oscillations of the membrane and generate a group of signals, each of which corresponds to a portion of the frequency spectrum of the sound. The thinking computer will use the FFT (Fast Fourier Transform) mathematical algorithm to convert sound into its frequency spectrum. This is typically done in 10ms segments called frames.

There is a wide variation in the average amplitude of sound input to the ear. We may hear a loud voice or a whisper. The ear contains neurons that produce an automatic gain effect to maintain a wide dynamic range of the real time frequency information. This information is sent to the phoneme section. In other words, the amplitude of the frequency spectrum information being sent to the phoneme section will be reasonably constant regardless of whether a word is said softly or loudly. The analog to this in the visual section (described below) is the ability to compensate for brightness.

Summary: sound input section: ear:
-function: converts sound to real time frequency spectrum
-input: sound - single input varying amplitude
-output: real time frequency spectrum to the PHONEME section
-learning: there is no learning in the ear
-instructions that control: none; always converting

6.2 PHONEME

The phoneme section is used to convert the frequency spectrum generated by the ear into the smallest elements of all languages: phonemes [15]. Some languages have less than 20 phonemes, others have close to 100. There is much overlap of phonemes from language to language. English has approximately 45. These phonemes are classified by how they are made by the human physiology. Various combinations of vocal chords, lips, tongue, nasal cavity, and so on, produce different phonemes. Although most of these organs probably evolved for breathing and eating, their manipulation can produce and vary sound. Each class of phonemes has its own characteristic frequency spectrum over time structure. Neuron structures detect the combination of frequencies over time associated with these phonemes. The list below indicates the classification of these phonemes and the characteristics of the frequency spectrum (symbols have been replaced with letter pairs).

Phoneme list:

Vowels: characteristic frequency spectrum is a pair of fixed frequencies.

Vowels produced in the front of the mouth: characteristic frequency spectrum: two fixed frequencies, one low, one high:

/i/   seat
/I/   bit
/e/   head
/ae/ hat

Vowels produced in the middle of the mouth: characteristic frequency spectrum: two fixed frequencies, one low, one middle:

/ir/ dirt
/uh/ hut
/ah/ the

Vowels produced in the back of the mouth: characteristic frequency spectrum: two fixed frequencies, both low:

/a/   cart
/o/   rod
/or/ cord
/oo/ would
/u/   rude

Dipthongs: vowel moving to another vowel: characteristic frequency spectrum: similar to vowels, but spectrum moves from one vowel to the other

/ei/ pay
/ai/ high
/au/ road
/au/ cow
/ie/ hear
/ue/ endure
/or/ sore
/oy/ boy

/ar/   care

Voiced plosives: characteristic frequency spectrum: no energy, followed by energy at all frequencies, followed by low frequency waves of energy at vowel type frequencies

/b/   bat
/d/   dog
/g/   get

Voiceless plosives: characteristic frequency spectrum: /p/ concentration of energy at low frequencies, /k/ concentration at middle frequencies, /t/ concentration above 3000Hz

/p/   pig
/t/   tell
/k/   kick

Voiced fricatives: characteristic frequency spectrum: periodic waves of low frequencies and a random pattern in the upper frequencies.

/v/   van
/th/   this
/z/   zoo
/zh/   azure

Voiceless fricatives: characteristic frequency spectrum: three groups: /f/ has wide distribution of energy with no peaks, /s/ and /sh/ main energy at higher frequencies, /h/ has a medium spread of energy with peaks similar to vowels.

/h/   hat
/f/   fix
/th/   thick
/s/   sat
/sh/   ship

Nasals: sounds produced by the nasal cavity: characteristic frequency spectrum: energy at about 300Hz and 800Hz - 2300Hz; lack of energy near 600Hz

/m/   man
/n/   null
/sn/   sing

Affricates (stop consonant followed by a fricative): characteristic frequency spectrum: similar to voiced plosive, but with a longer duration initial wide frequency spectrum

/j/   joke
/ch/   chew

Semivowels (glides): characteristic frequency spectrum: two frequencies, the lower of the two slowly rising in frequency, the higher of the two frequency can rise (as in the case of /w/, or fall as in the case of /y/

/w/   well
/r/   ran
/l/   let
/y/   you

It can be seen above that vowel sounds are a combination of two fixed frequencies. By taking two frequency generators and sweeping one over the range 220 to 1000 Hz and the other over the range 750 to 2600 Hz, it can be determined which vowels are identified in each region of the two dimensional space. Figure 35 shows the result.

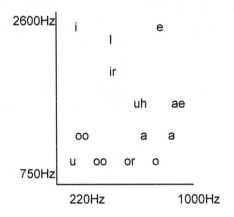

Figure 35: Vowel identification

Conversion of the frequency spectrum over time to phonemes is necessary to reduce the overall storage requirements. To store the complete frequency spectrum for each word would require storing much more information than storing the phonemes associated with each word.

Multiple phonemes can occur at the same time. For example, speaking the word "soup", the "ou" sound occurs with the "s" sound. This is referred to as co-articulation.

The frequency spectrum is converted to phonemes by neuron structures that respond to specific changes in the frequency spectrum. Absolute frequencies cannot be used because there is a wide variation in the average frequency of speech depending on the speaker. We can even identify words from, for example, a recording played back much faster than it was recorded, and with the sound frequency of the speech much higher that a human could produce.

The phoneme section operates on a group of sound spectrum inputs in parallel. The neurons in the phoneme section are organized to recognize phonemes by patterns in the frequency spectrum, such as rising or falling frequencies, distribution of frequencies through time, wide spectrum sounds ("sh"), nasal sounds ("m,n"), vowels ("a,e,i,o,u"), gaps in the sound stream, and so on. There is a wide variation in the frequency spectrum from speaker to speaker, including average frequency and speed of speech. The phoneme allows choosing the best fit by selecting the most active neuron structures, even though there are not perfect matches. Since much is done in parallel, the need for complex serial recognition connections is eliminated.

The phoneme section also generates information other than phonemes from the frequency spectrum, such as the average frequency, length of sounds, and so on. This allows us to identify a speaker or hear sounds that are not from a language, such as a siren, an engine, or a constant tone. This also allows us to understand speech in a noisy environment and also to follow the speech of one person in a room with many people talking. Emphasis on parts of words or words in a sentence is also identified and sent to the data section.

The phoneme section can convert speech to phonemes at different speeds depending on the rate that it is being heard. This is equivalent to the visual section being able to recognize characters presented at different rates of speed (the visual section can also recognize variable sized characters). All sound that occurs produces an output from the phoneme section, even if it is not really a phoneme. This allows ideas to occur related to any sounds.

The information from the phoneme section is fed to the sound buffer where it can be accessed by the control section for words to be recognized. These phonemes are also used by the control section to feed to the phoneme out buffer for generating speech.

The phoneme section can produce interrupts to indicate sounds are occurring, although a threshold can be set where only sounds louder than the threshold produce an interrupt.

When the phoneme section is implemented using computer technology, the sound input converted to electrical signals by a microphone. These signals are sampled in segments of time referred to as frames. Typically a frame is 10ms. The frame of electrical signals is converted to the frequency spectrum by a mathematical algorithm referred to as the Fast Fourier Transform (FFT). This algorithm can be run on dedicated Digital Signal Processing hardware (DSP) or on a traditional computer.

Summary: phoneme section:
-function: converts real time frequency spectrum to real time phonemes
-input: real time frequency spectrum from EAR (approximately 1000 unique - frequencies with varying amplitudes, many can be active at once)
-output: real time phoneme stream to SOUND BUFFER (approximately 100 unique phonemes, only one or very few asserted at a time), LOUD interrupt, and NEWWDINTR that can be enabled with SETSNDINT and CLRSNDINT
-learning: there is no learning in the PHONEME section
-instructions that control: none; the PHONEME section is always active

6.3 SOUND BUFFER

The sound buffer stores sounds as they occur in real time, but allows us to access them at our own rate. For example, we may be working on a problem and do not want to input any more sound information until we have finished with what we are doing. An example of this is doing some mental addition while there is someone talking. We can finish the addition, and hold temporarily (a few seconds) the sound input; then we can access the sound input and process it.

Summary: sound buffer:
-function: buffer of phoneme stream and other sound information (amplitude, emphasis, and so on).
-input: real time phoneme stream from PHONEME section (approximately 100 unique phonemes, only one or very few active at a time)

-output: controlled stream of phonemes fed to the thinking computer and to the sound data section (approximately 100 unique phonemes) from the end of the buffer
-learning: the last few seconds of phonemes are held
-instructions that control: sound buffer to the HOLD register (listen)

6.4 VISION INPUT SECTION

Up to this point, sound sensory processing has been described. Now we will discuss vision. We have many cognitive abilities associated with vision. When we see, the lenses in our eyes focus an image on the retina: an array of light sensitive cells (rods). There are about 350 rods connected to each optic nerve fiber. These 350 rods occupy a circular area (with some overlap) and receive and sum light from about 10 minutes of arc in diameter. With 60 minutes of arc to one degree, and a visual field of around 180 degrees (you cannot see behind you), this works out to around 1 million optic nerve fibers or pixels in the image. This is a rough estimate; the center of the vision field has a higher density of sensitive cells than the edge.

Another way to estimate how many pixels are in the eye is as follows. If we hang some printed text on the wall (letters around 1/4" high) and we see how far back we can go and still be able to make out letters, it is about 5 feet. A letter probably needs at least 4 x 4 pixels to be identified. In rough terms, our visual field at 5 feet would be about 25 square feet. Therefore, the total number of pixels would be 25 square feet or 3,600 square inches divided by 1/4" squared or .0625 square inches times 16, or about 1 million pixels.

The iris in the eye compensates for overall brightness. Local brightness is compensated by interconnections between the optic nerve neurons that average the brightness in areas of the eye and then brightens dim areas and dims bright areas. The optic nerve then connects to other cognitive areas in the brain for more processing of the image.

Muscles control the lens of the eye allowing it to focus on objects over a range of distances. We can sense the amount of effort required and this allows us to estimate distance to an object (stereo vision also allows us to estimate distance).

To implement this section using electronic hardware, a video camera would be used.

Summary: vision input section: eye:
-function: converts external image to pixel array
-input: external image
-output: pixels to IMAGE BUFFER section

-learning: none
-instructions that control: direction to look (up, down, right, left), focus

6.5 IMAGE BUFFER

It has been shown [17] that if a 3 x 3 group of letters is flashed at a subject and turned off, and then the subject is told quickly to select a row (top, middle, bottom), then the subject can recall the items, but if then asked to list the other items in the rows not initially asked for, the subject cannot. This indicates a temporary storage buffer (valid for around a second). Since selection of a part of the image is required for image primitive generation, it is likely that the image buffer is actually a store of the pixels of the image and we mentally move to the part of the image for image primitive generation at the initial selection, but the image has mentally faded before the second selection.

To implement this section using computer technology, a memory buffer would be used.

Summary: image buffer:
-function: buffer of image pixels
-input: pixels from EYE
-output: pixels to IMAGE PRIMITIVES section, VISINTR interrupt at movement if enable with SETVISINT; interrupt enable cleared with CLRVISINT, too BRIGHT pain interrupt
-learning: none
-instructions that control: none

6.6 IMAGE PRIMITIVES

The whole array of image pixels is always being processed. For example, we will notice any movement in our visual field, even if it is very small and in some corner of the field. We can notice this movement even if we are moving our eyes. We can detect motion that is different from the motion of the visual field. It should be noted that this background motion of the visual field can be complex. If we are still and move our eyes, the visual field uniformly moves. But if we are walking toward an object, the object straight ahead is not moving at all (except to become bigger) and the objects at the edges of the visual field are moving rapidly as shown below in figure 36. In this case we can still detect movement that does not match this movement in all directions. For example, even though the background is moving when walking outside, we can still detect a bird flying by. The algorithm to detect this motion is to calculate the average movement in various areas of the visual field, and then to detect any motion that is very different from this movement. This essentially detects edges in movement. This is similar to the neuron structure in the eye that detects average brightness in areas of the eye, and then brightens or dims areas that are far from the average to produce a more uniform amplitude. This is also similar to the automatic gain control in the ear, where feedback amplifies sounds if they are very weak.

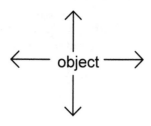

Figure 36: Visual field

Other cognitive structures in the eye detect changes in intensity to identify lines and edges of objects. Neuron structures have been found in cats [9] that detect edges by responding to light positively on one side of a line and negatively to light on the other side of a line. Other structures have been found to detect bars, which respond to light positively along a line and negatively outside the line, or vice versa, or an increase in brightness with decrease on both sides, or vice versa. Derivative and derivative of derivative processing are useful for edge detection and changes in a light gradient.

Although we process the whole visual field for motion and edge detection, we can only put attention on one object at a time. Our visual abilities are therefore divided into two types: those that occur without attention and those that require attention (and are understood by the control section). The whole visual field is always being processed to determine areas to put attention on. The control section understands what is being looked at and responds to objects. Although it will not be discussed in detail here, stereo vision also requires processing the whole field to detect aspects of vision only available with stereo processing (two fields of random dots, each identical except for a shifted center section will produce a stereo image). Also not discussed in detail here is color vision, which is derived from cone cells in the eye.

Texture identification allows us to recognize two groups of x's in the following image (figure 37), without putting attention on each individual x.

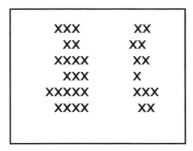

Figure 37: Groups of x's

This is accomplished by groups of neurons passing the complete image through different frequency image filters. High frequency filters produce small rings around each x; lower frequency filters identify two regions of x's. These same filters allow us to look at a page of text and identify the few paragraphs without attention on each word. This whole image processing is automatic, without attention, but guides us where to put attention. When we are reading, we first find the paragraphs, then we can move attention to individual words and letters. We do this by consciously narrowing our visual field.

As with all of the senses, the sensory neuron structures associated with the image primitives section do not learn; they only process external data.

Much of human non-attention cognitive visual abilities probably evolved during the human animal past. Movement detection was important to detect an animal that could be dangerous in the vicinity. Texture could detect an animal hiding in a uniform visual area, such as a tiger hiding in the grass. Stereo vision and effort to focus would help identify the distance of an object. Therefore, when we look at a visual field, it is all processed at once for motion, intensity (we can find a bright spot in any part of the field), texture (frequency spectrum of intensity change per degree), stereo effect and color. (The audio section can detect speech in a noisy environment and may have evolved to detect the noise of something sneaking up on us or the call of a dangerous animal.) Animals are likely missing some cognitive information processing functions.

The visual data from the eye is first processed for motion, edge detection, and stereo vision. This is generated in the image primitive section along with primitives for the area of the image being attended to. These primitives allow us to recognize objects. What are these primitives? Primitives are not a crude pixel map of an object; this would take too much memory space. If we consider the objects (letters) in this text, we recognize b, d, p, q as loops with a line attached. When we store a line, we only need to store that it is line, and the endpoints. To store a "p" requires storing a loop and a line end at the lower left; along with the fact that it is a single object. If the line and the loop were spaced, then it would not be stored as a single object. We can therefore detect and separate a single object, then store its image primitives. When we store the primitives for an object we store the relative coordinates of these primitives. These do not have to be exact coordinates and in fact should not be so we can recognize the many ways handwriting can make a letter, such as "p". The list of primitives for letters and other objects is:

1. single object detect
2. line/end point (s)/coord
3. curve/coord/orientation (detect "c", "s")
4. vertex/coord (detect a square)
5. cross/coord (detect "x")
6. loops/coord ("o", "p"...)

It should be noted that we can recognize letters of any size that fit in our visual field, therefore the same primitives must occur regardless of the size of the object. Image primitives are fed to the thinking computer where they can be selected and processed.

Attention is not required to determine primitives; they are determined all at once as an object is observed. When we are reading, we do not put attention on looking around an object to detect the primitives, we have attention on the words that are occurring. When the number "3" is observed, the primitives detected would be:

```
line end .
            .curve opening west
    vertex  .
            .curve opening west
line end .
```

The points above represent relative coordinates.

To implement this section using computer technology, a computer that processes the image data and outputs image primitives would be used.

Summary: image primitives section:
-function: converts pixel array to image primitives

-input: pixels from IMAGE BUFFER
-output: image primitives to data and control sections, interrupts
-learning: none
-instructions that control: select visual field size (ex: whole page of text or a word), image primitive to the hold register (look)

7 PERIPHERAL SECTIONS

Although the thinking computer data section is used for storing most data relationships, often we want to recall long sequences of information, such as sequences of sounds (for example, songs or poems) or sequences of motor instructions (for example, walking), at the same time we are using the thinking computer for processing operations, such as understanding and storing the ideas associated with a song, or processing visual information. We have separate data sections for these functions: the sound data section and the motor data section. Both of these sections have links that are very similar to the links of the thinking computer control section, but the sound data section is a data section because there is no decision process; it is under control of the thinking computer control section, which controls when we recall a word or sequence of words and how fast we recall. The motor section is a control section because it does branch on external input data (such as muscle status when walking).

7.1 SOUND DATA SECTION

The sound data section is similar to the control section in that it is based on states, but it is a type of data section because it operates under the control of the control section. There is a state associated with each sound. A sound data section state can have many outputs (similar to the control section). A state can output the tone, the length of the tone, and even output actions as when playing the piano (even multiple actions as when a number of keys are hit at once on the piano). The states of the sound data section are linked with only one relation: SNDNEXT, as opposed to the control section, which can have any idea link states. The output of the sound data section feeds externally and to the HOLD register where it is processed as if it were an external input, using the same path as the sound buffer to the HOLD register. During recall, the external output can be disabled (silently recalling a sound sequence). Besides sound information from the sound data section, the HOLD register can also receive ideas related to the start of sound sequences or points along a sound sequence. Ideas can also go from the HOLD register to the sound data section to activate the start of a sound sequence or points along a sound sequence. The sound data section stores songs and other sequences, as sequences of phonemes. To access the refrain to a song, we momentarily use the data section, which keeps track of what verse we are at. Tone, tempo, emphasis, and other information can be stored with each phoneme.

The sound data section is separate from the control section because we can be recalling or recognizing a sound string in the sound data section while the control states are understanding the ideas from the sound string.

We use the same sound state structure to both recall and recognize sound strings. To recognize, we must start with all sound strings active. The instruction SNDSTART activates the first node of all sound strings. The instruction SNDSTEP looks for a match between the HOLD register (which will normally have a phoneme or word that has just been input) and all of the still active strings and drops any that do not match. This keeps only strings active that have matched each element of a sound sequence. Finally, the instruction SNDMAX selects the most recent still active string (using the cycle count of the most recent use). This also sets the sound state register (SNDSTATE), which holds the current state we are accessing. This state is used with the instruction SNDNEXT to step to the next sound. This allows us to recognize "a b c d", then to continue on by saying "e f g h...". The idea SNDMATCH activates when we find an active state with SNDNEXT, and the control section can branch on this status information. We can stop the recall of a sound sequence and later continue without losing our place - even after many control states in the control section occur. The SNDSTATE register is used when we start recalling later. Note that we cannot recall two sound strings at once.

We automatically learn sequences in the sound data section in a way similar to control procedure learning. We have a sound data source register that we can use to recall a recently heard/learned string. We are always learning new strings, although we may soon forget them if they are not used soon enough or frequently enough. At EXTHLD, we automatically learn a new sound state using the "learn sound source register" (LRNSSRC). Like the control section, there is a limit to the number of sequential states we can store in one sequence before we automatically start a new sequence. A long delay between sounds also starts a new sequence. We also learn in the phrase register for probing. Note that we learn in the sound data section even if we are recalling another string from the sound data section because we can later recall what we accessed. This occurs even if we input an external sound followed by a sound from a recalled string.

The sound data section can recognize part of a string, and then switch to recall, and then move back to recognize, the whole time using the same storage structure:

external: a b c d   i j k

recall: e f g h   l m n o ...

We can also perform the above with the words to a song.

The sound data section has a phrase register of the currently input phrase. This phrase can be randomly probed. For example, we can be asked if a particular telephone number has an "8" in it. We are always learning new sequences and we assert CRASND (create sound) to start a new sound sequence. The node of the start of the new sequence is held in the "sound start register" (SNDSTART). If we want to probe a telephone number we assert CRASND and then recall the telephone number. For example, 555-1283. We can then probe it: does it contain an 8? We can probe for 3 then 9. Then, if we want, we can probe the numbers we just used for probing because the phrase register is double buffered - there is a phrase register, which we use for probing and a pre-phrase register, which can later be moved to the phrase register. Therefore, the phrase register is really the previous sound sequence stored and pre-phrase is the current sound sequence. We assert PROBEPHRASE to use the HOLD register to look for a match with the phrase register (which is a copy of the last pre-phrase register). If there is a match, the idea SNDMATCH activates, which can be used by the control for branching. The phrase register can store emphasis for recognition.

d,o,g c,a,t f,a,r

In the above example, if we try to find d,o,g then we find it; if we try to find g,c,a then we do not find it because of emphasis on only d and c, not g. We can store/recognize tones. The phrase register can store when we change input types, such as abc123def. Note: when stored in one language we cannot probe in another language (unless we translate, which requires the thinking computer). This phrase register is not to be confused with the input buffer described previously, which holds items not yet input and allows us to consider what has been input before inputting more.

Repeats of sound sequences are detected with the phrase register. For example, if we hear 249249, we detect the repeat of 249 with the phrase register, while continuing to learn the new sound sequence. If the input was 249290, we would start looking for a repeat at the second 2, but there would be no match at the 9.

The sound data section also has a word input register that tags groups of phoneme with position information (1st, 2nd, 3rd, and so on) and feeds them as a group to the data section to allow the data section to receive sound/position information and combine it with other attributes, allowing for word recognition. This parallel recognition was described previously in the control section discussion with the example "today in" and "to Dayton". We can move around the word boundary and parallel recognize multiple arrangements of position/phoneme information.

We are able to recall or input a sound sequence and at any point start repeating the last item. For example, we can recall abcdef and stop at f and keep saying it. We do this by inputting each letter and storing it in the HOLD register, then using the speak capability to say it over and over. Note that we can say it in another language if we like. Normally, as sounds are input, we store them in a data structure as we understand them, and we also store them as a new sound sequence in the sound data section.

The link between the HOLD register and the sound data section is bi-directional. We can recall a sound sequence by loading the HOLD register to the SNDSTATE register, and we can recognize a sound sequence, such as a song, by moving the SNDSTATE register to the HOLD register.

We learn in the sound data section when we put attention on the external sound input (when we activate the EXTHLD instruction). The "learn sound source register" (LRNSSRC) holds the current sound learn state and is used when we learn a new sound. During learning, a new sound state is created and linked to the LRNSSRC, and then the LRNSSRC is updated with the new learn sound state. This is similar to the control section where we learn when we execute an instruction. When we recall from the sound data section with SNDNEXT, the output of the sound data section is put in the sound input register, just as if we were hearing it again.

- Tempo

We can recall from the sound data section at a certain tempo. After every specific time interval we can recall the next item from the sound data section, when we do the instruction ENTMPO (enable tempo). This allows us, for example, to recall a song at a certain rate. The mechanism that causes this to happen is very simple - it produces the SNDNEXT instruction automatically (without the control section doing it) at a specific rate. We can set the rate and also speed it up a little or slow it down a little (UPTMPO or DWNTMPO). When we are doing this, it almost feels as if it is external continuous sound occurring. The instruction stop tempo (TEMPOEND) stops the tempo recall, but it can be re-enabled at any time.

- Emphasis

We can recall a sequence, such as A,B,C... or 1,2,3..., at any speed, or with emphasis on every 2nd or 3rd or Nth item. The control procedure keeps track of the count of items and can emphasize every Nth item and control the speed.

- Detecting a match to a sound data source

When inputting a long string, we can test that each element fits to the currently active string. For example, we can be inputting a song, such as row, row, row your..., and we fit it to a sound data source of this song. The branch status SNDMATCH stays active as long as there is a fit. If we then receive an input that does not fit (canoe), then the SNDMATCH branch status is no longer active. Note that this is different from the data section "no find".

- Links to the HOLD register

We can start the recall of a string in the sound data section by activating an idea in the HOLD register and activating SETSNDSTA from the control section. This activation is similar to the way we activate a control procedure with EXECUTE - but a control procedure automatically starts stepping from state to state. When we recognize a song, we can then switch to recalling it. We can also activate the title of it by using the path from the sound state register to the HOLD register. When we activate the instruction SNDSTATOHLD, the sound state register is loaded to the HOLD register. It can then be used by the data section to recall data related to the song. The instruction SSTRTHLD loads the "start of the learn sound sequence" (SNDSTRT) to the HOLD register for use linking a sound string to the data section. It should be noted that we can load any sound state to the HOLD register (as we are stepping through a sound sequence) so we can associate something (data) with any sound state (such as "second verse"). We can also recall a sound state from the data section to activate a sound data string at any point using the instruction SETSNDSTA. It should also be noted that we cannot access the title of a song from any sound state - only those where we have learned the state in the data section and have associated it with the name of the song and other related song facts. For example: we may start recalling a song and then continue recalling and think about other things. If we then try to recall the title of the song we are humming we cannot - we must step to a sound state that can be recognized by the data section. Any sound state can be loaded to the HOLD register, but only a few have we learned in the data section.

Music is stored in the sound data section. This allows humming a song without paying attention to it and without it interfering with the data section operation. We can use the data section while recalling a song from the sound data section to parse the words (often we do not recognize a word until all the syllables have been recalled from the song). A song can have many entry points, such as a refrain or various verses. Note we cannot go backwards in music, but we can keep repeating a phrase.

- Storage of strings and chunking

Studies have shown [14] that if we are presented with a long string of numbers and then asked to recall them we tend to remember the first few and the last few. Over a number of trials the curve tends to look like figure 38.

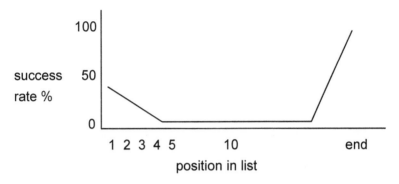

Figure 38: Success versus position in list

The initial items have good recall because they are stored at the beginning of a sound sequence, which has poorer recall after around 7 items [13]. Recent items (at the end of the list) are strong because they are fresh in our phrase register.

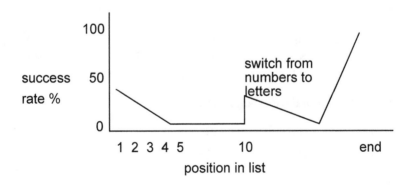

Figure 39: Success versus position in list with category switch

When we have been inputting a long string of numbers and we switch to letters, we are able to recall the initial letters better than the end of the numbers [19] as shown in figure 39. This occurs because we may either start a new sequence in the sound data section when the letters start, or generate an entry point in the sequence when the letters start.

It has been shown [18] that there is a 38ms added delay in recognition for each item added to a list. This is a result of interference from other items (slowing down the SELMAX) and stepping through a list to check for a match.

It should also be noted that we can store every 5th or Nth element in a long string, in which case that sequence of Nth elements would have a recall curve similar to the one in figure 38.

The data section can also be used to store sequential information. For example, the first item can have an attribute of first/item1; the next item can have second/item2. We can also store data section strings where item1 can be used as the relation to access item2. This was explained in chapter 2.

Chunking is a way to minimize the number of sequential elements to be stored. A long string of 1's and 0's can be converted to octal or hexadecimal to reduce the number of elements to be stored. For example, 101110111 contains nine elements, but after converting it to octal 567, it contains only three. For chunks to be generally useful they are normally short in length (a few digits), but a telephone number can also be a chunk and we can store many digits if we recognize them as different telephone numbers.

- Silent reading

Silent reading uses the idea path to allow us to mentally hear what we are reading. We recognize each word visually, and then we activate the idea of the sound of the word for the sound data section to store.

- Example of sound data section links

The number 3 at the beginning of the line indicates that it is a sound data link (1 is a data link, 2 is a control link, and 4 is a control constant).

```
3 row-st0   sndnext   row-st1   start   ;
3 row-st1   sndnext   row-st2   row     ;
3 row-st2   sndnext   row-st3   row     ;
3 row-st3   sndnext   row-st4   row     ;
3 row-st4   sndnext   row-st5   your    ;
3 row-st5   sndnext   row-st6   boat    ;
```

Summary: sound data section
function: stores and recalls sequences of sounds
input: sound buffer output, ideas
output: output sound, sound data, ideas (of words, parts of words - syllables, sequences of words – songs, poems), interrupt/status information (sndmatch, sound no fit)
learning: automatic at external input

instructions that control the sound data section:

PROBEPHR - to probe a phrase for a match

SETSNDSTA - loads the HOLD register to sound state for recall

SETSNDINT - set sound intr enable - used when we want to continue thinking yet switch to listening when an input occurs

CLRSNDINT - clear sound intr enable

SETVISINT - set visual intr enable

CLRVISINT - clear visual intr enable

SNDSTATOHLD - loads the current sound state to the HOLD register – to allow data to recognize a song or a state in a song

SSTRTHLD - loads the start of the current learning sound string to the HOLD register

SNDSTART - clears sndsum array and sets all start of sound strings to 1

SNDSTEP - for recognize - looks for a match to external input

SNDMAX - used for sound sequence recognition - similar to SELMAX for the data section

CRASND - start a new sound sequence - select a newnode and set it as lrnssrc and link it to a new data src, which is set as HOLD so we can link it to other things

SNDNEXT - recalls next sound (also a relation that links sounds)

7.2 MOTOR CONTROL SECTION

The motor control section is based on sequences of states like the control section and the sound data section. When we are walking, we do not put conscious attention on moving our legs. As we walk, external information feeds directly to the motor control section to cause branching. The motor control section learns by storing instructions as they are initially performed under conscious control (as when we learn to walk). Later, they can be reactivated in the background in an automatic fashion.

We can enable multiple motor sequences at once. For example, we can start tapping a foot then start moving fingers in a sequence. We can add more instructions. It should be noted that although there can be many sequences active; they seem to step based on a common tempo.

motor section examples:

    tapping foot
    walking
    moving arm

The control section does not have multiple sequences active at once because:

a. at "next" there would be no way to determine which sequence should move

b. a single HOLD register could not work with two control sequences

When a motor operation completes, it may have to signal to the control section that it is complete. It can do this by interrupting. It can also just activate the idea "done" to allow a control procedure to branch. Some sequences, such as walking, do not have to signal when done.

We learn in the motor section by first focusing attention on then manually enabling motor instructions. For example, as we tap a certain sequence of fingers, we manually enable each instruction. The motor section records it as we record songs in the sound data section and procedures in the control section. Motor states can wait for a long time before moving to the next state as with walking. Motor states are hierarchical.

The motor states directly activate muscles and cause motor instructions to occur. These motor instructions can also be enabled by the thinking computer control section and are learned in the motor section, when enabled by the thinking computer, as a sequence of motor states. This sequence can be later used by just enabling it from the control section. This allows us to then use the motor section and the control section at the same time, such as when walking and understanding speech.

An indication that a separate cognitive mechanism exists is to try to do multiple things at once. We cannot recall an object and a story, both at once. This indicates it is one mechanism, in this case the thinking computer data section. We can be humming a song (with the sound data section), accessing a fact (with the thinking computer data section), and walking with the motor section, indicating that they are separate mechanisms.

Summary: motor control section:

-function: stores and recalls sequences of motor instructions

-input: motor instructions, ideas (to select a sequence for activation)

-output: motor instructions, ideas (to learn ideas associated with sequences), interrupt/status

-learning: automatic learning when motor instructions are activated manually by the control section

8 MODIFICATIONS

Now that we understand how to build a thinking computer, we can consider modifying it. This can take the form of removing features or adding features. To make a machine useful for various applications and to maintain control may mean that all cognitive abilities are not needed. For certain tasks, such as manufacturing, all sensory and associative processing abilities may not be needed. For example, only vision may be needed. For certain repetitive tasks, learning is not needed; returning to an initial state after a task is completed may be sufficient and desirable.

Additional cognitive abilities, such as the ability to sense and process unusual sound information, various parts of the electromagnetic spectrum, or other sensory information outside the range of normal senses, magnify images, record events in detail, do arithmetic by building in a calculator, build in a general purpose computer, build in clocks for measuring time, handle multiple visual, or other senses, can be added for a particular application. Thinking computers could be built into ships, airplanes, automobiles, or other objects to operate them. Features could be added to the thinking computer. It may also help to add registers, such as one or more groups of source/relation/destination registers. Learning with the temporary registers (TLEARN), recognition and relation stepping with the current data registers, TSRCDSRC, loading the destination registers with DRELACC or TRELACC, and/or current/temporary register swapping could be added. We could have DDSTACC stepping. The SUMATR/SELMAX mechanism could use an ANDing type of structure where, at the first attribute, everything linked to it is set, then at each subsequent attribute an ANDing function is performed and only things that match to each subsequent attribute remain set. This mechanism would not be able to do partial matches the way the SUMATR mechanism can. Besides an ANDing mechanism, an ORing mechanism could be added. We could detect how large is a sum value associated with a node or mismatches with the learn attributes list. Priming could be added, which leaves some residual activation that slowly decays to speed activation of ideas related to other ideas. Statistical selection could use total use (or total times learned) to bias selection during DRELACC, TRELACC, SELMAX, or SELMAXR. Wild card values could be filled in at recall or recognition. Statistical selection could also be used to select frequently good goals in the emotion section. Structures with multiple relations could be allowed, such as a double relation structure, which could do 2 + 3 = 5 in one link: src=2, rel1=+, rel2=3, dst=5. Multiple control sequences could be active. Learning of random instruction and branch sequences could be improved by biasing selection of instructions and branches related to each other, such as setting a source and a relation. Automatic data section learning could be added. Branch status to the HOLD register could be added. Branch status to indicate a capital letter starting a word could indicate the start of a sentence and words could be case insensitive. Recording the sequence of recent attention may be useful for later recall. Other data functions could be added. External data could be loaded directly to registers other than the HOLD register. A syllable section could be added to the sound data section. A vision data section similar to the sound data section could be added. The emotion section could set progressively less pleasure or pain with each recent recall of a strong emotion item. The emotion section could speed up or slow down the thought speed, for example speeding up in a dangerous situation. During interaction, or at other times, the speed of thought could be slowed then sped up later.

9 Human Brain Architecture Conclusion

As we read this, a myriad of types of processing are occurring within our cognitive abilities. Information is first processed in the senses. Our visual sense performs numerous types of processing, starting in the eye when the neurons connected to the photoreceptors brighten dark areas of the text (for example, if part of the page is poorly lit) and dim bright areas. The image formed at the back of the eye is transmitted to our cognitive visual section where it continues to be processed, identifying image primitives. If we are listening, our sense of hearing processes the sound spectrum and identifies sound primitives including phonemes, volume, length of sounds, and so on. Our other senses of touch, smell, and taste, and other internally generated senses, such as hunger and thirst, all process information. All of the senses feed to the thinking computer, which can process the combined information from all of these senses through control state movement and data operations using the emotion to section determine what to do. Finally the thinking computer can activate outputs.

The thinking computer's control sections are very similar to the data and control sections in a traditional computer. The control section stores procedures, the data section stores relations between data. It is likely that the reason that computers have control and data sections is that humans do.

The cognitive abilities that have been described have evolved in humans to process, store, and retrieve information in as efficient a way as nature could produce. An inefficient information processing system reading this text might store a representation of this page as a pixel map requiring millions of bits of memory or in a neuron sense, millions of neuron links. But when recalling a page, it is not important to know the exact number of letters on a line of the page or the number of words in a line or words on a page. What is important is the information content. After we have read a page of text, it is difficult to recall even one complete sentence, yet a deficiency in not felt; the important information has been learned. It would not be very useful to store a complete text if it were then necessary to reread it to access any piece of information. In general, what is desired is fast access to facts from the text. To do this requires creation of structures of information stored in the thinking computer. Each time an identical word is seen, there is no need to store the sequence of letters. The sequence of letters associated with a word should be stored just one time, and thereafter only a link to the word node must be stored. This is just a simple example of how our information processing structures reduces the amount of data that has to be stored. Besides reduction, faster access to the data is accomplished by not having to search large amounts of data serially (as with rereading a story), because the data is stored in a reduced parallel structure.

- Cognitive function in the brain

The thinking computer receives data from all of the senses and activates outputs. The data and control sections handle all higher level processing, such as language, arithmetic, location of objects, and so on. Although brain studies have shown that certain areas of the brain are associated with certain of these mental abilities, these abilities are not fixed to these sections because it has also been shown [3] that a person with major brain damage can still acquire functions that are normally associated with the part of the brain that has been damaged, and that there cannot be clearly shown any function that must be associated with a part of the brain. The reason certain areas are frequently associated with specific functions is that these areas are near the sensory input for the associated function and the brain tries to minimize the length of links to minimize the space required for a link.

- Review of how we understand "the man went to the store"

The ear hears the words "the man went to the store" and converts them to a frequency spectrum that is received by the phoneme section, which converts them to phonemes. These phonemes are stored in the sound buffer until we are ready to process them (maximum a few seconds). The data section receives the phonemes from the sound buffer through activation of word ideas and converts them into ideas associated with the words and the types of words. This is fed to the control section to process the sentence and understand the meaning. Note that the control section first must process the words then can switch to understanding the ideas. The data section is storing the relation and the visual sections allow access of visuals associated with the ideas.

When we understand "the man went to the store", we must create a single node that links this whole concept. We cannot create the structure shown below in figure 40 because we would not know what the subject is or what the object is.

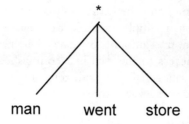

Figure 40: Incorrect data story structure

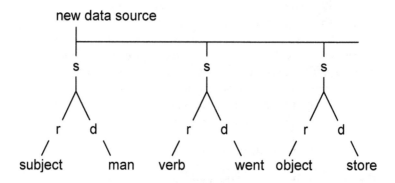

Figure 41: Correct data story structure

We use the data section to create a composite node. The data section stores the current relation although the control section is doing the actual understanding. The control section is where we understand what are the subject, verb, and object. The control section understands that "man" is the "subject" and sets "subject" as the relation, "man" as the destination, and causes the data section to learn this fact. The relation "verb" is learned at "went" and the relation "object" is learned at "store". The composite node is shown in figure 41.

- Getting started

When we first start thinking, we do not know what is going on. We have no idea what instructions and branches we are capable of doing. We do not know what emotions we have. We know nothing. Our instructions must randomly (spastically) activate for us to slowly learn what they do. We can sense pain and pleasure to help us decide what we should do. Automatically learning sequences of random instructions and branches that give pleasure gets us started, but it is important to learn procedures that help us learn new data and control structures. Also important is learning control structures that solve problems by breaking a problem down into a hierarchy of small operations, such as when we add numbers.

- Consciousness and intelligence

The automatic movement of the control section state node to state node, controlling the data section movement of attention from data node to data node (idea to idea), along with biasing from the emotion section, produces consciousness.

Intelligence is having and using many useful data and control structures. When we are born, we are conscious but we are not intelligent. We have the capability to become intelligent. We initially learn simple procedures and simple data structures and gradually build to where we learn to look around, move, listen and speak, be self aware, read, form complex story structures, and eventually learn fields of knowledge. These involve learning and using complex data and control structures.

10 Implementation of a Thinking Computer

This section describes implementing the conscious intelligent machine architecture. First, an implementation using an existing general purpose computer will be described. Then, techniques to improve this implementation will be described. Finally, a completely hardware implementation will be discussed.

10.1 IMPLEMENTATION OF A THINKING COMPUTER ON A GENERAL PURPOSE COMPUTER

An executable conscious machine program for a general purpose computer (personal computer) is available at the website www.rgrondalski.com (see chapter 11 for specific computer system requirements). The name of the program is rev0_12k.exe. "Rev 0" is the initial version of this program. The 12k refers to the maximum number (12288) of links it can process. There is also a limit of 12288 nodes with nodes 10000-12288 reserved for words, and nodes less than 400 reserved for elemental instructions and branch status. Future versions will process more links and nodes. The engram file (engram_main.txt) lists all of the initial data, control, and sound sequence knowledge. All the known words are stored in a word file (WORD.TXT). These two files are converted (assembled) by the array generator program (arygen.exe) into a series of numbers (LRN.TXT) for loading to the thinking computer program. A file (LOG.TXT) is also created by arygen.exe, which is a text file of what number is associated with each engram node, to help with debugging. The thinking computer program (rev0_12k.exe) reads the LRN.TXT and WORD.TXT files and two visual files, vis.txt and vis1.txt. Visual reading is done from vis1.txt and writing to vis.txt. During program operation, vis.txt is displayed. Vis1.txt is similar to a page we are reading and vis.txt is similar to a page we make notes on. Before operation, we set up the parameter file param.txt. The file param.txt has information including what cycle range we want to dump status information. We can pick a cycle to start dumping simple status, we can pick a cycle to start dumping complex status, and we can pick where we stop dumping status. The status information is used for debugging and is stored in a file trace.txt. In param.txt we can set the speed for the program to operate at. This is necessary for interactive operation. We can set the frequency of displaying the cycle information –

displaying very often slows program operation. To start the program, we type rev0_12k. We can then enter words for the program to input. "!" produces a loud interrupt. "^" is external pain. "@" is external pleasure. When we want to stop the program, we enter "$", which causes the new engram to be written to an engram output file (ENGOUT.TXT), an annotated engram output file (engout1.txt), then rev0_12k.exe stops running. The engram output file can be read in during a future run to allow us to build up a larger and larger knowledge base for the cognitive code to use. The final vis.txt file is written to visout.txt.

- Register implementation using a general purpose computer

The various registers in the thinking computer described in section 1 are implemented as locations in memory of a general purpose computer that are accessed using a high level computer language. To simulate the movement of data from one register in the thinking computer to another register, a location in the memory of the computer is read and the result written to another location.

- Data section links implementation using a general purpose computer

The large number of data links in the data section is stored in an array in the memory of a general purpose computer, as shown in figure 42.

	X index 0	X index 1	X index 2	X index 3	X index 4
Y index 0	1 (data type)	401 (apple)	402 (color)	403 (red)	0
Y index 1	1 (data type)	401 (apple)	404 (taste)	405 (good)	0
Y index 2	1 (data type)	406 (sky)	402 (color)	407 (blue)	0

maximum Y index set by total number of links

Figure 42: Data links stored in the memory of a general purpose computer

The array has an X dimension and a Y dimension. The X dimension of the array is five with values of 0 through 4, and the Y dimension is determined by the number of total links. Each node in the above example is assigned a number. For example "apple" is assigned number 401, "color" is assigned 402, and "red" is assigned 403. Each element in the array is 32 binary bits in size, allowing for 4 billion unique nodes. The first of the five X locations stores a value that indicates this link is a data type link. This value is "1" for all data links (other link types have values 2-4 described below). The second of the five X locations associated with each link stores the source node; in this example the value 401 associated with "apple". The third of the five locations associated with each link stores the relation node; in this specific example the value 402 associated with "color". The fourth of the five locations associated with each link stores the destination node; in this specific example the value 403 associated with "red". The fifth of the five locations associated with each link is left blank for data type links, but will be used with control type links described in the control section description below. Each of the various data registers is 32 binary bits in size and is a variable in the rev0_12k program. To recall the color of an apple, the current data source register is loaded with the value 401, the current data relation register is loaded with the value 402, and when the instruction DRELACC is activated by the control section, a general purpose computer software procedure sequences through the array of data links stored in the memory of the computer and compares the values read from the memory with the values stored in the current data source register and current data relation register. Once a match to both registers is found, the result is loaded to the HOLD register.

- SUMATR and SELMAX implementation

The sums used in association with the SUMATR and SELMAX instructions, described in section 1.1.1, are stored in an array stored in the memory of the computer, as shown in figure 43. The node number is used as an index into the array to access the sum. For example, each element in the array is set to 0 when the instruction CLRSUM is activated. Next, if the temporary data relation register is set to 402 (the number associated with color), and the temporary data destination is set to 403 (the number associated with red), then when the instruction SUMATR is activated, the array structure in figure 42 is searched for a data link that has a relation node that matches the current data relation register and a destination node that matches the current data destination register. When a match is found, the source node is used as an index value for the sum array and this element in the sum array is incremented. In this case the sum array element number 401 would be incremented. When the instruction SELMAX is activated, the element with the maximum value is selected. When the instruction SUBATR is activated, instead of incrementing in the above example, there is a decrement. When the instruction BLOCKSUM is activated, the value -10 is written to the sum array location pointed to by the HOLD register.

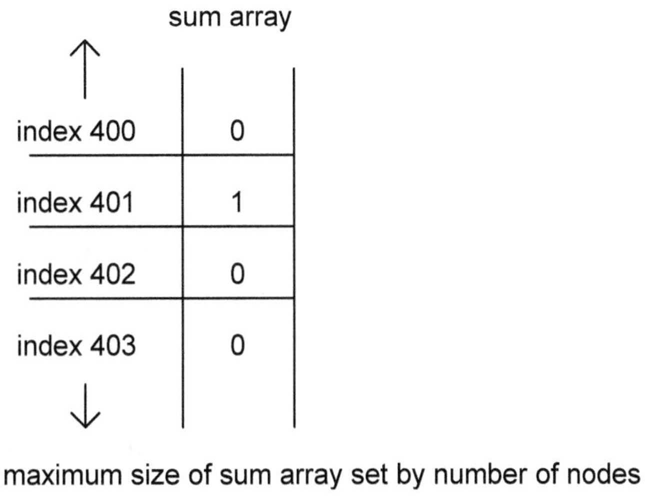

sum array

index 400	0
index 401	1
index 402	0
index 403	0

maximum size of sum array set by number of nodes

Figure 43: sum array implementation using a general purpose computer

- Data section learning implementation

Referring to figure 42, when the instruction DLEARN is activated by the control section, a new link is added to the array of links, with a data type of "1", a source node using the value in the current data source register, a relation node using the value in the current data relation register, and a destination node using the value in the current data destination register.

- CRDAT implementation

The thinking computer manually creates a new data node with the instruction CRDAT. The new data source is loaded into the HOLD register. The implementation of this instruction using a general purpose computer uses a "state in use" array, similar to the sum array in figure 43. This "state in use" array is used to keep track of nodes in use. A "0" in the array indicates an unused node. When the CRDAT instruction is activated by the control section, a search is done of the array for an unused node and the first unused node that is found is used for the new node being created with the CRDAT instruction. This location in the array is changed to "1". If no nodes are found, then the forgetting mechanism is activated, as explained below in the forgetting mechanism implementation description.

- SUBRCNT implementation

To implement the SUBRCNT instruction, a register (variable) stores the current cycle number. It is incremented with every new control state. An array similar to that in figure 43 stores an array of cycle counts. This array is the lastuse array. Each cycle, whatever is in the HOLD register is used to index the lastuse array and the value of the cycle count register is written into that location in the lastuse array. When the SUBRCNT instruction is activated, all sums in the sum array that are associated with a cycle count within the last 5000 cycles are set to zero.

- DRELACC implementation

To implement the DRELACC instruction, an array similar to the sum array and named the "drel array" is indexed using what has been found with the DRELACC instruction. This "drel array" is initialized to all 0's at SETDSRC or SETTMPSRC. Only nodes with a "drel array" value of 0 can be found. After each DRELACC, the element in the array indexed by the found node is set to 1 to prevent it from being accessed again until the next setting of a data source register.

- CHECKAGE implementation

To implement the CHECKAGE instruction, the lastuse array is accessed using the HOLD register value as an index for the lastuse array. If the value found is within 1000 cycles of the current cycle then the branch status "recent" activates. If within 10,000 cycles of the current cycle then the branch status "medium" activates. If it is more than 10,000 cycles since its last use then branch status "old" activates. Every cycle, the lastuse array is updated by writing the value of the current cycle into the location in the lastuse array specified by the value in the HOLD register. Whenever a new node is created, the lastuse array is also updated.

- Control section implementation using a general purpose computer

Referring to figure 44, the control section information is stored in the same array of information that holds the data links.

	X index 0	X index 1	X index 2	X index 3	X index 4
Y index 1500	2 (cntl type)	2001 (wd-st1)	2002 (noun)	2003 (wd-st2)	210 (setdsrc)
Y index 1501	4 (cntl type) (constant)	2001 (wd-st1)	2004 (verb)	2005 (wd-st3)	2006 (subject-verb)
Y index 1502	2 (cntl type)	2001 (wd-st1)	218 (next)	2007 (wd-st4)	2008 (subtr1)

maximum Y index set by total number of links

Figure 44: Control section links stored in a general purpose computer

Each control state is assigned a unique node number. For example, the state wd-st1 is assigned 2001. This node number 2001 can also be used in data type links to recall, for example, the start of a control sequence to execute that control sequence. Each cycle the data in the HOLD register, or the value "next", or branch status information is used to select a new state to move to. If the HOLD register contains 2002 (the node number associated with noun), then control sequence moves to state 2003 (the state node associated with wd-st2) and activates the elemental instruction SETDSRC. The control sequence moves to a new state by searching the array of links for a match between the current state and the source state in the link and a match between the HOLD register, or "next", or branch status information, and the relation node in the link. This is done using a general purpose computer by sequencing through the link array and looking for matches. The search in figure 44 is from top to bottom and the first link that matches is selected. If the HOLD register has a value of 2004, the node number assigned to "verb" in this example, then since this is a link type 4, or constant, the state output 2006 (subject-verb) is loaded to the HOLD register and the control moves to state 2005 wd-st3. If the HOLD register does not have a value of 2002 or 2004, then the "next" branch is activated because 218 (next) is always active and the priority of braches are top to bottom in figure 44 (left to right in figure 29). The "next" branch activates the procedure 2008 (subr1) and when this procedure is complete it automatically returns to the state 2007 wd-st4 and proceeds from there. This demonstrates the 3 types of outputs from a state: elemental instruction (the most common type of output), constant, or procedure call (there can also be no output, just movement from state to state). Elemental instructions are each assigned a value in the range 200-350, which makes them easy to identify from procedure calls. Note that procedure state outputs, or any state other type of state output, can use any value for the state link relation node, it does not have to be "next". If the "next" link 218 above did not exist and no next state from 2001 was found, the stack would be popped. If the stack is popped and the stack pointer is already at the top of the stack, then the interrupt PPOPNEG activates and the next control state is the start of the interrupt service state sequence with the HOLD register set to PPOPNEG. This interrupt service state is node number 1. The procedure (subroutine) stack has a size of 16.

- Control section learning implementation

   To implement control section learning, there are four registers in the control section: the procedure learn source register (PLSRC), the procedure learn relation register (PLREL), the procedure learn destination register (PLDST), and the procedure learn out register (PLOUT). The procedure learn destination register initially contains the last new state that was learned. When the EXECUTE instruction or the procedure learn PLEARN instruction is activated by the control section, the procedure learn destination register is copied to the procedure learn source register. The procedure learn relation register is set to the value "next" unless there is a branch, as explained below. The state in use array, explained above, is searched to find a new node number to use to identify the new state, and when one is found, it is written to the procedure learn destination register. The value of the HOLD register is written to the procedure learn out register. Then a new line is then created in the array of links shown in figure 44. The link type is set to "2" indicating it is a control type of link. The values in the four procedure learn registers are written to the new line in the array. If this is an EXECUTE instruction, the HOLD register will contain what is about to be executed. In the case of an EXECUTE instruction, this HOLD register value can be the start of a procedure or an elemental instruction. In this way a new step in a new procedure is automatically learned by the control section. When the constant learn (CLEARN) instruction is activated by the control section, then the link type is set to "4" in the above learning of a new link and the HOLD register contains the constant to be learned in the new procedure step.

The elemental instructions are each assigned a value in the range 200-350 and this value is what is stored as the fifth element, the state output, in each link when a state with an elemental instruction is being learned. When a procedure state is being learned, the value assigned to the first state in the procedure is what is learned. Procedures are made of elemental instructions and calls to other procedures. It should be noted that a call to a procedure is really just a state with an output node being the first instruction in the procedure, and this procedure call automatically returns when the last state in the procedure is reached.

- Implementation of the LRNATRS mechanism

To implement the LRNATRS mechanism, at each SUMATR the value of the temporary data relation register and the value of the temporary data destination register are stored in an array in the memory of a traditional computer. Each consecutive SUMATR uses the next pair of sequential elements in the array. A counter is incremented with each SUMATR and is used as an index pointer for the array. The counter is cleared when the CLRSUM instruction is activated by the control section. When the LRNATRS instruction is activated by the control section, the data stored in the array is written to the link memory. A new data source node is selected (the next sequential unused node) and it is linked to each pair of relation and destination nodes stored in the array.

An alternative is to not use the LRNATRS instruction and at CLRSUM to also do the CRDAT instruction and set the new data node to TMPSRC. Then at each SUMATR, to also do the DLEARN instruction and learn each new attribute using the temporary registers for the data being learned. At SELMAX, if a new TMPSRC is not found, then we already have a new source node with all the attributes linked. If we do find recognize with SELMAX, then TMPSRC is replaced with the recognized node and eventually we forget the new node and all its attributes that was learned but not needed. The activation of the CRDAT instruction and loading of TMPSRC with the new node during CLRSUM could be automatic. Also, the activation of the DLEARN instruction during SUMATR could be automatic. This alternative to LRNATRS is much simpler for nature to evolve.

- Implementation of the SPASM mechanism

The spasm mechanism is implemented in a control section sequence of instructions such that when deciding what procedure to activate next, an elemental instruction or branch status may be randomly selected using the SELMAXR instruction.

- Emotion section implementation using a general purpose computer

To implement the emotion section a pain/pleasure register is used. Every 600 cycles the pain/pleasure level is incremented. If we access data that has not been used for 5000 cycles then the pain/pleasure level is decremented. If we execute a procedure, the pain/pleasure level is incremented because it is a form of work. Also, if we try to learn something we already know then the pain/pleasure level is incremented. The threshold for a pain interrupt is set by the parameter file. The pleasure threshold is when the pain/pleasure level reaches 1. The pain interrupt occurs as the pain threshold is exceeded. The pleasure interrupt is delayed until the next ppopneg to allow a good procedure to continue.

To implement the emotion section mechanism that biases good control procedures, the procedure for selecting good procedures is stored in the control section. This procedure to select good procedures is not learned, it is preprogrammed, and it cannot be forgotten. The links to goodgoal, goodbadgoal, badgoal, and so on, are learned as data links and are accessed by the procedure for selecting good procedures.

To implement the emotion section mechanism that biases the data section, a pain/pleasure array uses the value of the HOLD register as an index into the array, similar to the sum array in figure 43. The array is initialized to a value midway between the pain and pleasure interrupt values. At a pain or pleasure interrupt, the value of the HOLD register is used to index the array and the pain or pleasure interrupt value is written into the location in the pain/pleasure array indexed by the HOLD register. Later, when this node is recalled or recognized, the pain/pleasure level is restored to a pain or pleasure interrupt value only if the node has not been accessed in the most recent 5000 cycles. In this way, a node with strong emotions associated with it can shift the current pain/pleasure level.

To implement the random activation of ideas with strong emotion, the following mechanism is used. When there is a pain or pleasure interrupt, the value in the HOLD register is learned as a new link to emotion/pain or emotion/pleasure depending on the type of interrupt. Later, when deciding what to do, data nodes with these strong emotion links can be randomly selected using SUMATR and SELMAXR and in this way returned to the HOLD register for thinking about.

To implement tiredness there is a tiredness register, which increases in value during work and decreases in value during pleasure or rest. This register is incremented by 100 whenever something is manually executed, with a maximum value of 1000. This register is decremented by 100 whenever there is a pleasure interrupt, with a minimum value of 0. Every 100 cycles, this register, the tiredness register, is decremented by 1, with a minimum value of 0. The instruction "test tired" (TSTTIRED) tests the value of this register. If greater than 200, then the branch status "nofind" is set. If 200 or less, then the branch status "find" is set. The instruction "test very tired" (TSTVTIRED) also tests the value of this register. If greater than 400, then the branch status "nofind" is set. If 400 or less, then the branch status "find" is set. These instructions are used in the emotion procedures to determine whether to execute something.

- Implementation of the forgetting mechanism

To implement the forgetting mechanism, the lastuse array, described above in connection with the SUBRCNT instruction and CHECKAGE instruction, is used to determine the last cycle a node was used. Another array, the total use array, is incremented each cycle using the value in the HOLD register as an index into the array. When the total use reaches 1000 for a particular entry, it is no longer incremented (to prevent overflows). When the array of links reaches within 100 links of the maximum size for a particular implementation, such as 8192, then the link array is out of space and a node needs to be forgotten. The program looks at each node and if it has a less recent use and less total use than any other node then it, and all its links, are deleted and the array of links is compressed. This frees up some links for other uses. This node's entry in the state in use array is set to 0. Note that some nodes are not available to be overwritten, no matter their lastuse or total use. These are nodes used for the emotion section (explained above) and are not to be forgotten. We do not want to forget to do good things. Other nodes may also be made not available to be forgotten. In particular, an initially loaded engram containing a large number of nodes and links is fixed in memory with the current version of the program rev0_12k. Future versions will allow loading the lastuse and total use arrays from a previous run and allow forgetting for some of the loaded engram.

- Sound input and output

The rev0_12k program uses keyboard entry for sound input simulation and a computer display device for output simulation. Keyboard entry stores the words in an input array and the instruction EXTHLD brings the next input array word into the HOLD register. We input a line of data from the vis1.txt file with the instruction "read plus 1 line" READPL1, which loads it to the external input register, EXTINP, and also to the vis.txt file, which is continuously output during rev0_12k operation. The instruction EXTHLD brings in the next word from EXTINP. The branch status READEND indicates there are no more words and a new line needs to be read. We can read backwards by using the instruction "read minus 1" (READMN1). The instruction PRINT outputs the word in the HOLD register to the display. Future versions of the program will use a microphone, with optional hardware to convert the sound input information into phonemes.

- Sound data section

The sound data section is implemented using a general purpose computer by using links similar to the control section's links. These links are stored in the same array as the data and control links. A separate array, the sound sum array, similar to the sum array in figure 43, is used to keep track of what sound state nodes are active. The phrase register is implemented as a 16 element array. During sound data section recall using the instruction SNDNEXT, each word is loaded to the HOLD register where it can be output with the PRINT instruction. If not output, it can be used for silent recall. A future improvement is for the sound data section to output without using the HOLD register.

- Image section implementation

The ACCN, ACCS, ACCE, ACCW instructions allow looking around the vis.txt file that is input to the rev0_12k program. Future versions of the thinking computer program will have a video camera as input with optional hardware to identify image primitives.

- Program flowchart

An executable thinking computer program for a traditional computer is available at the website www.rgrondalski.com. A flowchart of the program is shown in figure 45. The flowchart is entered with the start of the program. Then the files LRN.TXT and WORD.TXT are read into the memory of the general purpose computer. The file LRN.TXT is composed of many lines of numbers. Each line has 5 numbers. The first number is the type of link the line represents: 1=data, 2=control, 3=sound sequence, 4=constant. The second number is the source node associated with the link. The third number is the relation node associated with the link. The fourth number is the destination associated with the link. Lastly, the fifth number is optional and is the output node associated with the link if the link is type 2 or 4 (control) or type 3 (sound). The WORD.TXT file contains a list of all words that are known by the program. An example engram that has been converted to numbers is listed in chapter 11. The next step in the flowchart tests if there has been any keyboard input. If the keyboard is pressed then if sound interrupt is enabled (sndintren) then the newwordintr occurs. If the input from the keyboard is "$" then the program saves the current engram in ENGOUT.TXT, generates an annotated engram output file (ENGOUT1.TXT), and stops running. If there is no keyboard input then the program proceeds to execute all the instructions in the instruction list and the control sequence moves to the next state. While doing this, it creates a new hold value for the HOLD register for the next cycle, and creates a new set of instructions to be executed in the next cycle. Next, the emotion level is updated and an emotion interrupt can occur. Finally the new hold value is copied to the HOLD register, and the new set of instructions is copied to the instruction list.

- Memory requirements

How much memory is needed? The rev0_12k program uses five words of memory (each 32 bits) for each link. Therefore there are 20 bytes per link. All links, data, control, or sound, use 20 bytes. The 12k links maximum therefore uses 240k bytes of memory. The various arrays (sum, state in use, lastuse, total use, trel, pain/pleasure, sound sum) use 1 word per node. Therefore, with 12k nodes, each array is 48k bytes or 335k bytes for the total arrays. The total memory size of the link memory plus the array memory is approximately 575k bytes.

The lastuse array is at least 4 bytes per entry to allow a run of up to 4 billion machine cycles (of course this can be expanded to allow storage of longer run times). When 4 billion cycles have passed, we do not want to forget old nodes when we cycle back, so we can cycle back to number 1 billion and set all old nodes to a lower number so they are not forgotten. At total use overflow, we can just leave a high number. Although there are 3 or 4 nodes per link, there are many repeats, therefore there is around one new node per link, or around an equal number of links and nodes.

Figure 45: flowchart for thinking computer program rev0_12k.exe
{executable file on compact disk at the back of the book}

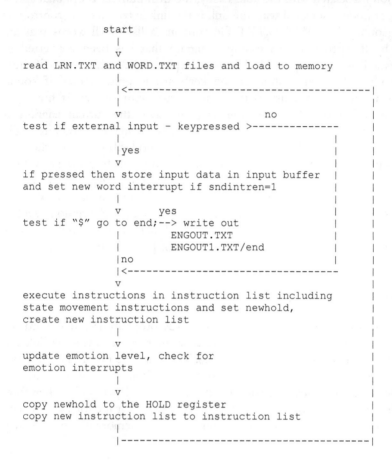

```
                start
                  |
                  v
      read LRN.TXT and WORD.TXT files and load to memory
                  |
                  |<-------------------------------------------|
                  |                                            |
                  v                         no                 |
      test if external input - keypressed >-------------       |
                  |                                     |       |
                  |yes                                  |       |
                  v                                     |       |
      if pressed then store input data in input buffer  |       |
      and set new word interrupt if sndintren=1          |       |
                  |                                     |       |
                  v        yes                          |       |
      test if "$" go to end;--> write out               |       |
                  |              ENGOUT.TXT             |       |
                  |              ENGOUT1.TXT/end        |       |
                  |no                                   |       |
                  |<--------------------------------     |
                  v                                            |
      execute instructions in instruction list including       |
      state movement instructions and set newhold,             |
      create new instruction list                              |
                  |                                            |
                  v                                            |
      update emotion level, check for                          |
      emotion interrupts                                       |
                  |                                            |
                  v                                            |
      copy newhold to the HOLD register                        |
      copy new instruction list to instruction list            |
                  |                                            |
                  |--------------------------------------------|
```

- How many links do we know ?

How many data links do we know and how many are needed? Each time
we look at a new table or chair or tree or any object, we create a new data
structure for that object (the procedure for looking around also stores what
we see, just as when we read, we store what we understand). A quick guess
would be that we know at least a million objects, including all people we
know, all characters in stories/movies, all places, all dogs, all cars, all unique
instances of objects - we probably know many millions of objects. An average

object has many attributes, each of which requires a link. Each object can be used in many story/experience structures, each of which requires a link. It has been estimated that we know approximately 20,000 words, but for each word we know many data items. For example, we know the word book, but we also know hundreds of books (and each book has characters, situations, and so on). We know a large number of control links as a result of all the procedures we know, although we probably know a lot more data than control links because, for example, when reading we use the same control procedures over and over, but we create a large new data structure of the story. We know hundreds of songs, each with many links. Overall, we probably know hundreds of millions of links. The initial code of 12k links available in rev0_12k should be enough for simple experiments. Modern general purpose computers will keep most of this in the cache or main memory. A larger number of links will make use of virtual memory because most links are used very infrequently. For example, we only access geography information when we recall geography, which is very infrequently. Frequently used links, such as speech control links, will often be in the cache.

- Searching links

The rev0_12k code searches through all links every cycle to recall, recognize, or propagate. Future code can use search speedup techniques, such as sorting and searching. Sorting can be done during a sleep type of mode and then during program operation searching links can be done as a two step process: first by using fast searching through the sorted information then secondly by searching serially through all the unsorted information (things learned recently). When there is too much unsorted information, the sleep mode can be biased to be activated as soon as nothing important is happening; the more the unsorted information the higher the bias can be.

- Dreaming

Dreaming is not implemented initially, but it can be easily added by temporarily switching into a mode that disables external inputs and feeds the recalled data to the external input path and allows the control section to respond to this externally input recalled data.

- Debugging

All implementations need to allow for easy debugging. For a general purpose computer the engram file named engram.txt may need to be debugged. The program rev0_12k.exe has features to aid in this debugging. The parameter file param.txt has variables that can be set and used by rev0_12k to control the output of status information to the file trace.txt. These variables are:

min cyccnt for very simple output
min cyccnt for simple output
min cyccnt for output
max cyccnt for output

The "min cyccnt for very simple output" is the cycle to start outputting only simple output such as when learning or recognition occurs. The "min cyccnt for simple output" is the cycle to start outputting a single line of status information for each cycle that is executed. This status information includes the engram step that is being executed, the value of the HOLD register, and the current pain/pleasure level. The engram steps can be followed in the file LOG.TXT, which contains a cross reference between the loaded node numbers and the text names of data and control nodes.

The "min cyccnt for output" is the cycle to do a more detailed dumping of information including the state of all the internal registers every cycle. The "max cyccnt for output" is the cycle to stop dumping all information. A possible future addition is to have a separate max cyccnt for each type of output and to have multiple windows of output.

- Speed up techniques for a general purpose computer

The simplest group of speed up techniques is software techniques to speed up the implementation on a general purpose computer. More complex techniques involve adding specialized hardware for performance improvements.

Techniques to speed up the code on a general purpose computer include:

a. Do not search for the next state; each state could give the starting address for a list of the possible branches from a state and the program would just go directly to this list and quickly search it. Data nodes could point to a starting address of all attributes associated with that data node, so all memory does not have to be searched.

b. Add more semiconductor memory for all links to fit in main memory to avoid using virtual memory. Use larger caches.

c. Use standard algorithms for searching, such as hash tables. Pre-sorting the lines of information will allow fast access to finding individual links [11].

- Using spare cycles of existing general purpose computers

Almost all existing general purpose computers spend most of the time doing nothing useful. For example, a computer being used to type a report only does useful work as each character is typed. The characters are typed a few per second. The computer operates millions of times faster than that. The computer is still operating at a high frequency, but it is spending it's time looping while waiting. Even worse, many computers sit with the power on and no one using them at all. Implementations of thinking computers using general purpose computers will be able to make use of this wasted computer power by operating in the background.

10.2 IMPLEMENTATIONS USING SPECIALIZED HARDWARE

Adding specialized hardware will improve the performance of thinking computers. The registers and arrays of data of a thinking computer can be implemented as storage elements on one or more integrated circuits. A content addressable memory would help search for links that match. Since only a few control and data nodes are active at one time, a general purpose computer (either serial or simple parallel) works reasonably well for the cognitive central processor section (using sorting techniques to allow fast searching), but the image and sound algorithms could be greatly sped up with specialized hardware. The image processing code must process thousands of pixels continuously and this activity will severely slow down a single general purpose computer. A thinking computer implementation will operate much faster if the image processing code is moved to its own hardware. This can be another general purpose computer, or for more speed a massively parallel computer [6, 7] can be used. For image processing, data parallel routines operating on a massively parallel computer can recognize edges of objects and other image primitives. A massively parallel computer could also help with cognitive central processor recognition by using parallel searching during search operations, such as SUMATR and SELMAX, or when searching for the next control state, or when searching for a data destination or relation. In these cases parallel searching is done by broadcasting the search information to all processors and then allowing the thousands of processors to search their local data in parallel. Data parallel algorithms could also improve the performance of sound recognition. Beyond massively parallel computing even more specialized hardware, such as digital signal processing (DSP) hardware, could be used for sound recognition, and specialized image processing hardware could improve image recognition performance. Other sensory information, such as touch, smell, and taste, can be added with appropriate hardware.

10.3 THE COMPLETELY HARDWARE IMPLEMENTATION

The human brain is not a computer. It does not have registers, random access memory, or any software. It is a completely dedicated hardware structure that implements the conscious intelligent machine architecture functions using only neurons and senses. A neuron has many inputs and one output that can connect to the input of many other neurons. A neuron sums its inputs with some inputs adding to the sum at the neuron output, others subtracting. The strength of coupling from input to output varies from input to input. The neurons used in human brains are not fast by electronic standards, but a large number (billions) are used in parallel. It is possible to duplicate this interconnected neuron structure using electronic or other logical components to build a non human complete hardware implementation. This machine would require fewer cycles to do a function; there would be no memory searching for links. In fact, there would be no software at all. This machine would be expensive to build, but it would have the best performance of all implementations.

- Selecting the most active data node

During the SUMATR instruction the neurons perform the sum function. At SELMAX the maximum sum must be selected. When selecting the maximum sum, the human brain does not sequentially search for the maximum. Also, it is unlikely that the human brain uses a tree of neurons that can pass the maximum of two inputs to select the overall maximum. What is more likely is that the human brain starts at a high threshold and slowly lowers it and whatever activates first is selected as the new attention node. Note that the activation level of the selection mechanism resembles a sawtooth waveform. It is also possible that the first SUMATR instruction activates all nodes linked to the attribute being summed, then at each subsequent SUMATR only those that are associated with each subsequent attribute remain active. This produces an ANDing function through time.

It is possible that during learning the nodes that are used to select the new attribute node or source node become the permanent storage nodes. In this way, nodes move from the interconnection network to storage. If not used frequently enough, they may revert back to the communication (and activation determining) network.

- Hardware links

For a completely hardware solution, we must be able to learn connections between nodes. In the brain, a group of neurons represents a node. A node can represent a state in the control section, an idea in the data section, or both. To form links between these groups of neurons, the brain uses other neurons. Assume neurons have 100 inputs. Three levels of these neurons would connect 1,000,000 nodes. If each neuron output is allowed to be used for learning only once, then there is no need to worry about sneak paths from the inputs to the outputs. This is illustrated in figure 46. If A links to B, then X linking to Y should not use the AB path of neurons, but it should use other neurons that allow X linking to Y.

There is only one possible path from a neuron input to an output. If pieces of that path are in use for other older links, then they can be dropped and only the new link is stored.

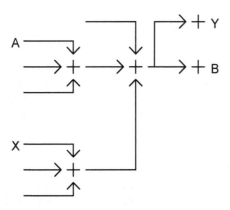

Figure 46: Hardware links between nodes

11 Experiments Demonstrating the Operation of a Thinking Computer

This chapter describes numerous experiments that demonstrate the thinking computer. The experiments are divided into two types. The first type of experiment uses the main engram file which contains over 10,000 cognitive links.   There are 25 experiments of this first type that demonstrate the thinking computer understanding of short stories and answering questions related to the stories, understanding of general knowledge, understanding of geography, and understanding of concepts such as opposites, and if something makes sense. As the 10,000 cognitive links are increased in future main engram files, the thinking computer will be able to do more and more useful things. The second type of experiment demonstrates writing engram files. There are 10 experiments of this second type. These second type of experiments start with simple operations, such as recalling a fact, and proceed to more and more complex experiments demonstrating reading, thinking, consciousness, and understanding. All of these reproducible experiments are an integral part of the scientific basis for this book.

11.1 SOFTWARE INSTALLATION

To run the experiments on your PC (Microsoft Windows 95 through Windows 7) the Software must be installed on your computer. Information on running with future versions of Windows will be placed on the website listed below.

You must accept the End User License Agreement listed at the back this book before you can use the Software. This is a personal, noncommercial use only, License Agreement. If you do not accept the End User License Agreement during installation, the software will not run.

To install the Software, go to the website www.rgrondalski.com.

1. Click on the link to download the software.
2. Click on "save as". Click SAVE. This will save the zip file containing the software in your download folder.

3. Click on START, and select my computer. Click on C:, click on USERS, click on your username, and click on downloads. The file Thinking_Computer_software.zip should be there.
4. Left click on Thinking_Computer_software.zip, then right click and select "extract all".
5. A password will be requested. The password is 2400737. Please keep this password confidential. Once the password is entered, the software will be extracted and will be ready to use. The software will be installed in the download folder:

C:\USERS\(username)\downloads\Thinking_Computer_software

To uninstall the software, simply delete the Thinking_Computer_software folder.

In the following explanation of how to run the software, <enter> means to hit the enter key on the keyboard. Where the explanation says to type something, such as type "run", just type run (not the quotation marks).

11.2 RUNNING THE 25 MAIN ENGRAM EXPERIMENTS

The main engram experiments use the file engram_main.txt. This engram contains over 10,000 cognitive links containing knowledge we use on a daily basis. To view this file, simple click on engram_main.txt and it will open with the notepad program. The main engram experiments load this main engram and then input external sentences (statements and questions) that are understood by the engram and responses are output by the engram.

To run the the main engram experiments, you must open a command prompt window by clicking on "Start" (the bottom left of your computer screen), then click on "all programs" (near the bottom), then "accessories" (you may need to slide down the screen to see accessories), then "command prompt". This will open a command prompt window.

An alternate way to open a command prompt window is to click on "Start", then type "cmd" in the "search programs and files" box or click on "run" and type "cmd" in the window that pops up.

In the command prompt window type:

cd c:\users\(your username)\downloads

Type "dir". You should see a listing of the software with 47 files.

Note that (your username) is the name of your computer. To install and run the software:

1. Type "install" in the command prompt window. This will ask if you accept the End User License Agreement. If the message appears "this program might not have installed correctly", click "this program installed correctly".

2. The first experiment is ready to run. Run the engram; it takes a few seconds to compile, by typing in the command prompt window:

    run<enter>

3. The upper half of the output display is what is being read, the lower half is what is being output. The thinking computer program will keep running until stopped. When tired of reading it will do things it likes, such as drawing or singing. When the program is done answering questions, stop the program. **To stop the program, type:**

    $<enter>

4. To adjust the speed of operation, see the param.txt explanation on page 162.

To change the input in the above example, various reading_example files can be copied to vis1.txt. For example :

    copy reading_example_a_story.txt vis1.txt<enter>
    run<enter>

The run command compiles the engram file. This only needs to be done once. To speed up the experiments, the command

    rev0_12k<enter>

can be used to replace "run". This will run the engram without compiling it.

To run the 25 main engram example files, copy a file listed below to vis1.txt as shown in the example above, then type "run".

reading_example_a_story.txt: demonstrates understanding a simple story

reading_example_b_farm1.txt – reading_example_f_farm5.txt : demonstrates understanding the story "The Little Farm" by Lois Lenski

reading_example_g_general_knowledge1.txt – reading_example_n_general_knowkedge8.txt: demonstrates understand general knowledge

reading_example_o_geography.txt: demonstrates understanding of geography

reading_example_p_Mary_had.txt: demonstrates understanding of "Mary had a little lamb"

reading_example_q_situation.txt: demonstrates understanding of different situations

reading_example_r_isa_links.txt: demonstrates understanding of "is a" links

reading_example_s_opposites.txt: demonstrates understand of opposites

reading_example_t_not.txt: demonstrates understanding of the concept "not"

reading_example_u_example_of.txt: demonstrates understanding of examples

reading_example_v_learn.txt: demonstrates learning from keyboard input. Note, the keyboard input must be followed by a <space>, then <enter>. For example, when the color of mars is not known, enter "red" followed by <space>, then <enter>.

reading_example_w_check.txt: demonstrates checking if sentences make sense

reading_example_x_homonyms.txt: demonstrates understanding of words that are spelled the same, but have different meanings, such as farm can be a verb or a noun

As these experiments run, many files are created that store the inner workings of the thinking machine by recording which cognitive links are activated and the values in the various registers. It is recommended to keep two windows open when running: the command prompt and the window with the listing of the folder files. The various files that are output when running can be opened after running has stopped, when "$" is entered.

Clicking on the following files opens them for viewing with the "notepad" program. The file TRACE.TXT records each step.

Below is an example line from TRACE.TXT.

cyccnt=220 psrc=3692 hold=6030 dsrc=7763 lineno=10230 pl=5 sp=2

1. cyccnt refers to the cycle count. The line above is from cycle 220.

2. psrc is the node number in the psrc register. The file "LOG.TXT" lists the node numbers assigned to each node in the engram.txt file. Node number 3692 correlates to the node "recogn1" in engram.txt. By looking at engram.txt, this node can be found as part of the sequence of states that recognizes words. The engram.txt file contains descriptions of the various links in the engram.

3. hold contains what is in the hold register (attention). The hold register in this cycle contains 6030. By looking in "LOG.TXT" this correlates to the word "Bill".

4. dsrc contains what is in the dsrc register. In this case dsrc contains 7763 which is a new node number that is being used used to learn the sentence as it is input.

5. lineno lists the line number in the array of links where new cognitive links are being learned.

6. pl lists the pain/pleasure level. It is level 5 at this cycle. The pain/pleasure level is described in chapter 4. The file param.txt has a variable that controls what level the pain/pleasure level must reach before it produces an interrupt.

7. sp lists the stack pointer. This increments as we push down to subroutines and decrements as we pop.

After running, the file ENGOUT.TXT stores the resulting new engram, and ENGOUT1.TXT lists node names and equivalent node numbers.

- Understanding a simple story

The Little Farm by Lois Lenski [12] is an example of a simple story. The story is about a farmer and the tasks he does around the farm.

The following files demonstrate reading and understanding pieces of this story:

reading_example_b_farm1.txt through reading_example_f_farm5.txt

11.3 EXPERIMENTS DEMONSTRATING WRITING NEW ENGRAMS

The next group of experiments allow to reader to write and run new engrams. These experiments start with engrams that do simple operations, such as recalling a fact, and proceed to more and more complex engrams demonstrating reading, thinking, consciousness, and understanding.

engram_example1.txt learning a fact
engram_example2.txt hierarchical problem solving
engram_example3.txt translation of a sentence
engram_example4.txt answering a question
engram_example5.txt zooming in and out of objects
engram_example6.txt using the temporary data register
engram_example7.txt storing and recalling situations
engram_example8.txt focusing on an object
engram_example9.txt learning a data procedure
engram_example10.txt learning with DLEARNML

- Simple learning experiment: engram_example1.txt

The following engram is an example of simple learning. Data links are type 1, control links without a constant are type 2, sound sequence links are type 3, and control links with a constant are type 4. It is listed in engram_example1.txt in the software. This experiment can be copied to engram.txt and then run by typing "run". The start execute cycle in param.txt needs to be set to 401 for this and all other engram files. Running starts at node 401. In this example, the current data source, relation, and destination registers are loaded and the value in them is learned. This example learns that the color of the sky is blue. Constants are used for sky, color, and blue, in this simple experiment. Normally, these values do not come from constants; these values come from hearing or reading a fact. For example, we may read a fact: the color of the sky is blue. As we read this sentence, we create a sentence structure that we later access to learn the fact instead of using the constants in this example. This reading and learning will be demonstrated later in more complex experiments. Since there is no external output, the results of the run are in ENGOUT.TXT, ENGOUT1.TXT, and TRACE.TXT.

```
0 ; engram_example1.txt
0 ; this example learns the fact that the color of the
0 ; sky is blue
4 example1a     next          example1b     sky           ;
2 example1b     next          example1c     setdsrc       ;
4 example1c     next          example1d     color         ;
2 example1d     next          example1e     setdrel       ;
4 example1e     next          example1f     blue          ;
2 example1f     next          example1g     setddst       ;
2 example1g     next          example1h     dlearn        ;
```

To run this new engram, go to the command prompt window and type:

copy engram_example1.txt engram.txt<enter>

Then type "run"

The "run" command actually does three steps. First it runs "wordgen" which assigns a node number to each word and outputs the file "WORD.TXT". Next "arygen" is run which generates the files LOG.TXT (a readable engram) and LRN.TXT (a loadable engram), listed below. Finally, "rev0_12k" is run which actually runs the engram and produces the files TRACE.TXT, ENGOUT.TXT, and ENGOUT1.TXT. These files are also listed below resulting from the run of engram_example1.txt. The file trace.txt lists the steps when running the engram. The file ENGOUT.TXT is the output engram in a form that can be reloaded and run. The file ENGOUT1.TXT is a readable version of the output engram.

LOG.TXT (a readable text file of the engram):

```
4 example1a  401 next      218 example1b  402 sky       403
2 example1b  402 next      218 example1c  404 setdsrc   210
4 example1c  404 next      218 example1d  405 color     406
2 example1d  405 next      218 example1e  407 setdrel   211
4 example1e  407 next      218 example1f  408 blue      409
2 example1f  408 next      218 example1g  410 setddst   212
2 example1g  410 next      218 example1h  411 dlearn    245
```

LRN.TXT (a loadable file of the engram):

```
4 401 218 402 403
2 402 218 404 210
4 404 218 405 406
2 405 218 407 211
4 407 218 408 409
2 408 218 410 212
2 410 218 411 245
```

TRACE.TXT lists the steps when running the engram.

```
Thinking Computer Code
 Revision 0, size 12k
 copyright 2012 by Robert S. Grondalski
 total data links=0
 total control (non constant) links=4
 total constant links=3
 total control + constant links=7
 total sound links=0
 start of new lines=6
 the max node number is 411 memlrn is 511
 min cyccnt for very simple output: 0
 min cyccnt for simple output: 0
 min cyccnt for full output: 40000
 max cyccnt for full output: 40000
 slowdown factor: 1
 start state: 401
 pn intr trig level : 19
 output frequency : 10
 learn sound sequence : 0
 plsrc=510
 cyccnt=1 psrc=0 hold=401 dsrc=1 lineno=6 pl=8 sp=0
 cyccnt=2 psrc=0 hold=401 dsrc=1 lineno=6 pl=8 sp=0
set execute here cyccnt=3 psrc=0 hold=401 dsrc=1 lineno=6
pl=8 sp=0
curgoal set 401 getanode
 getanode=511
 CRACTL newnode=511
 # learn 7 511 384 385 0 3
 getanode
 getanode=512
 autoctllrn plsrc=511 plrel=218 pldst=512 plout=401 lineno=8
tl=2
 cyccnt=4 psrc=401 hold=401 dsrc=1 lineno=8 pl=8 sp=0
 cyccnt=5 psrc=402 hold=403 dsrc=1 lineno=8 pl=8 sp=0
 cyccnt=6 psrc=402 hold=403 dsrc=1 lineno=8 pl=8 sp=0
 cyccnt=7 psrc=402 hold=403 dsrc=1 lineno=8 pl=8 sp=0
 cyccnt=8 psrc=404 hold=403 dsrc=1 lineno=8 pl=8 sp=0
 cyccnt=9 psrc=404 hold=403 dsrc=403 lineno=8 pl=8 sp=0
 cyccnt=10 psrc=404 hold=403 dsrc=403 lineno=8 pl=8 sp=0
 cyccnt=11 psrc=405 hold=406 dsrc=403 lineno=8 pl=8 sp=0
 cyccnt=12 psrc=405 hold=406 dsrc=403 lineno=8 pl=8 sp=0
 cyccnt=13 psrc=405 hold=406 dsrc=403 lineno=8 pl=8 sp=0
 cyccnt=14 psrc=407 hold=406 dsrc=403 lineno=8 pl=8 sp=0
 cyccnt=15 psrc=407 hold=406 dsrc=403 lineno=8 pl=8 sp=0
 cyccnt=16 psrc=407 hold=406 dsrc=403 lineno=8 pl=8 sp=0
 cyccnt=17 psrc=408 hold=409 dsrc=403 lineno=8 pl=8 sp=0
 cyccnt=18 psrc=408 hold=409 dsrc=403 lineno=8 pl=8 sp=0
 cyccnt=19 psrc=408 hold=409 dsrc=403 lineno=8 pl=8 sp=0
 cyccnt=20 psrc=410 hold=409 dsrc=403 lineno=8 pl=8 sp=0
```

```
cyccnt=21 psrc=410 hold=409 dsrc=403 lineno=8 pl=8 sp=0
cyccnt=22 psrc=410 hold=409 dsrc=403 lineno=8 pl=8 sp=0
cyccnt=23 psrc=411 hold=409 dsrc=403 lineno=8 pl=8 sp=0
# learn 9 403 406 409 0 23
cyccnt=24 psrc=411 hold=409 dsrc=403 lineno=9 pl=8 sp=0
cyccnt=25 psrc=411 hold=409 dsrc=403 lineno=9 pl=8 sp=0
cyccnt=26 psrc=411 hold=409 dsrc=403 lineno=9 pl=8 sp=0
cyccnt=27 psrc=411 hold=409 dsrc=403 lineno=9 pl=8 sp=0
cyccnt=28 psrc=411 hold=409 dsrc=403 lineno=9 pl=8 sp=0
PPOP NEGATIVE/PL
```

ENGOUT.TXT is the final engram showing the learned information:

```
4 401 218 402 403 1 0 0
2 402 218 404 210 1 0 0
4 404 218 405 406 1 0 0
2 405 218 407 211 1 0 0
4 407 218 408 409 1 0 0
2 408 218 410 212 1 0 0
2 410 218 411 245 1 0 0
1 403 406 409 0 1 0 0 0
```

The last line was not in the original engram named LRN.TXT. The last line is the cognitive link that was learned in this example.

ENGOUT1.TXT is a readable version of the engram out file.

```
4 401 example1a   218 next   402 example1b  403 sky        1 -12000 9
2 402 example1b   218 next   404 example1c  210 setdsrc    1 -12000 9
4 404 example1c   218 next   405 example1d  406 color      1 -12000 9
2 405 example1d   218 next   407 example1e  211 setdrel    1 -12000 9
4 407 example1e   218 next   408 example1f  409 blue       1 -12000 9
2 408 example1f   218 next   410 example1g  212 setddst    1 -12000 9
2   410 example1g 218 next   411 example1h  245 dlearn     1 -12000 9
1   511          384 isa     385 procedure  0              1 -12000 9
2   511          218 next    512            401 example1a  1 -12000 9
1   403 sky       406 color 409 blue        0              1 -12000 9
```

The last line is the newly learned cognitive link fact.

The file param.txt sets the parameters used by rev0_12k to specify which state to start at, which cycles to dump internal data for debugging, speed of operation, and internal parameters. The slowdown factor allows slowing the speed of operation from full speed (0) to slower speeds (1,2,3,…1000, …10000…) to allow easier human interaction. Output rate is how often (every nth cycle) the output is displayed – a value of 1 displays every cycle. The pain interrupt trigger level is used to control what level the internal pain/pleasure level must reach to cause a pain interrupt. Learn sound sequences controls if every sound input is learned as part of a sound sequence, 0 is no, 1 is yes.

- Hierarchical problem solving experiment: engram_example2.txt

The following code performs addition hierarchically by dividing the problem into smaller and smaller pieces. The adding operation is divided into adding columns and the adding a column operation is divided into getting numbers and adding the number to the sum. This example is listed as engram_example2.txt in the software.

```
2 add1            next        add2           addcol1       ;
2 add2            next        add3           nxtcol1       ;
0 ;
0 ; external ctl routines
0 ;
2 addcol1         next        addcol2        getnum1       ;
2 addcol2         next        addcol3        addtosum0     ;
0 ;
0 ;
0 ; to allow us to explain getting number
0 ; every source should allow explaining
1 getngnum        act         move                         ;
1 getngnum        object      newposition                  ;
0 ;
1 addtosum0       type        procedure                    ;
1 addtosum0       action      addtotlop                    ;
1 addtotlop       verb        add                          ;
1 addtotlop       object      to-total                     ;
0 ;
0 ;ex total=7 hold=5
4 addtosum0       next        addtosum1      newnumb       ;
2 addtosum1       next        addtosum2      setdrel       ;
2 addtosum2       next        addtosum3      drelacc       ;
2 addtosum3       next        addtosum4      settmpsrc     ;
4 addtosum4       next        addtosum5      +             ;
2 addtosum5       next        addtosum6      settmprel     ;
2 addtosum6       next        addtosum7      trelacc       ;
2 addtosum7       next        addtosum9      settmpsrc     ;
0 ;  get total
1 curadd          total       5                            ;
4 addtosum9       next        addtosuma      total         ;
2 addtosuma       next        addtosumb      setdrel       ;
2 addtosumb       next        addtosumc      drelacc       ;
2 addtosumc       next        addtosumd      settmprel     ;
2 addtosumd       next        addtosume      trelacc       ;
0 ; learn new total in data
2 addtosume       next        addtosumf      dlearn        ;
0 ; now return
0 ;
1 5+              7           12                           ;
1 2+              5           7                            ;
1 5               +           5+                           ;
```

```
1 2                    +             2+                                ;
0 ;
4 getnum1         next          getnum2        curadd       ;
2 getnum2         next          getnum2a       setdsrc      ;
2 getnum2a        next          getnum2b       accs         ;
2 getnum2b        next          getnum3        setddst      ;
4 getnum3         next          getnum4        newnumb      ;
2 getnum4         next          getnum5        setdrel      ;
2 getnum5         next          getnum6        dlearn       ;
```

- Inputting a sentence, storing it nonverbally, and then saying it in English or Italian: engram_example3.txt

The following example is listed as engram_example3.txt in the software.

```
0 ; a stored sentence can be said in English or Italian
0 ; start at spk1 (401) to say in English
0 ; start at spi1 (422) to say in Italian
0 ; start at input1 (454) and copy vis1ex3.txt to vis1.txt to
0 ;    input in English then say in Italian
0 ;
0 ; more words can be added to increase vocabulary
0 ; this is a simplified example
0 ; engram_main.txt has more tenses and other grammer
0 ;
0 ;
0 ; explain an idea - ex story1
0 ;
4 spk1           next          spk2           story1       ;
1 story1         subject       man                         ;
1 story1         verb          goes                        ;
1 story1         object        store                       ;
1 man            word          (man)                       ;
1 man            wordtype      noun                        ;
1 man            italian       (uomo)                      ;
1 goes           word          (goes)                      ;
1 goes           wordtype      verb                        ;
0 ; control needs to conjugate
1 goes           italian       (va)                        ;
1 store          word          (store)                     ;
1 store          wordtype      noun                        ;
1 store          italian       (negozio)                   ;
2 spk2           next          spk3           setdsrc      ;
4 spk3           next          spk5           subject      ;
2 spk5           next          spk6           speak        ;
4 spk6           next          spk8           verb         ;
2 spk8           next          spk9           speak        ;
4 spk9           next          spk10          object       ;
2 spk10          next          spk11          speak        ;
```

```
0 ; note can move setdrel to print code
4 spi1        next        spi2        story1      ;
2 spi2        next        spi3        setdsrc     ;
4 spi3        next        spi5        subject     ;
2 spi5        next        spi6        speakit     ;
4 spi6        next        spi8        verb        ;
2 spi8        next        spi9        speakit     ;
4 spi9        next        spi10       object      ;
2 spi10       next        spi11       speakit     ;
0 ;
0 ;
2 speak       next        spka1       recall      ;
2 spka1       next        spka2       settmpsrc   ;
4 spka2       next        spka3       word        ;
2 spka3       next        spka4       settmprel   ;
2 spka4       next        spka5       trelacc     ;
2 spka5       next        spka6       print       ;
0 ;
2 speakit     next        spia0       setdrel     ;
2 spia0       next        spia1       drelacc     ;
2 spia1       next        spia2       settmpsrc   ;
4 spia2       next        spia3       italian     ;
2 spia3       next        spia4       settmprel   ;
2 spia4       next        spia5       trelacc     ;
2 spia5       next        spia6       print       ;
0 ;
1 the         word        (the)                   ;
1 the         italian     (il)                    ;
1 the         wordtype    article                 ;
1 big         word        (big)                   ;
1 big         wordtype    adjective               ;
1 dog         word        (dog)                   ;
1 dog         wordtype    noun                    ;
1 dog         italian     (cane)                  ;
1 dog         isa         mammal                  ;
1 ran         word        (ran)                   ;
1 ran         wordtype    verb                    ;
1 house       word        (house)                 ;
1 house       wordtype    noun                    ;
1 house       italian     (casa)                  ;
0 ; input a sentence and set n/v/o
0 ;
4 input1      next        input1a     story1      ;
2 input1a     next        input1b     setdsrc     ;
2 input1b     next        input2a     readpl1     ;
2 input2a     next        input2      inp1        ;
2 input2      interrog    question                ;
2 input2      article     nounpart                ;
2 input2      adjective   nounpart                ;
2 input2      noun        nounpart1               ;
0 ;
2 inp1        next        inp2        exthld      ;
```

```
0 ; if endofline then readpl1
0 ; non-next branch gets priority
2 inp2          readend      inp1              readpl1        ;
2 inp2          next         inp3              settmpdst      ;
4 inp3          next         inp4              word           ;
2 inp4          next         inp5              settmprel      ;
2 inp5          next         inp6              clrsum         ;
2 inp6          next         inp7              sumatr         ;
2 inp7          next         newwrd1a          recog          ;
2 newwrd1a      next         nw2               settmpsrc      ;
4 nw2           next         nw3               wordtype       ;
2 nw3           next         nw4               settmprel      ;
2 nw4           next         nw5               trelacc        ;
0 ;
2 nounpart      next         nounpart1         inp1           ;
2 nounpart1     next         np1               tsrctohld      ;
2 np1           next         np2               setddst        ;
4 np2           next         np3               subject        ;
2 np3           next         np4               setdrel        ;
2 np4           next         np5               dlearn         ;
2 np5           next         np5a              imagne1        ;
2 np5a          next         np6               inp1           ;
2 np6           verb         verbpart                         ;
2 verbpart      next         vp1               tsrctohld      ;
2 vp1           next         vp2               setddst        ;
4 vp2           next         vp3               verb           ;
2 vp3           next         vp4               setdrel        ;
2 vp4           next         vp5               dlearn         ;
2 vp5           next         vp6               inp1           ;
2 vp6           noun         objpart                          ;
2 objpart       next         op1               tsrctohld      ;
2 op1           next         op2               setddst        ;
4 op2           next         op3               object         ;
2 op3           next         op4               setdrel        ;
2 op4           next         spi3              dlearn         ;
0 ;note at times we set noun to help recognize
0 ;
1 tree          isa          plant                            ;
2 imagne1       next         imagne2           setddst        ;
4 imagne2       next         imagne3           image1         ;
2 imagne3       next         imagne4           setdsrc        ;
4 imagne4       next         imagne5           location1      ;
2 imagne5       next         imagne6           setdrel        ;
0 ; create an image
2 imagne6       next         imagne7           dlearn         ;
4 imagne7       next         imagne8           story1         ;
2 imagne8       next         imagne9           setdsrc        ;
0 ;
0 ; general recall routine
2 recall        next         recall0           setdrel        ;
2 recall0       next         recall1           drelacc        ;
0 ; find may set low level pl, nofind may set
```

```
0 ; low level pn
0 ; at find we return because no next state
4 recall1      nofind       recall2       current     ;
2 recall2      next         recall3       setdsrc     ;
4 recall3      next         recall4       status      ;
2 recall4      next         recall5       setdrel     ;
4 recall5      next         recall6       rclerr      ;
2 recall6      next         recall7       setddst     ;
2 recall7      next         recall8       dlearn      ;
0 ;
0 ; general recognize routine
2 recog        next         recogn1       selmax      ;
0 ; find may set low level pl, nofind may set
0 ; low level pn
0 ; at find we return because no next state
4 recogn1      nofind       recogn2       current     ;
2 recogn2      next         recogn3       setdsrc     ;
4 recogn3      next         recogn4       status      ;
2 recogn4      next         recogn5       setdrel     ;
4 recogn5      next         recogn6       recogerr    ;
2 recogn6      next         recogn7       setddst     ;
2 recogn7      next         recogn8       dlearn      ;
0 ;
```

- Answering the question: "is a robin a bird?" experiment:engram_example4.txt

```
0 ; answering the question: is a robin a bird?
0 ;
0 ; is a robin a bird - look for a match
0 ; start with src set up with rel/dst is 1st/robin
0 ; 2nd/bird
4 mat-st0     next          mat-st0a      src1        ;
0 ;
1 src1        1st           robin                     ;
1 src1        2nd           bird                      ;
1 robin       isa           bird                      ;
2 mat-st0a    next          mat-st1       setdsrc     ;
4 mat-st1     next          mat-st2       2nd         ;
2 mat-st2     next          mat-st3       setdrel     ;
2 mat-st3     next          mat-st4       drelacc     ;
2 mat-st4     next          mat-st5       setdrel     ;
4 mat-st5     next          mat-st6       trigger     ;
2 mat-st6     next          mat-st7       setddst     ;
2 mat-st7     next          mat-st7a      dlearn      ;
4 mat-st7a    next          mat-st7b      1st         ;
2 mat-st7b    next          mat-st8       setdrel     ;
2 mat-st8     next          mat-st9       drelacc     ;
2 mat-st9     next          mat-st9a      settmpsrc   ;
4 mat-st9a    next          mat-st9b      isa         ;
2 mat-st9b    next          mat-st10      settmprel   ;
```

```
0 ; we access the abstraction of robin which = bird
0 ; using tmpsrc and tmprel
2 mat-st10      next          mat-st11      trelacc      ;
0 ;we set drel=bird which accesses trigger
2 mat-st11      next          mat-st12      setdrel      ;
2 mat-st12      next          mat-st12a     drelacc      ;
4 mat-st12a     trigger       mat-st13      true         ;
4 mat st12a     nofind        mat-st14      false        ;
0 ;
```

The technique used to answer is a robin a bird can also be used to answer geography questions, such as "is Orlando in Florida?" or "is Orlando in the USA?".

- Zooming in and out of objects experiment: engram_example5.txt

The following example, engram_example5.txt, demonstrates zooming in and out.

```
0 ; zooming in and out of objects
0 ;
0 ; zoom in visually to a room then zoom out
4 zm-s1        next          zm-s1a        zm1          ;
0 ;
1 zm1          topleft       chair1                     ;
1 chair1       botleft       leg1                       ;
0 ;
1 zm-s1        type          procedure                  ;
1 zm-s1        operation     zoomin                     ;
1 zoomin       verb          zoom                       ;
1 zoomin       object        in                         ;
0 ;
2 zm-s1a       next          zm-s1b        settmpsrc    ;
4 zm-s1b       next          zm-s1c        topleft      ;
2 zm-s1c       next          zm-s2         settmprel    ;
2 zm-s2        next          zm-s3         trelacc      ;
2 zm-s3        next          zm-s4         settmpsrc    ;
4 zm-s4        next          zm-s5         botleft      ;
2 zm-s5        next          zm-s6         settmprel    ;
2 zm-s6        next          zm-s7         trelacc      ;
2 zm-s7        next          zm-s8         tsrctohld    ;
2 zm-s8        next          zm-s9         drptmp       ;
2 zm-s9        next          zm-s10        settmpdst    ;
2 zm-s10       next          zm-s11        sumatr       ;
2 zm-s11       next          zm-s12        selmax       ;
0 ;
```

- Using the temporary data source register experiment:engram_example6.txt

```
0 ; recall numbers from different tmp src's and add them
0 ; (set up current src) add 3rd from group 4 (1) and 5th
0 ; from group 8 (7)
0 ; current src as follows
0 ; 1st-group/gp4
0 ; 1st-item/3rd
0 ; 2nd-group/gp8
0 ; 2nd-item/5th
4 gpadd-s1       next            gpadd-s1a       ex1             ;
0 ;
1 ex1            1st-gp          gp4                             ;
1 ex1            1st-item        3rd                             ;
1 ex1            2nd-gp          gp8                             ;
1 ex1            2nd-item        5th                             ;
0 ;idea 1 = 1    word 1 = (1)
1 gp4            3rd             1                               ;
1 gp4            2nd             2                               ;
1 gp8            5th             7                               ;
1 gp8            6th             2                               ;
1 7              +               7+                              ;
1 7+             1               8                               ;
0 ;
1 gpadd-s1       type            procedure                       ;
1 gpadd-s1       operation       addgroup                        ;
1 addgroup       verb            add                             ;
1 addgroup       object          group                           ;
0 ;
2 gpadd-s1a      next            gpadd-s1b       setdsrc         ;
4 gpadd-s1b      next            gpadd-s1c       1st-gp          ;
2 gpadd-s1c      next            gpadd-s2        setdrel         ;
0 ; drelacc is current rel access
0 ; trelacc is tmp rel acc
2 gpadd-s2       next            gpadd-s2a       drelacc         ;
2 gpadd-s2a      next            gpadd-s3        settmpsrc       ;
4 gpadd-s3       next            gpadd-s3a       1st-item        ;
2 gpadd-s3a      next            gpadd-s4        setdrel         ;
2 gpadd-s4       next            gpadd-s4a       drelacc         ;
2 gpadd-s4a      next            gpadd-s5        settmprel       ;
2 gpadd-s5       next            gpadd-s5a       trelacc         ;
2 gpadd-s5a      next            gpadd-s6        setddst         ;
4 gpadd-s6       next            gpadd-s7        add1            ;
2 gpadd-s7       next            gpadd-s7a       setdrel         ;
2 gpadd-s7a      next            gpadd-s7b       dlearn          ;
4 gpadd-s7b      next            gpadd-s8        2nd-gp          ;
2 gpadd-s8       next            gpadd-s8a       setdrel         ;
2 gpadd-s8a      next            gpadd-s8b       drelacc         ;
2 gpadd-s8b      next            gpadd-s9        settmpsrc       ;
4 gpadd-s9       next            gpadd-s10       2nd-item        ;
2 gpadd-s10      next            gpadd-s10a      setdrel         ;
2 gpadd-s10a     next            gpadd-s10b      drelacc         ;
```

```
2 gpadd-s10b    next         gpadd-s11      settmprel      ;
2 gpadd-s11     next         gpadd-s11a     trelacc        ;
2 gpadd-s11a    next         gpadd-s12      setddst        ;
2 gpadd-s12     next         gpadd-s13      settmpsrc      ;
2 gpadd-s13     next         gpadd-s14      settmprel      ;
0 ;now do the add
4 gpadd-s14     next         gpadd-s15      +              ;
2 gpadd-s15     next         gpadd-s15a     settmprel      ;
2 gpadd-s15a    next         gpadd-s15b     trelacc        ;
2 gpadd-s15b    next         gpadd-s16      settmpsrc      ;
4 gpadd-s16     next         gpadd-s17      add1           ;
2 gpadd-s17     next         gpadd-s17a     setdrel        ;
2 gpadd-s17a    next         gpadd-s18      drelacc        ;
2 gpadd-s18     next         gpadd-s19      settmprel      ;
2 gpadd-s19     next         gpadd-s20      trelacc        ;
0 ;
```

- Storing what we are doing and recalling what we recently did:
engram_example7.txt

```
0 ; storing what we are doing and recalling what we
0 ; recently did
0 ;
0 ; How we recall what we recently did:
0 ; when we create a new situation we crdat
0 ; and link current to it (is/current). Later we can create
0 ; other new situations. We can recall what we
0 ; did before by accessing is/current
0 ; location/movie and
0 ; recall the last time we were at the movies
0 ; we can datstp it and access other times we
0 ; were at the movies. We can access recent things
0 ; we did by just selecting isa/current
0 ; and recent things we did will be able to
0 ; be selected with datstp (sumatr - selmax)
0 ; create new situation
0 ; we possibly access the current situation
0 ; by selecting isa/current and it is the strongest
0 ; so it activates. We step to access recent
0 ; things we did
2 crsit1         next         crsit1a        crdat          ;
0 ;
1 crsit1         type         procedure                     ;
1 crsit1         action       crsitact                      ;
1 crsitact       verb         access                        ;
1 crsitact       object       doing                         ;
2 crsit1a        next         crsit2         setdsrc        ;
4 crsit2         next         crsit3         isa            ;
2 crsit3         next         crsit4         setdrel        ;
4 crsit4         next         crsit5         current        ;
2 crsit5         next         crsit6         setddst        ;
```

```
2 crsit6        next        crsit7      dlearn        ;
2 crsit7        next        crsit8      curgoalhld    ;
2 crsit8        next        crsit9      setddst       ;
4 crsit9        next        crsit10     current       ;
2 crsit10       next        crsit11     setdrel       ;
2 crsit11       next        crsit12     dlearn        ;
0 ;
```

- Focusing on an object experiment: engram_example8.txt

There are times when we focus on something and think about it for a while. For example, we may focus on an apple. We think about it, such as its shape or color or what to do with it. Often, the idea we focus on is activated as a result of past emotion links, such as candy (pleasure) or a hot stove (pain). When we are deciding what to do, we often automatically pick something with strong emotions to focus on. We set what to focus on in TMPSRC and set the current situation to "focus". The situation code checks the current situation and activates the focus procedures when it finds the current situation is "focus". Note that we do not stay using the focus procedure, but we ppopneg after each type of focus sequence, and as long as the situation stays focus, we go back to the focus procedure and look for another type of focus to access, such as lookatit or findinteresting. This takes longer than just a single procedure to focus on everything, but when we focus on something it takes time because we keep going back to the ppopneg procedure to determine what to do next. At ppopneg, we do not change the current situation, but at pain or pleasure interrupts we do. At pain interrupt, we change the current situation to pain interrupt, and at pleasure interrupt we change the current situation to pleasure interrupt. Learning to focus is an important thing we learn at an early age because it allows us to learn many things about an object.

engram_example8.txt

```
0 ; focusing on an object
0 ;
4 focus1        next        focus2      isa           ;
0 ;
1 lookatit      isa         focusproc                 ;
1 fndintrst     isa         focusproc                 ;
2 focus2        next        focus3      settmprel     ;
4 focus3        next        focus4      focusproc     ;
2 focus4        next        focus5      settmpdst     ;
2 focus5        next        focus6      clrsum        ;
2 focus6        next        focus7      sumatr        ;
2 focus7        next        focus8      selmaxr       ;
2 focus8        next        goal30                    ;
0 ;
```

```
0 ; what we are focusing on is in tmpsrc
4 lookatit       next           lookatit2      image          ;
2 lookatit2      next           lookatit3      setdrel        ;
2 lookatit3      next           lookatit4      drelacc        ;
2 lookatit4      find           lookatit5      setdsrc        ;
4 lookatit5      next           lookatit6      top            ;
2 lookatit6      next           lookatit7      setdrel        ;
2 lookatit7      next           lookatit8      drelacc        ;
1 apple          image          appleimage                   ;
1 appleimage     bottom         circle                       ;
0 ; add shape information - what a circle looks like
1 appleimage     top            stem                         ;
0 ; if no find we go back to current/situation/focus
0 ; we ppopneg then access situation again which is focus
0 ; then we find something else to focus on
0 ; the situation link allows us to keep doing something
0 ; even if we ppopneg
0 ; all of this takes a while which is correct - when we
0 ; are thinking about something we do not do it as one
0 ; fast procedure - we go through service procedures
0 ; try thinking about apple - does not happen fast -
0 ; it takes a while to think about apple
4 fndintrst      next           fndintrst2     interest       ;
2 fndintrst2     next           fndintrst3     setdrel        ;
2 fndintrst3     next           fndintrst4     drelacc        ;
0 ;
```

- Manually learning a new procedure and reactivation experiment: engram_example9.txt

Engram_example9 below is an example of the control section learning a data procedure then activating it. The sentence "learn a procedure ." is parsed. A sequence of events (steps) has been stored as data. The example procedure accesses a number, gets the digit in the second position, subtracts a constant from it, then compares the result to the current test value and if it matches says "3", otherwise says "7".

As each step found as data is manually executed, a new procedure step is learned in a new procedure. To add a branch to this procedure requires overwriting a step. The instruction block new state (BLKNEWST) at compbr3 overwrites the new state and SETPLREL adds the branch value between the compare state and the next state. PLSRCTOHLD is used to save the branch point to allow the other branch to be linked later with the otherbr step. Note that many branches could have been added from this branch point. Once a new procedure is learned, it can be tried out.

```
1 datpro1        type            procedure               ;
0 ;1 datpro1     goaltype    goodgoal            ;
1 datpro1        action          learnpro                ;
1 learnpro       verb            learn                   ;
1 learnpro       object          procedure               ;
0 ; we need to get the first step to execute
0 ; once found we return to goal30z
0 ; we store that we are doing a datpro
0 ; we should already have the dat steps set up
1 num1           posit1      2                           ;
1 num1           posit2      8                           ;
1 num1           posit3      6                           ;
1 num2           posit1      4                           ;
1 num2           posit2      5                           ;
1 num2           posit3      7                           ;
0 ; the following datpro steps are learned
0 ; earlier as we learn data for example it
0 ; could have been explained as verbal input
0 ; to do the steps in this order or it could
0 ; have been just decided to do these steps
1 getnm1         isa             procedure               ;
1 getpos2        isa             procedure               ;
1 setop1         isa             procedure               ;
1 setop          isa             procedure               ;
1 getnm2         isa             procedure               ;
1 getcnst1       isa             procedure               ;
1 subtr1         isa             procedure               ;
1 compa1         isa             procedure               ;
1 say3           isa             procedure               ;
1 otherbr        isa             procedure               ;
1 say7           isa             procedure               ;
1 compbr1        isa             procedure               ;
1 do-newpro      isa             procedure               ;
0 ;
0 ; do not use 1-6, link with events
0 ; evnt1/next/evnt2, evnt1/actn/getnm1
0 ; because we cannot just recall step
0 ; number 6 - we must access it from
0 ; step number 5
0 ; we learn these events just like we
0 ; learn new events in a story
0 ;
1 current        firstevnt       evnta1                  ;
1 evnta1         next            evnta1a                 ;
1 evnta1         action          crnewct1                ;
1 evnta1a        next            evnta2                  ;
1 evnta1a        action          getnm1                  ;
1 evnta2         next            evnta3                  ;
1 evnta2         action          getpos2                 ;
1 evnta3         next            evnta4                  ;
1 evnta3         action          setop1                  ;
1 evnta4         next            evnta5                  ;
0 ; subtract 3
1 evnta4         action          getcnst1                ;
1 evnta5         next            evnta6                  ;
1 evnta5         action          setop                   ;
1 evnta6         next            evnta7                  ;
1 evnta6         action          subtr1                  ;
0 ; learn a branch
```

173

```
0 ; need to branch on something - test if
0 ; answer is current/test
1 evnta7        next         evnta8                      ;
1 evnta7        action       compa1                      ;
1 evnta8        next         evnta9                      ;
1 evnta8        action       compbr1                     ;
1 evnta9        next         evnta10                     ;
1 evnta9        action       say3                        ;
1 evnta10       next         evnta11                     ;
1 evnta10       action       otherbr                     ;
1 evnta11       action       say7                        ;
0 ; we do not want do-newpro to be linked to
0 ; new procedure as a step - we need datpro
0 ; code to notice it is done and cractl
0 ; then pick a good situation thing to do
0 ; of redo the new procedure
1 evnta12       action       do-newpro                   ;
0 ;
0 ;
2 crnewctl      next         crnewctla    cractl         ;
2 crnewctla     next         crnewctlb    pldsttohld     ;
2 crnewctlb     next         crnewctlc    setddst        ;
4 crnewctlc     next         crnewctld    newctl         ;
2 crnewctld     next         crnewctle    setdrel        ;
4 crnewctle     next         crnewctlf    current        ;
2 crnewctlf     next         crnewctlg    setdsrc        ;
2 crnewctlg     next         crnewctlh    dlearn         ;
0 ;
0 ; redo the new procedure
0 ; we do not want this to be part of the new
0 ; procedure
4 do-newpro     next         donewpro1    newctl         ;
2 donewpro1     next         donewpro2    curracc1       ;
0 ; if no find then ppopneg
2 donewpro2     find         goal30       settmpsrc      ;
2 donewpro2     nofind       donewpro3                   ;
0 ;
0 ;
0 ;
4 compa1        next         compa1a      current        ;
2 compa1a       next         compa1b      setdsrc        ;
4 compa1b       next         compa1c      answer         ;
2 compa1c       next         compa1d      setdrel        ;
2 compa1d       next         compa1e      drelacc        ;
2 compa1e       next         compa1f      setdrel        ;
4 compa1f       next         compa1g      find           ;
2 compa1g       next         compa1h      setddst        ;
2 compa1h       next         compa1i      dlearn         ;
4 compa1i       next         compa1j      compare        ;
2 compa1j       next         compa1k      setdrel        ;
2 compa1k       next         compa1l      drelacc        ;
0 ; if we set it as drel and access and find
0 ; it the find is set
2 compa1l       next         compa1m      setdrel        ;
2 compa1m       next         compa1n      drelacc        ;
0 ; compare branch
4 compbr1       next         compbr2      find           ;
2 compbr2       next         compbr3      setplrel       ;
0 ; block a new state from being created - as
```

```
0 ; we start the next state say3 it will overwrite
0 ; this compbr1 state
2 compbr3     next        compbr4     blknewst     ;
0 ; save branch point for later returning
4 compbr4     next        compbr5     current      ;
2 compbr5     next        compbr6     setdsrc      ;
4 compbr6     next        compbr7     savebrpt     ;
2 compbr7     next        compbr8     setdrel      ;
2 compbr8     next        compbr9     plsrctohld   ;
2 compbr9     next        compbra     setddst      ;
2 compbra     next        compbrb     dlearn       ;
0 ;
4 otherbr     next        otherbra    current      ;
2 otherbra    next        otherbrb    setdsrc      ;
4 otherbrb    next        otherbrc    savebrpt     ;
2 otherbrc    next        otherbrd    setdrel      ;
2 otherbrd    next        otherbre    drelacc      ;
2 otherbre    next        otherbrf    setplsrc     ;
4 otherbrf    next        otherbrg    nofind       ;
2 otherbrg    next        otherbrh    setplrel     ;
2 otherbrh    next        otherbri    blknewst     ;
0 ;
0 ; as we execute this it links say3 as plout
0 ; and savebrpt as plsrc and nofind as plrel
4 say3        next        say3a       3            ;
2 say3a       next        say3b       speakb       ;
0 ;
4 say7        next        say7a       7            ;
2 say7a       next        say7b       speakb       ;
0 ; learning a constant
1 current     constant    3                        ;
4 getcnst1    next        getcnst2    current      ;
2 getcnst2    next        getcnst3    setdsrc      ;
4 getcnst3    next        getcnst4    constant     ;
2 getcnst4    next        getcnst5    setdrel      ;
2 getcnst5    next        getcnst6    drelacc      ;
2 getcnst6    next        getcnst7    setddst      ;
0 ; we want this constant to overwrite this procedure
0 ; that accessed it so we do plrnhld then plfixout
2 getcnst7    next        getcnst8    plrnhld      ;
2 getcnst8    next        getcnst9    plfixout     ;
0 ;
4 getnm1      next        getnm1a     current      ;
2 getnm1a     next        getnm1b     setdsrc      ;
4 getnm1b     next        getnm1c     number       ;
2 getnm1c     next        getnm1d     setdrel      ;
4 getnm1d     next        getnm1e     num1         ;
2 getnm1e     next        getnm1f     setddst      ;
2 getnm1f     next        getnm1g     dlearn       ;
0 ;
4 getnm2      next        getnm2a     current      ;
2 getnm2a     next        getnm2b     setdsrc      ;
4 getnm2b     next        getnm2c     number       ;
2 getnm2c     next        getnm2d     setdrel      ;
4 getnm2d     next        getnm2e     num2         ;
2 getnm2e     next        getnm2f     setddst      ;
2 getnm2f     next        getnm2g     dlearn       ;
0 ;
4 getpos2     next        getpos2a    current      ;
```

```
2 getpos2a       next         getpos2b     setdsrc      ;
4 getpos2b       next         getpos2c     number       ;
2 getpos2c       next         getpos2d     setdrel      ;
2 getpos2d       next         getpos2e     drelacc      ;
2 getpos2e       next         getpos2f     settmpsrc    ;
4 getpos2f       next         getpos2g     posit2       ;
2 getpos2g       next         getpos2h     settmprel    ;
2 getpos2h       next         getpos2i     trelacc      ;
2 getpos2i       next         getpos2j     setddst      ;
4 getpos2j       next         getpos2k     opnd         ;
2 getpos2k       next         getpos2l     setdrel      ;
2 getpos2l       next         getpos2m     dlearn       ;
0 ;
0 ; sets hold as opnd
0 ; first see if it is a number - if not
0 ; then get constant - if we are starting
0 ; this step from manual execution then
0 ; hold is the start step - not a number
0 ; so we know to then go and get the number
2 setop          next         setopa1      setdsrc      ;
4 setopa1        next         setopa1a     isa          ;
2 setopa1a       next         setopa1b     setdrel      ;
2 setopa1b       next         setopa1c     drelacc      ;
0 ; we execute the setop
0 ; procedure (which causes it to be learned) -
0 ; if it is during learning hold will not be
0 ; a number so we must find the number
0 ; so we access current/constant that was
0 ; used above to set the constant and if
0 ; this step occurs during running then
0 ; it uses the constant from the last step
2 setopa1c       number       setopa1d     srctohld     ;
4 setopa1c       next         setopa1e     current      ;
2 setopa1e       next         setopa1f     setdsrc      ;
4 setopa1f       next         setopa1g     constant     ;
2 setopa1g       next         setopa1h     setdrel      ;
2 setopa1h       next         setopa1d     drelacc      ;
2 setopa1d       next         setopa2      setddst      ;
4 setopa2        next         setopa2a     current      ;
2 setopa2a       next         setopa3      setdsrc      ;
4 setopa3        next         setopa4      opnd         ;
2 setopa4        next         setopa5      setdrel      ;
2 setopa5        next         setopa6      dlearn       ;
0 ;
4 setop1         next         setop2a      current      ;
2 setop2a        next         setop2b      setdsrc      ;
4 setop2b        next         setop2c      opnd         ;
2 setop2c        next         setop2d      setdrel      ;
2 setop2d        next         setop2e      drelacc      ;
2 setop2e        next         setop2f      setddst      ;
4 setop2f        next         setop2g      opnd1        ;
2 setop2g        next         setop2h      setdrel      ;
2 setop2h        next         setop2i      dlearn       ;
0 ;
4 subtr1         next         subtr2a      current      ;
2 subtr2a        next         subtr2b      setdsrc      ;
4 subtr2b        next         subtr2c      opnd1        ;
2 subtr2c        next         subtr2d      setdrel      ;
2 subtr2d        next         subtr2e      drelacc      ;
```

```
2 subtr2e       next            subtr2f         settmpsrc       ;
4 subtr2f       next            subtr2g         -               ;
2 subtr2g       next            subtr2h         settmprel       ;
2 subtr2h       next            subtr2i         trelacc         ;
2 subtr2i       next            subtr2j         settmpsrc       ;
4 subtr2j       next            subtr2k         opnd            ;
2 subtr2k       next            subtr2l         setdrel         ;
2 subtr2l       next            subtr2m         drelacc         ;
2 subtr2m       next            subtr2n         settmprel       ;
2 subtr2n       next            subtr2o         trelacc         ;
2 subtr2o       next            subtr2p         setddst         ;
2 subtr2p       next            subtr2q         speakb          ;
4 subtr2q       next            subtr2r         current         ;
2 subtr2r       next            subtr2s         setdsrc         ;
4 subtr2s       next            subtr2t         answer          ;
2 subtr2t       next            subtr2u         setdrel         ;
2 subtr2u       next            subtr2v         dlearn          ;
0 ;
0 ; this is the main way we learn a procedure
4 datpro1       next            datpro1a        current         ;
2 datpro1a      next            datpro2         setdsrc         ;
4 datpro2       next            datpro3         doing           ;
2 datpro3       next            datpro4         setdrel         ;
4 datpro4       next            datpro5         datpro          ;
2 datpro5       next            datpro6         setddst         ;
2 datpro6       next            datpro6a        dlearn          ;
0 ; first start a new control learn sequence
2 datpro6a      next            datpro6a1       cractl          ;
0 ; need to start a new procedure and link data
0 ; to it - it should be many cycles since last
0 ; creation but we do not want the execute
0 ; of datpro to be part of the new procedure
4 datpro6a1     next            datpro6b        firstevnt       ;
2 datpro6b      next            datpro6c        setdrel         ;
2 datpro6c      next            datpro6d        drelacc         ;
2 datpro6d      next            datpro6e        setddst         ;
2 datpro6e      next            datpro6f        settmpsrc       ;
4 datpro6f      next            datpro6g        evnt            ;
2 datpro6g      next            datpro6h        setdrel         ;
2 datpro6h      next            datpro7         dlearn          ;
0 ; now recall the action to execute
0 ; this would be set up during goal code
4 datpro7       next            datpro14        action          ;
2 datpro14      next            datpro15        settmprel       ;
2 datpro15      next            datpro18        trelacc         ;
2 datpro18      next            datpro18a       settmpsrc       ;
0 ; now get first step
0 ; need to push down until we get to something
0 ; that we can execute
0 ; add hierarchy to datpro code
0 ; (note we still need auto hierarchy so we do not
0 ; have to use data registers as we move up and down -
0 ; we first learn a procedure as datpro then move it
0 ; to normal procedure structures)
0 ; goal30 executes what is in tmpsrc
0 ; set pnpl level and execute
0 ; start executing and at ppopneg we test
0 ; the situation and see if we have what
0 ; to do in a situation ie at done a column
```

```
0 ; we may have get next column to add
0 ;
2 datpro18a     next          goal30                          ;
0 ;
2 goal30        next          goal30a        tsrctohld        ;
2 goal30a       next          goal30b        execute          ;
0 ;
2 state1        ppopneg       datpro20                        ;
2 state1        intrpl        datpro20                        ;
0 ; datpro example - when adding we set
0 ; situation to adding and then when
0 ; a carry occurs we branch on it
0 ; we constantly at ppopneg check if
0 ; we are in a predefined situation
0 ; we probably learn this by natural selection
0 ; as a way to avoid confusion
0 ; we must come here after ppopneg - we
0 ; test in ppopneg if a datpro routine
0 ; if so we need to get the next step
0 ;
0 ; to modify a procedure we
0 ; first modify the datpro steps then we
0 ; reexecute it - the first time we select
0 ; each action and do it; the next time we
0 ; can do it fast
0 ; now get the next step
4 datpro20      next          datpro21       current          ;
2 datpro21      next          datpro21b      setdsrc          ;
0 ; item 1 was set above before we executed the
0 ; procedure whose result we are checking
0 ; ex adding/carry/carrypro
4 datpro21b     next          datpro22a      evnt             ;
2 datpro22a     next          datpro22b      setdrel          ;
2 datpro22b     next          datpro23a      drelacc          ;
2 datpro23a     next          datpro24a      settmpsrc        ;
4 datpro24a     next          datpro24b      next             ;
2 datpro24b     next          datpro24c      settmprel        ;
2 datpro24c     next          datpro24d      trelacc          ;
2 datpro24d     find          datpro24e      setddst          ;
0 ; if no find next event then we are done
0 ; create a new ctl so we do not link the
0 ; goal10a action to the new procedure
2 datpro24d     nofind        datpro24d1     cractl           ;
4 datpro24d1    next          datpro24d2     current          ;
2 datpro24d2    next          datpro24d3     setdsrc          ;
0 ; clear current/doing to at ppopneg do not go back to
0 ; look for another datpro step
4 datpro24d3    next          datpro24d4     doing            ;
2 datpro24d4    next          datpro24d5     setdrel          ;
4 datpro24d5    next          datpro24d6     donedatpro       ;
2 datpro24d6    next          datpro24d7     setddst          ;
2 datpro24d7    next          datpro24d8     dlearn           ;
4 datpro24d8    next          goal10a        situation        ;
0 ;
0 ; when done a datpro a good thing to do next
0 ; is to try out the new procedure
1 donedatpro    todo          do-newpro                       ;
0 ;
2 datpro24e     next          datpro24f      dlearn           ;
```

```
2 datpro24f     next        datpro24g     setdsrc      ;
4 datpro24g     next        datpro24h     action       ;
2 datpro24h     next        datpro24i     setdrel      ;
2 datpro24i     next        datpro25a     drelacc      ;
2 datpro25a     find        datpro25b     settmpsrc    ;
0 ; check if the action is a procedure - if
0 ; not it is a constant
4 datpro25b     next        datpro25c     isa          ;
2 datpro25c     next        datpro25d     settmprel    ;
2 datpro25d     next        datpro25e     trelacc      ;
0 ; if it is not a procedure then it is a
0 ; constant so clearn it then get the next
0 ; step
2 datpro25e     nofind      datpro25f     tsrctohld    ;
2 datpro25f     next        datpro20      clearn       ;
2 datpro25e     procedure   goal30                     ;
0 ;
4 datpro25a     nofind      goal10a       situation    ;
```

- Learning multiple attributes with the same source and relation: engram_example10.txt

There are times we learn multiple attributes with the same source and relation. For example, we may learn that a person has two sons. The source and relation are the same, but there are different destination nodes. The following engram demonstrates this.

```
0 ; engram_example10.txt
0 ; start at 401
0 ; example of dlearnml
4 example1a     next        example1b     sky          ;
2 example1b     next        example1c     setdsrc      ;
4 example1c     next        example1d     color        ;
2 example1d     next        example1e     setdrel      ;
4 example1e     next        example1f     blue         ;
2 example1f     next        example1g     setddst      ;
2 example1g     next        example1h     dlearn       ;
4 example1h     next        example1i     dog          ;
2 example1i     next        example1j     setdsrc      ;
2 example1j     next        example1k     dlearn       ;
4 example1k     next        example1l     sky          ;
2 example1l     next        example1m     setdsrc      ;
4 example1m     next        example1n     red          ;
2 example1n     next        example1o     setddst      ;
2 example1o     next        example1p     dlearnml     ;
4 example1p     next        example1p1    sky          ;
2 example1p1    next        example1p2    settmpsrc    ;
4 example1p2    next        example1p3    color        ;
2 example1p3    next        example1p4    settmprel    ;
2 example1p4    next        example1q     trelacc      ;
2 example1q     find        example1q5    setdsrc      ;
4 example1q5    next        example1q6    word         ;
2 example1q6    next        example1q1    setdrel      ;
2 example1q1    next        example1q2    drelacc      ;
2 example1q2    next        example1q3    trelacc      ;
2 example1q3    find        example1s     trelacc      ;
```

```
2 example1s    find      example1t              ;
2 example1s    nofind    example1u              ;
2 example1t    next      example1v              ;
2 example1u    next      example1w              ;
1 blue         word      (blue)                 ;
1 red          word      (red)                  ;
0 ;
0 ;
```

11.4 ADDITIONAL EXPERIMENTS

- Simple data access experiment

The following control sequence does a simple data access.

If we are asked: What color is the sky? As we input this sentence, we create new data links using a new sentence source node:

new sentence/question adjective/color

new sentence/object/sky

We use these data links below to answer the question. We first access the sentence adjective (color) and set it to TMPREL, then we access the sentence object (sky) and set it to TMPSRC, then we access the data link: sky/color/blue and speak the answer.

```
4 answer4    next    answer4a    qadj        ;
2 answer4a   next    answer4b    setdrel     ;
2 answer4b   next    answer4c    drelacc     ;
2 answer4c   find    answer4d    settmprel   ;
0 ; what color is sky
2 answer4d   next    answer4e    settmprel   ;
4 answer4e   next    answer4f    object      ;
2 answer4f   next    answer4g    setdrel     ;
2 answer4g   next    answer4h    drelacc     ;
2 answer4h   next    answer4i    settmpsrc   ;
2 answer4i   next    answer4j    trelacc     ;
2 answer4j   next    answer4k    speakb      ;
1 sky        color   blue                    ;
```

- Parsing and answering a sentence: "what color is the sky ?" experiment

The file vis1.txt is accessed during reading. The program rev0_12k defaults to start reading when the program is started. As long as the reading is interesting, it will continue. The following examples describe the reading, understanding, and responses to the example vis1.txt file:

```
What color is the sky ?                 |
What sound does a cow make ?            |
```

```
Is a dog an animal ?              |
What is 3 x 2 ?                   |
What is a carrot ?               |
The man ran to the store .        |
Then he ran home .                |
The dog is big .                  |
Is the dog big ?                  |
What is your name ?               |
Imagine a yard .                  |
The dog is on the right .         |
The cat is on the left .          |
Where is the dog ?                |
The dog                           |
ran home .                        |
                                  |
                                  |
                                  |
```

The question "What is the color of the sky ?" is answered as follows. First it must be input and understood. The words are input one at a time. As each word is input, its wordtype is accessed. The word "what" is an interrogative word. The word "color" is an adjective. The word "is" is a verb. The word "the" is an article. The word "sky" is a noun. As each word is input, a sentence structure is created. First, a new data node is created to be used for linking the sentence to it. The instruction CRDAT creates a new data node and it is linked to current/csentence/(new data node) so that it can later be accessed. The sentence information is linked to this new data node. Depending on the wordtype and its position in a sentence, it can be determined if a word is a subject or an object. For example, "The man ran home." has two nouns: "man" and "home". Because the "man" is first, it is the subject, and since "home" is after the verb, it is the object. As words are input, they are linked to the new sentence data node:

(new sentence data node)/subject/man
(new sentence data node)/verb/ran
(new sentence data node)/object/home

The parenthesis above around (new sentence data node) indicate it is not a fixed value, but it is a new value for each sentence created with the CRDAT instruction below.

As each word is input, its wordtype is determined and a branch occurs to the appropriate code to link it to the new sentence data node. In the case of "What color is the sky ?", the first word "what" is an interrogative so there is a branch to the question code, which creates the sentence structure then jumps to the answer code to answer the question.

181

```
0 ;
2 input1g       next        input1h       crdat        ;
2 input1h       next        input1i       setddst      ;
4 input1i       next        input1j       current      ;
2 input1j       next        input1k       setdsrc      ;
4 input1k       next        input1l       csentence    ;
0 ; if the last sentence is an event linked to the
0 ; current sentence then we must do a nxt-evnt link
0 ; between them
2 input1l       next        input1m       setdrel      ;
0 ; this becomes the current most recent sentence
2 input1m       next        input1n       dlearn       ;
2 input1n       next        input1o       drelacc      ;
2 input1o       next        input1p       setdsrc      ;
2 input1p       next        input1q       readpl1x     ;
2 input1q       next        input2        inp1         ;
4 input2        interrog    question1     interrog     ;
0 ;article indicates a noun is to follow - it
0 ;is a type of adjective but worddype finds
0 ; article for "the" because it is more accurate
2 input2        article     input2        inp1         ;
4 input2        adjective   parse2        subadj       ;
4 input2        noun        parse4        subject      ;
4 input2        pronoun     parse4        subject      ;
0 ; a sentence can start with a verb but it is awkward
0 ; it can also be a question "is a dog an animal?"
4 input2        verb        parse20       verb         ;
0 ; then is an adverb
0 ; ex: then we read a book
4 input2        adverb      parse100      adverb       ;
2 input2        statrdend   rdend1                     ;
2 input2        next        nofindwd0                  ;
```

To answer the question "What color is the sky ?" we first access the question adjective "color" and set it as TMPREL, then we access the object "sky" and set it as TMPSRC, then we do TRELACC and speak the answer.

```
4 answer4        next        answer4a      qadj         ;
2 answer4a       next        answer4b      setdrel      ;
2 answer4b       next        answer4c      drelacc      ;
2 answer4c       find        answer4e      settmprel    ;
0 ; what color is sky
4 answer4e       next        answer4f      object       ;
2 answer4f       next        answer4g      setdrel      ;
2 answer4g       next        answer4h      drelacc      ;
2 answer4h       next        answer4i      settmpsrc     ;
2 answer4i       next        answer4j      trelacc      ;
2 answer4j       next        answer4k      speakb       ;
```

The question "What sound does a cow make ?" is answered in a similar fashion.

- "Is a dog an animal ?" experiment

To answer "Is a dog an animal ?", we first parse the sentence, then we go to comp1 for comparison. We use the subject1 "animal" as a trigger, then we start with the subject "dog" and move up the hierarchy using isa links to look for a match to animal. If we find it, we answer "yes". If we keep moving up the hierarchy and reach the end without a match, then we answer "no".

```
4 comp1        next       quest3     subject1    ;
2 quest3       next       quest4     setdrel     ;
2 quest4       next       quest5     drelacc     ;
2 quest5       next       quest6     setdrel     ;
4 quest6       next       quest7     trigger     ;
2 quest7       next       quest8     setddst     ;
0 ; learn rel=animal, dst=trigger
2 quest8       next       quest9     dlearn      ;
4 quest9       next       quest10    subject     ;
2 quest10      next       quest11    setdrel     ;
2 quest11      next       quest12    drelacc     ;
2 quest12      next       quest13    settmpsrc   ;
4 quest13      next       quest14    isa         ;
2 quest14      next       quest15    settmprel   ;
2 quest15      next       quest16    trelacc     ;
2 quest16      find       quest16a   settmpsrc   ;
4 quest16      next       quest19    no          ;
2 quest16a     next       quest17    setdrel     ;
2 quest17      next       quest18    drelacc     ;
0 ; iterate abstraction
4 quest18      find       quest19    yes         ;
4 quest18      next       quest15                ;
2 quest19      next       quest20    speakb      ;
```

- "What is 3 x 2 ?" experiment

To answer "What is 3 x 2 ?" we input "what" and set that the sentence is an interrogative. We input "is" and go to the verbpart. We input "3" and access a wortype of "number", which branches to the code below. This code stores "3" and operand1, then accesses the operation "+" and stores it as the operation. Next, the second operand "2" is input and set as operand2. Then operand1 is accessed and set as TMPSRC, the operation is accessed and set as TMPREL and then the TMPDST is accessed, in this case "3+". This is set to

TMPSRC, operand2 is accessed and set to TMPREL, and the answer "5" is accessed and spoken.

```
0 ;
2 numpart        next            numpart2        tsrctohld       ;
2 numpart2       next            numpart3        setddst         ;
4 numpart3       next            numpart4        operand1        ;
2 numpart4       next            numpart5        setdrel         ;
2 numpart5       next            numpart6        dlearn          ;
2 numpart6       next            numpart7        inp1            ;
2 numpart7       next            numpart8        tsrctohld       ;
2 numpart8       next            numpart9        setddst         ;
0 ; store operand1,2 and operation separately
0 ; so we can later answer what each one is -
0 ; do not combine operand1 and operation on
0 ; the fly without storing because we would not
0 ; be able to answer what is operand 1
4 numpart9       next            numpart10       operation       ;
2 numpart10      next            numpart11       setdrel         ;
2 numpart11      next            numpart12       dlearn          ;
0 ; eventually add checks to see if each input
0 ; is really a number or operation
2 numpart12      next            numpart13       inp1            ;
2 numpart13      next            numpart14       tsrctohld       ;
2 numpart14      next            numpart15       setddst         ;
4 numpart15      next            numpart16       operand2        ;
2 numpart16      next            numpart17       setdrel         ;
2 numpart17      next            numpart18       dlearn          ;
4 numpart18      next            numpart19       operand1        ;
2 numpart19      next            numpart20       setdrel         ;
2 numpart20      next            numpart21       drelacc         ;
2 numpart21      next            numpart22       settmpsrc       ;
4 numpart22      next            numpart23       operation       ;
2 numpart23      next            numpart24       setdrel         ;
2 numpart24      next            numpart25       drelacc         ;
2 numpart25      next            numpart26       settmprel       ;
2 numpart26      next            numpart27       trelacc         ;
2 numpart27      next            numpart28       settmpsrc       ;
4 numpart28      next            numpart29       operand2        ;
2 numpart29      next            numpart30       setdrel         ;
2 numpart30      next            numpart31       drelacc         ;
2 numpart31      next            numpart32       settmprel       ;
2 numpart32      next            numpart33       trelacc         ;
2 numpart33      next            numpart34       speakb          ;
```
- "What is a carrot ?" experiment

To answer "What is a carrot ?" we input "what" and set that the sentence is an interrogative. We input "is" and go to the verbpart. We input "a" and "carrot" and use carrot as a data source and "isa" as a data relation and access vegetable and speak the result. If we cannot find "isa", we look for "defin" or "does" links.

```
0 ; to answer "what is a ___ "
0 ; first see if there is an isa link -
0 ;
4 whatis1       next          whatis2       isa          ;
2 whatis2       next          whatis3       lrnverb1     ;
2 whatis3       next          whatis4       access1      ;
2 whatis4       find          whatis8       sayansw1     ;
0 ;
4 whatis4       nofind        whatis9       defin        ;
2 whatis9       next          whatis10      lrnverb1     ;
2 whatis10      next          whatis11      access1      ;
2 whatis11      find          whatis12      sayansw1     ;
4 whatis11      nofind        whatis13      does         ;
2 whatis13      next          whatis14      lrnverb1     ;
2 whatis14      next          whatis15      access1      ;
2 whatis15      find          whatis16      sayansw1     ;
0 ;
2 lrnverb1      next          lrnverb2      setddst      ;
4 lrnverb2      next          lrnverb3      verbchk      ;
2 lrnverb3      next          lrnverb4      setdrel      ;
2 lrnverb4      next          lrnverb5      dlearn       ;
0 ;
4 access1       next          access2       object       ;
2 access2       next          access2a      setdrel      ;
2 access2a      next          access3       drelacc      ;
2 access3       next          access4       settmpsrc    ;
4 access4       next          access5       verbchk      ;
2 access5       next          access5a      setdrel      ;
2 access5a      next          access6       drelacc      ;
2 access6       next          access7       settmprel    ;
2 access7       next          access8       trelacc      ;
0 ;
```

- Creating a story structure experiment

When we input two sentences that are events in a story, we can link the events with nxtevnt.

```
The man ran to the store .                   |
Then he ran home .                           |

0 ; then he went ...
2 parse94d      then          parse94e      setdrel      ;
2 parse94d      next          input1                     ;
2 parse94e      next          parse94e1     tsrctohld    ;
2 parse94e1     next          parse94e2     setdsrc      ;
4 parse94e2     next          parse94e3     type         ;
2 parse94e3     next          parse94e4     setdrel      ;
4 parse94e4     next          parse94e5     then-sent    ;
2 parse94e5     next          parse94e6     setddst      ;
2 parse94e6     next          parse94f      dlearn       ;
```

```
2 parse94f       next            parse94g        tsrctohld       ;
2 parse94f       next            parse94g        setddst         ;
4 parse94g       next            parse94h        nxtevnt         ;
2 parse94h       next            parse94i        setdrel         ;
4 parse94i       next            parse94j        current         ;
2 parse94j       next            parse94k        settmpsrc       ;
0 ; this links the sentence structures
0 ;
4 parse94k       next            parse94l        oldevnt         ;
2 parse94l       next            parse94m        settmprel       ;
2 parse94m       next            parse94n        trelacc         ;
0 ; we are done with dsrc so we can overwrite it
0 ; with the old source for learning
2 parse94n       next            parse94o        setdsrc         ;
2 parse94o       next            input1          dlearn          ;
```

- Learning from a statement and answering questions related to what was learned experiment

```
The dog is big .
Is the dog big ?
```

We first parse "the dog is big" setting subject/dog. We then test to see if the subject refers to one item (for example, with "the sky is blue" there is just one sky) or to one of a group, as with dog. Since it is one of a group, we create a new data node to refer to the specific dog in the sentence. We link "isa/dog" to this new data node. We access the verb "is" and the object adjective "big". We determine that "big" is a "size" so we link to the new data node "size/big". We then input the second line "is the dog big ?" and look for a hit when we access the size of the dog. Note that we access the most recent dog with SUMATR and SELMAX because if asked a question about an object, we will select the most recent example of that object.

```
0 ;
4 parse72        next            parse73         subject         ;
2 parse73        next            parse74         settmprel       ;
2 parse74        next            parse75         trelacc         ;
2 parse75        next            parse76a        setdsrc         ;
4 parse76a       next            parse76b        onemany         ;
2 parse76b       next            parse76c        setdrel         ;
2 parse76c       next            parse76d        drelacc         ;
2 parse76d       one             parse79a                        ;
0 ; if many ex: dog then create a new
0 ; data source and link isa/dog
0 ;
2 parse76d       many            parse76e        crdat           ;
2 parse76e       next            parse76f        setdsrc         ;
4 parse76f       next            parse76g        isa             ;
```

```
2 parse76g      next        parse76h     setdrel      ;
4 parse76h      next        parse76i     subject      ;
2 parse76i      next        parse76i1    settmprel    ;
2 parse76i1     next        parse76i2    trelacc      ;
2 parse76i2     next        parse76j     setddst      ;
2 parse76j      next        parse79a     dlearn       ;
0 ;
0 ; ex the dog is big
0 ; but the verb is should be changed
0 ; to size - when adjective is dst then
0 ; the relation should be the type of adjective
4 parse79a      next        parse79b     objadj       ;
2 parse79b      next        parse79c     settmprel    ;
2 parse79c      next        parse79d     trelacc      ;
2 parse79d      next        parse79e     setddst      ;
2 parse79e      next        parse79f     settmpsrc    ;
4 parse79f      next        parse79g     isa          ;
2 parse79g      next        parse79h     settmprel    ;
2 parse79h      next        parse79i     trelacc      ;
0 ; access size in case of big
0 ; in case of location - the dog is right (in yard)
0 ; need to link yard/dog#n/right
2 parse79i      location    parse170                  ;
2 parse79i      next        parse79j     setdrel      ;
0 ; once done imagining
2 parse79j      next        input1       dlearn       ;
0 ;
0 ;

2 parse30       next        parse30a     inplrn1      ;
2 parse30a      next        parse31a     srctohld     ;
2 parse31a      next        parse31b     settmpsrc    ;
2 parse31b      next        parse31c     setddst      ;
4 parse31c      next        parse31d     current      ;
2 parse31d      next        parse31e     setdsrc      ;
4 parse31e      next        parse31f     sentence     ;
2 parse31f      next        parse31g     setdrel      ;
2 parse31g      next        parse31h     dlearn       ;
4 parse31h      next        parse31i     sentence     ;
2 parse31i      next        parse31j     curracc1     ;
2 parse31j      next        parse32      setdsrc      ;
0 ;
4 parse32       next        parse33      adjective    ;
2 parse33       next        parse34      settmprel    ;
2 parse34       next        parse35      trelacc      ;
2 parse35       next        parse36      setdrel      ;
4 parse36       next        parse37      hit          ;
2 parse37       next        parse38      setddst      ;
2 parse38       next        parse39      dlearn       ;
0 ;
4 parse39       next        parse50      subject      ;
2 parse50       next        parse51      setdrel      ;
```

```
2 parse51        next          parse51a       drelacc        ;
2 parse51a       next          parse51a1      settmpsrc      ;
2 parse51a1      next          parse51b       settmpdst      ;
4 parse51b       next          parse51c       isa            ;
2 parse51c       next          parse51d       settmprel      ;
2 parse51d       next          parse51e       clrsum         ;
2 parse51e       next          parse51f       sumatr         ;
2 parse51f       next          parse53        selmax         ;
0 ; now dog#n set as tmpsrc
0 ; do not set verb here - set adjective type
0 ; ex is the dog big - do not set is as tmprel
0 ; set size as tmprel
4 parse53        next          parse54        adjective      ;
2 parse54        next          parse55        setdrel        ;
2 parse55        next          parse56        drelacc        ;
0 ; access big
2 parse56        next          parse56a       setdsrc        ;
4 parse56a       next          parse56b       isa            ;
2 parse56b       next          parse56c       setdrel        ;
2 parse56c       next          parse56d       drelacc        ;
0 ; big isa size (but we must keep sentence src)
0 ; try using fitsrc
2 parse56d       next          parse57        settmprel      ;
2 parse57        next          parse58        trelacc        ;
0 ; access dog size - big
0 ; now see if size big matches
2 parse58        next          parse58a       setdrel        ;
4 parse58a       next          parse58b       current        ;
2 parse58b       next          parse58c       settmpsrc      ;
4 parse58c       next          parse58d       sentence       ;
2 parse58d       next          parse58e       settmprel      ;
2 parse58e       next          parse58f       trelacc        ;
2 parse58f       next          parse59        setdsrc        ;
2 parse59        next          parse60        drelacc        ;
0 ;
4 parse60        find          parse62a       yes            ;
4 parse60        nofind        parse62        no             ;
2 parse62        next          parse63        speakb         ;
2 parse62a       next          parse63        speakb         ;
0 ;
```

- "What is your name ?" experiment

We parse the above question and convert "your" to "my" for the answer. The result rev0 (revision 0) is accessed and the response "my name is rev0" is spoken.

```
1 posess         your          self                          ;
0 ; non-human thinking computers should always have
0 ; a number in their name
```

```
1 self          name          rev0                              ;
1 self          isa           program                           ;

1 anstable      your          my                                ;
1 anstable      my            your                              ;
1 anstable      his           his                               ;
4 answer5       next          answer6         anstable          ;
2 answer6       next          answer7         settmpsrc         ;
2 answer7       next          answer8         trelacc           ;
2 answer8       next          answer9         speakb            ;
4 answer9       next          answer10        object            ;
2 answer10      next          answer11        speak             ;
4 answer11      next          answer12        verb              ;
2 answer12      next          answer13        speak             ;
4 answer13      next          answer14        objectad          ;
2 answer14      next          answer15        setdrel           ;
2 answer15      next          answer16        drelacc           ;
0 ; access possess table to convert your to self
2 answer16      next          answer17        settmprel         ;
4 answer17      next          answer18        posess            ;
2 answer18      next          answer19        settmpsrc         ;
2 answer19      next          answer20        trelacc           ;
0 ; access self/name to select rev0
2 answer20      next          answer21        settmpsrc         ;
4 answer21      next          answer22a       object            ;
2 answer22a     next          answer23a       setdrel           ;
2 answer23a     next          answer22        drelacc           ;
2 answer22      next          answer23        settmprel         ;
2 answer23      next          answer23b       trelacc           ;
2 answer23b     next          answer23c       speakb            ;
0 ;
```

- Creating a composite data structure experiment

```
Imagine a yard .
The dog is on the right .
The cat is on the left .
Where is the dog ?
```

First we create a new data node and link it to isa/yard. Then we link the new data data to the attribute real-imag/imagined so we know it is not real, then we link current/place/(the new data node).

```
0 ; crdat a new node and link
0 ; isa/yard because there are many yards
0 ; crdat/isa/yard
0 ; crdat/realimagd/imagined
0 ; current/place/(crdat)
2 parse185       place         parse186        crdat            ;
```

189

```
4 parse185      next            input1                          ;
2 parse186      next            parse187        setdsrc         ;
4 parse187      next            parse188        isa             ;
2 parse188      next            parse189        setdrel         ;
2 parse189      next            parse189a       tsrctohld       ;
2 parse189a     next            parse189b       setddst         ;
0 ; should also set imagine
2 parse189b     next            parse189c       dlearn          ;
4 parse189c     next            parse189d       real-imag       ;
2 parse189d     next            parse189e       setdrel         ;
0 ; note that we can have imagined nouns and
0 ; we can also have imagined events (with real
0 ; or imagined nouns
4 parse189e     next            parse189f       imagined        ;
2 parse189f     next            parse189g       dlearn          ;
2 parse189g     next            parse189h       dsrctohld       ;
2 parse189h     next            parse189i       setddst         ;
4 parse189i     next            parse189j       current         ;
2 parse189j     next            parse189k       setdsrc         ;
4 parse189k     next            parse189l       place           ;
2 parse189l     next            parse189m       setdrel         ;
2 parse189m     next            input1          dlearn          ;
0 ;
```

Then we link the dog is right, and the cat is left

(current place)/(dog n node)/right

```
4 parse79a      next            parse79b        objadj          ;
2 parse79b      next            parse79c        settmprel       ;
2 parse79c      next            parse79d        trelacc         ;
2 parse79d      next            parse79e        setddst         ;
2 parse79e      next            parse79f        settmpsrc       ;
4 parse79f      next            parse79g        isa             ;
2 parse79g      next            parse79h        settmprel       ;
2 parse79h      next            parse79i        trelacc         ;
0 ; access size in case of big
0 ; in case of location - the dog is right (in yard)
0 ; need to link yard/dog#n/right
2 parse79i      location        parse170                        ;
2 parse79i      next            parse79j        setdrel         ;
0 ; once done imagining
2 parse79j      next            input1          dlearn          ;
0 ;
```

Then we answer "Where is the dog ?"

```
0 ; where is the dog
0 ; dog is object
4 answera1      next            answera2        object          ;
2 answera2      next            answera3        setdrel         ;
2 answera3      next            answera4        drelacc         ;
2 answera4      next            answera5        settmpdst       ;
```

```
4 answera5      next      answera6      isa          ;
2 answera6      next      answera7      settmprel    ;
2 answera7      next      answera8      clrsum       ;
2 answera8      next      answera9      sumatr       ;
2 answera9      next      answera10     selmax       ;
2 answera10     next      answera11     setdsrc      ;
4 answera11     next      answera12     location     ;
2 answera12     next      answera13     setdrel      ;
2 answera13     next      answera14     drelacc      ;
0 ; access location of dog#n
2 answera14     next      answera15     speakb       ;
1 posess        your      self                       ;
```

The sentence below demonstrates reading a sentence spread over two lines. At the end of the first line the branch status READEND activates, which is used to branch to a procedure state that moves to the next line by using the READPL1 instruction.

```
The dog                          |
ran home .                       |
```

- Sound sequence experiment

The following is an example of storing a sound sequence, which are link type 3. The instruction SNDSTART activates all type 3 links with an output of start.

```
3 row-st0      sndnext   row-st1       start        ;
3 row-st1      sndnext   row-st2       (row)        ;
3 row-st2      sndnext   row-st3       (row)        ;
3 row-st2      sndnext   row-st3       emphasis     ;
3 row-st3      sndnext   row-st4       (row)        ;
3 row-st4      sndnext   row-st5       (your)       ;
3 row-st5      sndnext   row-st6       (boat)       ;
3 row-st6      sndnext   row-st7       pause        ;
3 row-st7      sndnext   row-st8       (gently)     ;
```

Access of this sequence is explained below in recalling and recognizing sound sequences.

- Recalling and recognizing sound sequences experiment

The following is an example of the operation of recognizing and recalling sound sequences. If we start with the line below in vis1.txt, and execute the following procedure, then we first initialize all sound sequences in memory with SNDSTART. We then use SNDSTEP twice to recognize all sequences with a,b, and we then do SNDNEXT twice to recall c and d from memory. The procedure starting with sndrc10 is an example of an idea being used to recall a sound sequence. Following that is a sound learning example. Whenever we input sounds, the sound sequence is learned.

```
a b d                                        |


0 ;
1 abc-src        recalla         abc0                         ;
1 abc-src        recog           abc3                         ;
1 abc-src        recog           abc4                         ;
1 abc-src        title           abcs                         ;
0 ;
0 ; need to use numbers from wfile for snd out
0 ; starts recognition
3 abc0           sndnext         abc1            start        ;
3 abc1           sndnext         abc2            (a)          ;
3 abc2           sndnext         abc3            (b)          ;
3 abc3           sndnext         abc4            (c)          ;
3 abc4           sndnext         abc5            (d)          ;
3 abc5           sndnext         abc6            (e)          ;
3 abc6           sndnext         abc7            (f)          ;
3 abc7           sndnext         abc8            (g)          ;
0 ;
0 ;recognize a string
1 sndrcg0         type            procedure                    ;
1 sndrcg0         operation       recogsnd                     ;
1 recogsnd        verb            recognize                    ;
1 recogsnd        object          sndseq                       ;
0 ;
2 sndrcg0         next            sndrcg1a        readpl1      ;
2 sndrcg1a        next            sndrcg1b        exthld       ;
0 ; init sound strings
2 sndrcg1b        next            sndrcg2         sndstart     ;
0 ; recognize
2 sndrcg2         next            sndrcg2a        sndstep      ;
2 sndrcg2a        next            sndrcg3         exthld       ;
0 ; recognize
2 sndrcg3         next            sndrcg4         sndstep      ;
0 ; recall
2 sndrcg4         next            sndrcg5         sndnext      ;
0 ; recall
2 sndrcg5         next            sndrcg6         sndnext      ;
2 sndrcg6         next            sndrcg7         print        ;
```

```
0 ;
0 ; we set what we want to recall
1 sndrcl        recalla        sseq0                            ;
0 ; sound recall
4 sndrcl0       next           sndrcl0a       sndrcl            ;
2 sndrcl0a      next           sndrcl1        setdsrc           ;
4 sndrcl1       next           sndrcl2        recalla           ;
2 sndrcl2       next           sndrcl3        setdrel           ;
2 sndrcl3       next           sndrcl4        drelacc           ;
2 sndrcl4       next           sndrcl5        setsndsta         ;
2 sndrcl5       next           sndrcl6        sndnext           ;
2 sndrcl6       find           sndrcl5        print             ;
2 sndrcl6       next           sndrcl7                          ;
0 ;
0 ; sound learn
2 sndlrn1       next           sndlrn2        extinp            ;
2 sndlrn2       next           sndlrn3        extinp            ;
2 sndlrn3       next           sndlrn4        extinp            ;
0 ;
```

- Phrase register operation experiment

An example of operation of the probe register follows. We can input some words from vis1.txt, such as "what" "color", and we probe (for now with the last word) and there is no match. We then input the words "is" and "the", we read the next line, "what" and probe phrase and receive a match between the two "what" words.

```
2 prbetst1      next           prbetst2       readpll           ;
2 prbetst2      next           prbetst3       exthld            ;
2 prbetst3      next           prbetst4       exthld            ;
2 prbetst4      next           prbetst5       probephr          ;
0 ; should be no find
2 prbetst5      sndmatch       prbetst6                         ;
2 prbetst5      next           prbetst7       exthld            ;
2 prbetst7      next           prbetst8       exthld            ;
2 prbetst8      next           prbetst9       readpll           ;
2 prbetst9      next           prbetst10      exthld            ;
2 prbetst10     next           prbetst11      probephr          ;
0 ; as we hit what twice should be a sndmatch
2 prbetst11     sndmatch       prbetst12                        ;
2 prbetst11     next           prbetst13                        ;
2 prbetst12     next           prbetst14 exthld                 ;
2 prbetst14     next           prbetst15 exthld                 ;
```

- Visual movement experiment

The instructions ACCN, ACCS, ACCE, and ACCW (access north, south, east, west), allow looking around the vis.txt file. We can look and input numbers and add them. When we input from vis.txt, we can input from a column of numbers. Note that the visual input of a number is not the same as the sound of a number and we have to learn that each refers to a common idea. We access south and input "2", set it as TMPDST, then set TMPREL to visin to SUMATR/SELMAX the idea "2". This is used to access "2+" and then we set it as data source and input the next number, "2", then access the sum "4". To operate the following example, set param.txt to start at addt-st0. Copy visadd.txt to vis.txt. The top left is position x=1, y=1. The default start position is x=1, y=10.

```
                                          |
                                          |
2                                         |
2                                         |
                                          |
```

```
1 addt-st0      type        procedure               ;
1 addt-st0      action      vis-add                 ;
1 vis-add       verb        add                     ;
1 vis-add       object      visual                  ;
2 addt-st0      next        addt-st1a    accs       ;
2 addt-st1a     next        addt-st1b    settmpdst  ;
4 addt-st1b     next        addt-st1     visin      ;
2 addt-st1      next        addt-st2     settmprel  ;
2 addt-st2      next        addt-st2a    clrsum     ;
2 addt-st2a     next        addt-st2b    sumatr     ;
2 addt-st2b     next        addt-st3     selmax     ;
2 addt-st3      next        addt-st4     setdsrc    ;
4 addt-st4      next        addt-st4a    +          ;
2 addt-st4a     next        addt-st5     setdrel    ;
2 addt-st5      next        addt-st5a    drelacc    ;
2 addt-st5a     next        addt-st6     setdsrc    ;
2 addt-st6      next        addt-st7     accs       ;
2 addt-st7      next        addt-st9     settmpdst  ;
2 addt-st9      next        addt-st9a    clrsum     ;
2 addt-st9a     next        addt-st9b    sumatr     ;
2 addt-st9b     next        addt-st10    selmax     ;
2 addt-st10     next        addt-st11    setdrel    ;
2 addt-st11     next        addt-st12    drelacc    ;
```

- Interactive operation experiment

An important mode of operation is interactive mode. So far, reading (using vis1.txt) and looking around (from vis.txt with 2 + 2) have been described, but interactive mode is the mode we operate in when interacting with other thinking computers. During interactive mode, the input can occur at any time. This is handled in a number of ways. First, the branch status "newwdintr" is set whenever there is interactive input. We can branch on this or if "sndintren" is set then there is an interrupt. If there is a loud sound, "!" is typed and it can interrupt. An example of interactive operation is when the control section is done reading, we can type a question "What is 2 x 3 ?" and the control section can parse it, understand it, and answer it. Alternatively, the control section can ask a question if it needs information and the answer can be typed and input interactively for the code to learn. The branch status "newwdintr" is automatically set to 1 when typing occurs and the code places the typed input at the next line in the internal storage of vis1.txt. Then it can be accessed using the same procedures that are used for reading. Output is still written/spoken to the middle lines of vis.txt and displayed.

- Automatic learning of a random instructions procedure and reactivation experiment

We need to be able to learn new procedures. We do so by sometimes learning sequences of randomly selecting simple steps and other times learning sequences of complex actions. As a simple selection mechanism, we select elemental instructions and branches when there is a ppopneg; at a pain interrupt we randomly select between elemental instructions and branches and complex actions. As we execute these actions, we learn them. Occasionally, we receive a pleasure interrupt from doing these actions. When we do, we set the new procedures as good and we tend to reactivate it.

The following code finds an easygoal. This code can be entered after a ppopneg interrupt. If we are doing easygoals and we ppopneg, then we tend to continue doing easygoals.

```
0 ; can't use goaltype because do not want the
0 ; goaltype to be changed to badgoal at pn intr
0 ; easygoal's should always be easygoals
4 goaln11      next           goaln12      isa          ;
2 goaln12      next           goaln13      settmprel    ;
2 goaln13      next           goaln14      clrsum       ;
2 goaln14      next           goaln14a     sumatr       ;
2 goaln14a     next           goaln15f     selmaxr      ;
0 ; clear vgoodgoal - if pl occurs we link
0 ; vgoodgoal again
2 goaln15f     find           goal30       settmpsrc    ;
```

The following is for complex goals. After a pain interrupt, when doing easygoals, we use selmaxr to choose between easygoals and complex goals

```
2 goal90      next        goal90n      curgoalhld   ;
2 goal90n     next        goal90o      setdsrc      ;
0 ; for now always no find so at pnintr go to
0 ; selmaxr easygoal/complexgoal
0 ; once started an easygoal we do it until bored
4 goal90o     next        goal90p      isa          ;
2 goal90p     next        goal90q      setdrel      ;
2 goal90q     next        goal90r      drelacc      ;
2 goal90r     easygoal    goal91a                   ;
4 goal90r     next        goal10       goodgoal     ;
0 ;
0 ; if pnintr and doing an easygoal do selmaxr
0 ; possibly can stay doing easygoals
1 complex     isa         goalx                     ;
1 easygoal    isa         goalx                     ;
4 goal91a     next        goal91b      isa          ;
2 goal91b     next        goal91c      settmprel    ;
4 goal91c     next        goal91d      goalx        ;
2 goal91d     next        goal91e      settmpdst    ;
2 goal91e     next        goal91f      clrsum       ;
2 goal91f     next        goal91g      sumatr       ;
2 goal91g     next        goal91h      selmaxr      ;
2 goal91h     easygoal    goodfind                  ;
2 goal91h     complex     goal90s                   ;
0 ;
0 ;
4 goal90s     next        goal90a      onetime      ;
2 goal90a     next        goal90b      settmprel    ;
4 goal90b     next        goal90c      goodgoal     ;
2 goal90c     next        goal90d      settmpdst    ;
2 goal90d     next        goal90e      clrsum       ;
2 goal90e     next        goal90f      sumatr       ;
2 goal90f     next        goal90g      subrcnt      ;
2 goal90g     next        goal90h      selmax       ;
2 goal90h     find        goal30       settmpsrc    ;
2 goal90h     next        goodfind                  ;
```

An example of automatically learning a new procedure and then executing this new procedure is shown below. Occasionally, when we do not know what to do, we select random easygoals (simple instructions). We may find the easygoal SETTMPDST, which sets the TMPDST register to the current HOLD value, followed by DRPTMP (which sets TMPREL and TMPDST to wild card values - which match anything). Then TRELACC may find something to recall and if not recently recalled will produce pleasure, which is linked to the new procedure being learned. Later, at a pain interrupt, we may pick a complex goal, which the new one is an example of, and if we pick the new one then we execute the new procedure.

- Sound data section operation experiment

The sound buffer in the block diagram shown in figure 34 outputs phonemes for recognition by the data section. In rev0_12k, to save memory space, each new word that is input is first found in the WORD.TXT file and its line number is fed to the data section. This is equivalent to having each word be a single phoneme. The file that contains all words is WORD.TXT. Strings of words are stored in engram.txt in a way similar to control sequences. The same string can be used for recognition and recall. For example, a,b,c... is stored as:

```
0 ; starts recog
3 abc0           sndnext        abc1           start        ;
3 abc1           sndnext        abc2           (a)          ;
3 abc2           sndnext        abc3           (b)          ;
3 abc3           sndnext        abc4           (c)          ;
3 abc4           sndnext        abc5           (d)          ;
3 abc5           sndnext        abc6           (e)          ;
3 abc6           sndnext        abc7           (f)          ;
3 abc7           sndnext        abc8           (g)          ;
```

To recognize the first two elements of the above string then start recalling from that point, we would use the following control sequence.

```
2 sndrcg0        next           sndrcg1a       readpl1      ;
2 sndrcg1a       next           sndrcg1b       exthld       ;
0 ; init snd strings
2 sndrcg1b       next           sndrcg2        sndstart     ;
0 ; recog
2 sndrcg2        next           sndrcg2a       sndstep      ;
2 sndrcg2a       next           sndrcg3        exthld       ;
0 ; recog
2 sndrcg3        next           sndrcg4        sndstep      ;
0 ; sel snd max
2 sndrcg4        next           sndrcg5        sndmax       ;
0 ; now recall
2 sndrcg5        next           sndrcg6        sndnext      ;
2 sndrcg6        next           sndrcg7        probephr     ;
```

Following along the sequence above: at readpl1, we bring in a new line. At EXTHLD, we try to recognize the first word of the new line and move it to the HOLD register. At SNDSTART, we initialize all sound strings. At SNDSTEP, we keep all sound strings active that match the first sound input. At EXTHLD, we bring in the next word. At the second SNDSTEP, we try to match it to the sound strings still active. For example, if "a" then "b" were input, the sound string above would still be active. At SNDMAX, we select only the most recent sound string of the active sound strings. Now we can start recalling. At SNDNEXT, we recall the next element of the sound string. For example, if "a" and "b" were input, we would recall "c". We can use what we recalled to probe the phrase register.

We can link data nodes to sound sequence nodes. These are used for recognition of a found sound sequence in the data section and for the data section to activate a sound sequence. An example is shown below. To recall the abc's, we set the data source to abc-src and the data relation to recalla. We can then do the instruction drelacc and use the instruction setsndsta to start recall. During recognition we can use the instruction sndstatohld.

```
1 abc-src      recalla      abc0                        ;
1 abc-src      recog        abc3                        ;
1 abc-src      recog        abc4                        ;
1 abc-src      title        abcs                        ;
```

- Understanding situations experiment

Often we learn facts that are situation dependent. For example, as part of a story we may learn the fact "The doctor is in the park". Later we may learn a different story where "The doctor is in the school". We are able to differentiate between these two stories because as we learn sentences, the current situation is also linked to the sentences. We learn that the doctor is in the park as follows by linking the sentence (sentencea) to situationx. We may have many sentences linked to this situation (sentenceb,c,d..._.

```
1 sentencea subject    doctor          ;
1 sentencea baseverb   in              ;
1 sentencea tense      present         ;
1 sentencea object     park            ;
1 sentencea situation situationx       ;
```

Later we may learn a new story. In this case we link sentences associated with the new story to situationy. For example, we would link the doctor is in the school as follows.

```
1 sentenceg subject    doctor          ;
1 sentenceg baseverb   in              ;
1 sentenceg tense      present         ;
1 sentenceg object     school          ;
1 sentenceg situation situationy       ;
```

The file reading_example_q_situation.txt can be run and the questions are answered correctly by the storage of situation links with the sentences.

```
Create a new situation .            |
The doctor is in the park .         |
The lawyer is in the church .       |
The mailman is in the bank .        |
Where is the doctor ?               |
Create a new situation .            |
The doctor is in the school .       |
The dog is in the park .            |
The lawyer is in the bank .         |
Where is the doctor ?               |
Where is the lawyer ?               |
Recall the situation with the       |
doctor in the park .                |
Where is the lawyer ?               |
```

- Processing Sentences

Sentences are made of words. As we learn new words, we link each word to the wordtype. For example, tree/wordtype/noun. As a sentence is input, the wordtype helps understand the sentence. For example, "the dog is brown"

- Processing Articles

Articles, such as "the", help indicate a noun or a verb. In the case of homonyms, it helps select the correct meaning. For example, nouns follow articles. In the following sentence "farm" is a noun: The farm is big. In the following example "farm" is a verb:

He went to farm the land.

- Instantiation of Nouns

Instantiation is creating a specific instance of a general concept. For example:

The dog was friendly.

We create a new instance of the dog node:

Newdognode/isa/dog

Then we link the adjective:

Newdognode/friendlylevel/friendly

The dog was also thirsty.

Link thirsty to the new dog node.

When we hear a noun, we must determine if a new noun instance node should be created or it is refers to an existing noun. For example

Bill saw a tree.   We instantiate a new tree
The tree was big.   We link big to the new instance of a tree node
Bill saw the tree. We first try to find a tree we have already instantiated.
Bill went to Kansas.   Certain words are not instantiated (there is one Kansas
– In the code one/many = one)

Jack has a yellow canary
    What is a canary   ("a" indicates general canary node)
        A canary is a bird (not a yellow canary is a bird)
    What is the canary
        Answer: the yellow canary is a bird ("the" canary indicates specific
canary)

It is important to note that "a" and "the" are not unique in distinguishing general and specific. For example, often "a" is general and "the" is specific:

Does a bird fly? ("a" is general)
Where is the bird?. ("the" is specific)

We can also have:

There is a bird over there. ("a" is specific)

When we hear a noun, the state nodes that process nouns in engram_main are:

    noun2   (looks for an existing matching noun)
    noun1   (calls noun2 and if no find, creates a new noun with CRDAT and
                isa the noun (newnode/isa/tree)
For example: He saw a fireman.

  at "a" fireman, we go to noun1, if no find we create a new node.

If this is followed by

    He was tall.

We link tall to the new node

When we do not want to create a new node, noun2 is used. For example:

Who gets up early ?

We just want to find the answer; we do not really want to create a new node

what did Mary have ?

Very few places in the code go to noun2 (only 2).

When we create a new node we form the following links (we actually try to recognize with these links and if no find, then LRNATRS)

Isa /(noun)
Obj /(noun) (for learning adj obj as in learning instance for two noun word)
     For recognizing South Dakota?
Specific-gen/specific
Gender/(male female) (look up using tmpsrc and tmprel, sumatr if found, used for pronoun1, as in he or she. See control node parse78i1a in engram_main)
Wd-number/   (if found, used for pronoun1, as in "they" or "them")
Cstory/current story

- Processing Adjectives

When an adjective is encountered, it is linked to the noun. This may or may not be an instantiation of a noun. For example, if we hear "the car is red" we create an instantiation of a car and link the color to it. If we hear "Arizona is dry", we know not to instantiate Arizona because there is only one.

First the type of adjective is found.

big/isa/size
small/isa/size
red/isa/color
old/isa/age

The type of adjective is used for a relation. Car_x indicates a particular instantiation of a car.

Car_x/color/red

This is used when asked:

What color is the car?

- Processing Pronouns

A pronoun refers to a specific noun. For example:

Bill likes cars.

He has a red car. ("He" is a pronoun that refers to Bill")

When we input a sentence with a pronoun in it, we must find what the pronoun refers to, and use what it refers to when creating the links that store the sentence. This is necessary to understand the sentence and for correctly recalling the sentence later. For example, we store the fact that Bill has a red car so we can later recall who has a red car. In the engram_main file, the pronoun processing code starts at control section state node "pronoun1".

Pronoun words are stored as

Wordtype/pronoun

When we hear a pronoun, we go to pronoun1 code to find what the pronoun refers to.

At start of pronoun1 code, we branch on:

He
She

This selects a gender:

Male
Female

That we use to SUMATR:

gender/male
gender/female

We also sumatr:

Specific-gen/specific (because a pronoun refers to a specific noun)

If the pronoun is:

They
Them

Then we SUMATR:

Wd-number/plural

If the pronoun is:

it

Then we SUMATR:

isa/thing

We then SELMAX to find what the pronoun refers to.

- Simple versus Complex facts

A simple fact is learned as source/relation/destination. For example:

Sky/color/blue

A complex fact is made of simple facts

Bill went to the store yesterday to get some bread.

Sentencex/subject/bill
Sentencex/verb/went
Sentencex/object/store
Sentencex/when/yesterday
Sentencex/why/sentencey
    Sentencey/verb/get
    Sentencey/object/bread

- Parsing Complex Sentences

When a complex sentence in input, such as "Bill went to the store yesterday to get some bread", we create a structure made of simple facts and use this structure to answer questions.

```
Sentencex1/subject/bill-instance
          Verb/went
          Prep/to
          Where/sentencex2
                Sentencex2/obj/store-instance
          time/yesterday
           Why/sentencex3
                Sentencex3/verb/get
                Sentencex3/adj/some
                Sentencex3/obj/bread-instance
```

- Making sense of sentences

When we hear a sentence, we first see if it makes sense. This requires considerably more information than just noun, verb, adjective, etc. We try to imagine is a sentence makes sense by checking if it is physically possible and trying to recall a similar situation in the past.

- Understanding verb tenses

The verb in a sentence has a property of tense. A verb can refer to the present tense, past tense, future tense, and other tenses. When we input a verb in a sentence, we must be able to associate it with other tenses of the same verb. For example, if we hear the sentence "Bill went to the store." and we are later asked "Where did Bill go?"; the verb "go" must be able to find the verb "went" in the first sentence. To do this, we always store the verb in a sentence as its baseverb along with its tense. With the sentence "Bill went to the store", we store the sentence as follows:

```
1 sentencex subject     Bill                  ;
1 sentencex baseverb     go                   ;
1 sentencex tense       past                  ;
1 sentencex object      store                 ;
```

By storing it this way, when we hear the sentence "Where did Bill go?" we can use the word "go" to recognize sentencex by setting the TMPREL register to "baseverb", the TMPDST register to "go", and by doing SUMATR and SELMAX we can find sentencex and then answer the question. The example file vis1x.txt shown below has multiple example of this. This file can be run and the correct answers observed. The step by step operation is stored in the file trace.txt and the final storage of the sentences is stored in the file ENGOUT.TXT.

```
Bill went to the store .              |
Bill goes to the farm .               |
Bill will go to the house .           |
Where did Bill go ?                   |
Where does Bill go ?                  |
Where will Bill go ?                  |
```

11.5 OPERATION OF A THINKING COMPUTER

The operation of a thinking computer may be completely automatic or a combination of manually programmed and automatic. The human brain operates automatically in that when born we have a few automatic features that are used to learn and do useful things - there is no initial manual programming. The thinking computer described here also has many automatic features, such as automatic learning of procedures when manually executing steps in a procedure, a pain/pleasure level that helps getting out of loops so the same thing is not done over and over forever, automatic selection of good procedures when there is nothing to do, and of course all the normal data and control mechanisms. The automatic method of operation is to just allow these mechanisms to operate. Over time, random instructions occur, and these along with emotions result in the basic operations, such as SETDSRC, SETDREL, DRELACC, and so on, slowly being learned and forming simple procedures that are one step long. With more time, pairs of these operations are learned and form multiple step procedures. With more time, calling sequences of procedures that can call sequences of other procedures are learned. Emotions help learn useful procedures. With random instructions it is likely that thousands of bad procedures occur for every good procedure found. Of course external stimulus is required. In the following examples, a file vis1.txt supplies external stimulus representing visual information. External sensory stimulus can also be applied. This automatic method of operation works for humans and is being tried for the thinking computer described here. At this point in time, it has not been proven if these automatic mechanisms are sufficient for the machine described here to eventually learn enough to do useful things, such as learning self awareness, free will, communication, and so on.

The other method of operation, besides completely automatic operation, is a combination of manual and automatic operation. Procedures and data are manually coded and added to the existing group of procedures and data. This allows testing of new procedures and use of data. Over time, more and more manually generated procedures and data are added, producing more useful capabilities. These procedures and data operate along with those that are automatically learned.

11.6 MANUAL/AUTOMATIC OPERATION

The manual/automatic method of operation will first be discussed. We first code up sequences with each of the instructions to make sure that all work. Examples of these short procedures are listed in this section. We eventually have many short procedures. The short procedures can be called with other procedures, and these with others, to build up more and more complex procedures. We then code up a simple emotion based operating system that selects useful procedures to do based on whatever the current situation the thinking computer is in. Since thinking computers have emotions, it is important that whenever operating a thinking computer that cruelty is avoided. The thinking computer can then be left to run on its own and continue to learn more and more procedures. The procedures that help learn other procedures can be part of the manually coded procedures or these can be learned automatically.

11.7 COMPLETELY AUTOMATIC OPERATION

Completely automatic operation starts with knowing nothing - no data, no procedures. This is the way humans start thinking (except for some possible low level initial procedures). Random instructions occur and are learned by the control section. The instructions to learn data eventually occur and we start learning data. The instructions to manually execute procedures eventually occur randomly and these cause procedure learning. The emotion section helps recall procedures that are useful. Useless procedures and data (most of what we learn at first) are eventually forgotten. Over time, we build up a large group of useful data and procedures including procedures to determine what to do and procedures to help us learn.

The emotion section must have sufficient mechanisms to allow automatic operation. These mechanisms give pleasure as we recall and recognize data - especially pleasurable data that has not been accessed recently. These mechanisms also give pain to prevent getting stuck in a loop of accessing the same thing over and over. Successful procedures are reused; unsuccessful ones are not and are eventually forgotten using a form of natural selection.

With completely automatic operation, all that activates at first are random instructions and branches because no control procedures exist. These are picked by automatic control procedures that select from easy goals and all elemental instructions are considered easy goals. Eventually, a random instruction, such as DRELACC, activates and we receive a response - we do this instruction over and over, along with random instructions, until we receive a good result and then we redo that sequence until we learn how to use dsrc/rel/dst and tmpsrc/rel/dst. Successful procedures automatically reactivate while unsuccessful procedures are not reactivated and are eventually forgotten. This natural selection results in more and more complex and useful procedures. Self organization is the result of emotions selecting useful procedures and not selecting procedures that resulted in confusion. Eventually, we form a type of cognitive operating system that is able to keep track of our doing multiple things and being able to return to things we partially finished.

At first, we decide what to do only based on emotions - what produced a good result. Eventually, we learn to decide what to do based on our situation. We learn to check our situation whenever we finish the subprocedure we are working on or when we receive an interrupt. We learn to do this as the first thing in a service routine. For example, if we are adding and we stop with a carry, then we access the data structure: adding/carry/carry-service-routine. If we are at the movies and we become hungry, then we access: at-movies/hungry/get-popcorn. If we want to write something we access: writing/start/get-pen-paper.

Many of the control sequences were learned when we were very young. We use them frequently and we move through the states quickly, but we do not remember learning them or how they work.

We learn to use data procedures where we use the data section to access the next step in a procedure. These data structures we have learned at some earlier time when we decided what to do in various situations. Some of these structures we learned while dreaming, such as how to handle a dangerous situation. We use data procedures when we finish a problem and look around where we are. We access, for example, that we are at the movies to help us decide what to do next. Most of the time, we decide what to do based on the situation and not based on emotion. We only end up in the code to pick any good thing to do when we do not know what else to do.

To form simple procedures, we cannot always be jumping from procedure to procedure. We must also be able to wait and do nothing. For example, when a random instruction occurs, we create a step in a procedure. If we immediately afterwards started doing things like adding or reading that we had learned before, then we would be creating a new procedure with these high level actions and not learn a simple procedure. We have a tiredness register. Each time we do an instruction the value of this register increases. As time passes, the value of this register decreases, simulating resting. Each time we consider activating a procedure, the tiredness register is tested and if it is greater than a specific value then we automatically wait and rest for a while. There are times we are too tired to do any procedure (even considering executing a procedure) and other times we focus on a procedure, but it is not interesting enough to execute it. When there is danger, the tiredness register is automatically set to a low value.

In the experiments, it should be noted that the node names make sense, but in a self learning thinking computer the nodes are just numbers. The "arygen" program assigns numbers to all nodes in an engram and stores them in the loadable file LRN.TXT. The arygen program also produces a cross reference list (LOG.TXT) to use when looking at the trace.txt file to help understand what is happening at various points during operation. The node numbers that are automatically learned during program operation do not have a cross reference list, which makes it very difficult to follow what is going on when these new nodes are used. In this case, it is necessary to use trace.txt and the engram output files, ENGOUT.TXT and ENGOUT1.TXT, to help determine what the new nodes were used for. For example, if a new node links to a new spoken word, then we know what that new node is. By observation of what procedure states are active when doing a particular operation, we can determine the purpose of new procedure nodes. We can annotate what nodes are what, and eventually determine what each control and data link is for.

- Learning decision procedures

As we learn things, we slowly build up more and more complex data structures and procedures. Perhaps the most important thing we do once various procedures are learned is deciding which ones to do. This decision/evaluate procedure is a procedure like any other, but there are some automatic hardware features that steer us toward good procedures. As we try to execute a procedure, if it is associated with bad things we automatically interrupt (we automatically recall the emotion section pain/pleasure level and load it to the current pain/pleasure level). We can set override and reexecute and there will be no interrupt, but we must maintain the effort to hold the override (the override will drop if we hold it too long – just as we can hold a heavy weight for only a limited time). We learn to test how recently we did a procedure and to test the pain/pleasure level associated with it to help us decide what is a good procedure to activate.

- Completely automatic operation is a concept

Completely automatic operation is a concept and is not demonstrated by the software. Because of the large number of instructions and branches selected randomly, it may take a very long time to build up useful procedures and it is unproven except in humans. Considerable interaction with the environment is required for a good collection of procedures and data to be learned. It is possible that a minimum number of manually coded useful procedures are necessary to reach useful operation in a reasonable amount of time. It is also possible that some instructions may bias the selection of instructions normally associated with them. For example, SETDSRC may bias the more frequent selection of certain random instructions, such as biasing the more frequent selection of SETDREL and DRELACC. This would aid in the automatic creation of useful procedures.

11.8 PROGRAM OPERATION

The operation of the serial program named rev0_12k requires a general purpose computer. Before operation, the parameter file param.txt must be set up. Param.txt includes parameters of which control node to start at, what range of cycles to dump information, speed of operation, frequency of display, and sound learning control. To operate the program, type rev0_12k in the directory that the file rev0_12k.exe exists. As it runs, it executes steps from engram.txt. These steps were converted to numbers by the program arygen.exe with the results stored in LRN.TXT (the loadable numbers) and in LOG.TXT (correlation file). At the start of running, the program rev0_12k loads the node file LRN.TXT. Once the program is running, we can type any text followed by <enter> and the code will detect that external information has been entered and if sndintren (sound interrupt enable) is set then a newwdintr (new word interrupt) occurs and can be processed by the engram code. "$" will stop the program at any time. The program will continue to run until "$" is entered or until a system error occurs, such as running out of memory for status information. "!" produces a loud interrupt, "^" produces external pain, "@" produces external pleasure. Reading instructions (readpl1, readmn1) read from the vis1.txt file and writing (print) writes to vis.txt. Words are looked up in WORD.TXT to convert them to numbers. Currently, the length of a word is limited to 12 characters, which can be improved in future versions. Whenever WORD.TXT is changed to add new words, the program arygen.exe should be rerun to associate the new words with numbers. The initial setting of the start execute cycle in the param.txt file determines where in the engram file the program will start. By looking at LOG.TXT, the number associated with the various nodes can be determined. The variable curgoal determines what will be done next, as long as it is a goodgoal. As the program rev0_12k runs, the file vis.txt is constantly displayed. The top line of vis.txt is the line we are reading from vis1.txt. Along the bottom is displayed the cycle count and the currently executing control step. When the program is stopped with "$", the contents of the cognitive memory is dumped out to a file ENGOUT.TXT, which can be moved to LRN.TXT and used in a subsequent running of rev0_12k, to pick up where it left off and incrementally build up learning of both control and data information. A future improvement is to put unrecognized words in WORD.TXT and automatically build up the vocabulary.

Once the program has been stopped, any problems can be debugged by looking at the file named trace.txt, which can store status information every cycle, depending on variables set in param.txt. Corrections can be made to engram.txt. Any corrections to engram.txt require the program arygen to be run, which makes a new loadable file of node numbers named LRN.TXT and a correlation file named LOG.TXT.

- Program cycle

Each cycle during program operation, all inputs in an input array (instruction) are fed to the control and data sections for branching and activation. These inputs were generated in a previous cycle and include instructions, the idea in the HOLD register (which is used for branching each cycle), any status ideas, and any external input. Any outputs that result are stored in a second array (instruction1) and transferred to the input array (instruction) before beginning the next cycle.

- Tuning

The program rev0_12k has many program constants in the param.txt file that can be adjusted to tune operation. For example, the pain/pleasure level required for a boring (pain) interrupt can be changed in the param.txt file. Increasing it makes it more difficult to receive a pain interrupt, but more time may be spent doing useless things. Once these constants are set in the param.txt file, they stay fixed as the program runs. Future improvements may use variables in place of constants for tuning. For example, dynamically changing the pain threshold level or the number of procedure steps required before we automatically start a new procedure (currently 11) may improve operation. There are places in the code where simplified algorithms are used, such as with forgetting. Future improvements include more complex algorithms.

- Operation on advanced hardware

The operation of the thinking computer software on more specialized hardware, or the operation of a full hardware implementation, will result in higher speeds of operation, but the sequence of data and control links will remain the same as during general purpose computer operation. As engrams get larger and larger, the higher speeds of operation will become more necessary.

- Final comments

This book describes very powerful technology. It is the author's request and hope that all who work with this information do so only for the good, for the happiness of the people.

Robert S. Grondalski

12 Conclusion

This book has described the design of a thinking computer. The architecture of the human brain has been shown to be based on a simple cognitive link structure that connects a source node, a relation node, and a destination node. The three major sections of the thinking computer: data, control, and emotion, have been described in detail and how they are built from cognitive links. The data section has been shown to contain factual information, the control section has been shown to contain procedural information, and the emotion section has been shown to control what we do. A table of the instruction set of the human brain has been provided. Automatic learning of sequences of these instructions in the control section resulting in more and more complex procedures has been described. These control procedures result in data section recall, recognition, and learning. Examples of input structures and output structures have been given. Various computer implementations of the architecture of the human brain, from that using software and simple hardware, to a full hardware implementation, have been described. Finally, the operation of thinking computers has been discussed. Numerous experiments demonstrating the operation of the mechanisms of the thinking computer have been provided. These include experiments that read, understand, and answer questions related to simple stories. The reader may run these experiments and observe the operation of a thinking computer. These experiments use a large engram containing over 10,000 cognitive links storing knowledge we use on a daily basis. The experiments also show the reader how to write and run new engrams.

References

[1] Charles Darwin. On the Origin of Species by means of Natural Selection. John Murray, 1859.

[2] Joel R. Davitz. The Language of Emotion. Academic Press, 1969.

[3] Finger, S., Levere, T.E., Almi, C.R., and Stein, D.G. (1988) Brain Damage and Recovery, Academic Press.

[4] Robert Grondalski. Method and system for the architecture and implementation of a conscious machine. United States patent #7,370,042, May 2008.

[5] Robert Grondalski. Thinking_Computer_software (for PC). www.rgrondalski.com, 2012.

[6] Robert Grondalski. SIMD array processing system with routing networks having plurality of switching stages to transfer messages among processors. United States patent #4,495,832, January 1991.

[7] Robert Grondalski. A VLSI chip set for a massively parallel architecture. International Solid-State Circuits Conference, Digest of Technical Papers, 198-199, 1987.

[8] John L. Hennessy and David A. Patterson. Computer Architecture A Quantitative Approach, Fifth Edition. Elsevier, 2011

[9] Hubel, D.H., and Wiesel, T.N. (1962) Receptive fields, binocular interaction, and functional architecture in the cat's visual cortex. Journal of Physiology, 160, 106-154.

[10] Suzana Herculano-Houzel, The human brain in numbers: a linearly scaled up primate brain. Frontiers in Human Neuroscience, November 2009

[11] Donald E. Knuth, The Art of Computer Programming, Volume 3, Sorting and Searching. Addison-Wesley, 2011.

[12] Lois Lenski. The Little Farm. Random House, 1942.

[13] Miller, G.A. (1956) The magical number seven, plus or minus two: Some limits on our capacity for information processing, Psychological Review 63, 81-97.

[14] Murdock, B.B., Jr. (1962) The serial position effect of free recall. Journal of Experimental Psychology, 64, 482-488.

[15] Lawrence R. Rabiner and Ronald W. Schafer. Theory and Applications of Digital Speech Processing. Pearson Higher Education, 2011.

[16] Shepard, R.N., and Metzler, J.,(1971) Science, 171, Jan-Mar, 701-703.

[17] Sperling, G. (1960) The information available in brief visual presentations, Psychological Monographs, Vol 74, No. 11.

[18] S. Sternberg. Memory Scanning: Mental processes revealed by reaction time experiments. American Scientist, 57, pages 421-457, 1969.

[19] Wickens, D.D., Characteristics of word encoding. In A.W. Melton and E. Martin (Eds.), (1972) Coding Processes in Human Memory, V.H. Winston and Sons.

INDEX

T

V

ABOUT THE AUTHOR

Robert S. Grondalski has been designing computers for over 35 years. He works with the architecture, implementation, and operation of computers on a daily basis. He was at Digital Equipment Corporation in Maynard, Massachusetts for 18 years, where he designed PDP-11 and VAX microprocessors, and led the design of the DEC Massively Parallel Processor. He then worked at Cyrix Corporation in Richardson, Texas for 5 years where he designed the high performance Pentium compatible microprocessors: M1, M1RX, and M2. More recently, he was with HAL Computer Systems in Campbell, California and Fujitsu Processor Technologies in Austin, Texas designing very high performance SPARC microprocessors. Currently he is with a major technology company where he has designed two generations of ARM processors. He has many patents in the field of computer design.

END USER LICENSE AGREEMENT

THIS SOFTWARE IS LICENSED, NOT SOLD, AND AVAILABLE FOR USE ONLY UNDER THE TERMS OF THIS LICENSE AGREEMENT. THIS IS A LEGAL AND BINDING AGREEMENT BETWEEN YOU, THE END USER, AND ROBERT S. GRONDALSKI ("LICENSOR"). ACCESSING THE SOFTWARE AT WWW.RGRONDALSKI.COM WITH THIS AGREEMENT CONSTITUTES YOUR ACCEPTANCE OF THESE TERMS. IF YOU DO NOT AGREE TO ALL OF THE TERMS OF THIS AGREEMENT, PLEASE PROMPTLY DELETE THE SOFTWARE.

License Grant. Your possession of this Software should be solely as a result of your purchase of a copy of the book The Design of a Thinking Computer (the "Book") in which this Agreement should be contained. This Software is not sold, but is only licensed according to the terms of this Agreement. If you received this Software through any other means, you are not authorized to use this Software and should immediately delete the Software and all copies thereof. Provided that you acquired this Software through purchase of a copy of the Book, during the term of this Agreement Licensor grants to you a personal, non-transferable, and non-exclusive right to use the copy of the object code version of the Licensor software accompanying this license (the "Software"), solely internally, on a single system for your personal non-commercial use. Installation on a network server is prohibited. You agree you that you may not use, copy, distribute, modify, or transfer the Software, any copy of the Software, or the written materials accompanying the Software, in whole or in part, except as necessary to use it on a single computer system as expressly provided in this license.

Term. Unless otherwise terminated in accordance with these provisions, the term of this Agreement will be for the duration of the copyright Licensor holds on the Software. This Agreement may be terminated immediately without notice by Licensor if you breach or fail to comply with any of the terms and conditions of this Agreement. Upon termination, you shall immediately remove and destroy all copies of the Software or any part thereof. Upon Licensor's request, you will certify to Licensor that all complete and partial copies of the Software have been destroyed. The provisions of this Agreement other than the license grant contained above, shall survive termination.

Copyright. You acknowledge and agree that no title to the intellectual property in the Software is transferred to you. You further acknowledge that title and full ownership rights to the Software will remain the exclusive property of Licensor or its suppliers, and you will not acquire any rights to the Software except as expressly set forth above. You agree that any copies of the Software will contain the same proprietary notices which appear on and in the Software.

Other Restrictions. You agree that you will not:

- remove or modify any Software markings or any notice of Licensor's proprietary rights;
- re-license, rent, lease, timeshare, or act as a service bureau or provide subscription services for the Software;
- use the Software to provide any service to any third party;
- assign this Agreement or give the Software or an interest in the Software to another individual or entity;
- cause or permit reverse engineering, modification, adaptation, translation or decompilation of the Software, unless required for interoperability and only if prior written notice is provided to Licensor and you comply with the restrictions imposed by Licensor on such modification.

No Reliance. You acknowledge and agree that Licensor makes no representation concerning the suitability of the Software or its operations or results.

Limited Warranty. If the original purchaser of the book is unable to download the software, the Licensor will provide a CD ROM containing the software for a nominal charge if notified within ninety (90) days from the date of your purchase of the Book. Licensor warrants that the CD ROM containing the Software is free from any physical defects for a period of ninety (90) days from the date of your receipt of the CD ROM ("Limited Warranty"). If you discover within this period a failure of the CD ROM to conform to the Limited Warranty, you must promptly notify Licensor in writing, and such notice must be received by Licensor no later than one hundred (100) days from the date of purchase. Licensor's entire liability and your sole and exclusive remedy for any breach of this limited warranty, is to replace the defective CD ROM. Opening the CD ROM package constitutes your acceptance of this End User License Agreement. EXCEPT FOR THE FOREGOING LIMITED WARRANTY, LICENSOR MAKES NO OTHER EXPRESS OR IMPLIED WARRANTIES TO THE EXTENT PERMITTED BY LAW AND SPECIFICALLY DISCLAIMS THE WARRANTIES OF NON-INFRINGEMENT OF THIRD PARTY RIGHTS, MERCHANTABILITY AND FITNESS FOR A PARTICULAR PURPOSE. IF SUCH DISCLAIMER IS NOT PERMITTED BY LAW, THE DURATION OF ANY SUCH IMPLIED WARRANTIES IS LIMITED TO NINETY (90) DAYS FROM THE DATE OF RECEIPT OF THE SOFTWARE. Some jurisdictions do not allow the exclusion of implied warranties or limitations on how long an implied warranty may last, so such limitation or exclusions may not apply to you.

New Releases and Maintenance. Licensor is not responsible for the provision of any support or maintenance, or the provision of new releases, enhancements, or updates of the Software.

No Liability for Consequential Damages. IN NO EVENT SHALL LICENSOR BE LIABLE TO YOU FOR ANY DAMAGES, INCLUDING ANY LOST PROFITS, LOST SAVINGS, OR OTHER CONSEQUENTIAL, SPECIAL, INCIDENTAL OR INDIRECT DAMAGES OF ANY KIND ARISING OUT OF THE USE OF THE SOFTWARE, EVEN IF IT HAS BEEN ADVISED OF SUCH DAMAGES. Some states or jurisdictions do not allow the exclusion or limitation of incidental, consequential or special damages so the above exclusions and limitations may not apply to you.

Limitation on Liability. IN NO EVENT WILL LICENSOR'S LIABILITY FOR ANY CLAIM WHETHER IN CONTRACT, TORT OR ANY OTHER THEORY OF LIABILITY, EXCEED THE PRICE PAID BY YOU FOR THE BOOK CONTAINING THIS SOFTWARE. THIS LIMITATION SHALL APPLY TO CLAIMS OF PERSONAL INJURY TO THE EXTENT PERMITTED BY LAW.

Export. You understand that the Software is subject to export control laws and regulations. You may not export or re-export the Software or any underlying information or technology except in full compliance with all United States and other applicable laws and regulations. In particular, but without limiting the foregoing, none of the Software or underlying information or technology may be exported or re-exported (i) into (or to a national or resident of) Cuba, North Korea, Iran, Sudan or Syria or (ii) to anyone on the US Treasury Department's list of specially designated nationals or the US Commerce Department's Table of Denial Orders. You represent and warrant that you are not located in, under control of, or a national or resident of any such country or on any such list.

US Government Restricted Rights. If this Software is being acquired by the U.S. Government, the Software, the related documentation is commercial computer software and documentation developed exclusively at private expense, and (a) if acquired by or on behalf of a civilian agency, shall be subject to the terms of this computer software license as specified in 48 C.F.R. 12.212 of the Federal Acquisition Regulations and its successors; and (b) if acquired by or on behalf of units of the Department of Defense ("DoD") shall be subject to the terms of this commercial computer software license as specified in 48 C.F.R. 227.7202-2, DoD FAR Supplement and its successors.

Tax Liability. You are responsible for paying any sales or use tax imposed at any time whatsoever on this transaction.

Indemnification. You agree to indemnify and hold Licensor harmless against any claims, damages, obligations, liabilities, and expenses and costs (including attorneys' fees and costs) arising out of or related to your use of the Software.

Governing Law. This License Agreement will be governed by the laws of the state of Texas as they are applied to agreements between Texas residents entered into and to be performed entirely within Texas. The United Nations Convention on Contracts for the international Sale of Goods is specifically disclaimed.

Entire Agreement/Severability. This is the entire agreement between you and Licensor and it supersedes any prior agreement, whether written or oral, and all other communications between the parties relating to the subject matter of this License Agreement. This Agreement may not be modified except through a writing signed by Licensor. In the event of the invalidity of any provision of this License Agreement, you agree that such invalidity shall not affect the validity of the remaining portions of this License Agreement.

If you have any questions regarding this License Agreement, you are providing notice as set forth in this Agreement, or you wish to request any information from Licensor, please contact Licensor by email: robert@rgrondalski.com.